A NEW LITERACIES SAMPLER

new
literacies

AND DIGITAL EPISTEMOLOGIES

Colin Lankshear, Michele Knobel,
Chris Bigum, and Michael Peters
General Editors

Vol. 29

PETER LANG
New York • Washington, D.C./Baltimore • Bern
Frankfurt am Main • Berlin • Brussels • Vienna • Oxford

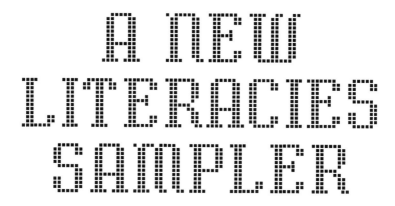

A NEW LITERACIES SAMPLER

Edited by
Michele Knobel and Colin Lankshear

PETER LANG
New York • Washington, D.C./Baltimore • Bern
Frankfurt am Main • Berlin • Brussels • Vienna • Oxford

Library of Congress Cataloging-in-Publication Data

Knobel, Michele.
A new literacies sampler / edited by Michele Knobel, Colin Lankshear.
p. cm. — (New literacies and digital epistemologies; vol. 29)
Includes bibliographical references and index.
1. Media literacy. 2. Mass media in education. I. Title.
P96.M4 N59   302.23—dc22   2006037193
ISBN 978-0-8204-9523-1
ISSN 1523-9543

Bibliographic information published by **Die Deutsche Bibliothek**.
Die Deutsche Bibliothek lists this publication in the "Deutsche
Nationalbibliografie"; detailed bibliographic data is available
on the Internet at http://dnb.ddb.de/.

Cover design by Joni Holst

The paper in this book meets the guidelines for permanence and durability
of the Committee on Production Guidelines for Book Longevity
of the Council of Library Resources.

Printed in the United States of America

To young (and not so young) digital insiders who inspire people like us

Table of Contents

Acknowledgements

The authors wish to thank the following for generously granting permission for their original work to be used in this book: the faculty and students at "Ridgeview Academy" (Chapter 2); Liz, Mike, Fran, Bill, Robert, Charles, Anne, Karl and Cassie for their insights into live action role-play games (Chapter 4); Nanako Tanako and her fanfic reviewers (Chapter 6); Tiana and Jandalf for their interview data, images and fanfic writing (Chapter 7); Jandalf for her sketch of Jemaei (Figure 7.3); and Mohawk/Limbert for permission to use the doll tea image appearing in Chapter 8 (Figure 8.3).

We would also like to thank the following for their permission to use their images on the cover of this book: Julia Davies and Guy Merchant for the screen shot from Blogtrax (blogtrax.blogsome.com); Zack Johnson for the image of Arwennie from the massively multiplayer online role playing game, Kingdom of Loathing (kingdomofloathing.com, © Asymmetric Publications, LLC); Jandalf for her sketch of Jemaei; Jay Maynard for the image of his Tron cosplay (Tronguy.com); and Rob Lewis for a webpage screenshot from Stickdeath (stickdeath.com).

The Editors thank the authors of the chapters for being part of this project. We thank them for being friends and colleagues who sustain, inspire, and encourage us and so many others in our collective endeavor to better understand "new literacies". We hope each and every one of them walks long and happily in this world—and all the other worlds they variously inhabit. We also thank everyone at Peter Lang Publishing for being so easy to work with on this project, and on the New Literacies series as a whole. In particular, we'd like to thank Sophie Appel and Chris Myers for their input, help and good humor.

CHAPTER ONE

Sampling "the New" in New Literacies

COLIN LANKSHEAR AND MICHELE KNOBEL

Sampling

This book "samples" work in the broad area of new literacies research on two levels.

First, it samples some typical examples of new literacies. These are video gaming, fan fiction writing, weblogging, using websites to participate in affinity practices, and social practices involving mobile computing. The question of what it is about these practices that makes us think of them as "new" and as "literacies" will occupy much of this introductory chapter.

Second, it samples from among the wide range of *approaches* potentially available for researching and studying new literacies. The studies assembled in this collection are all examples of what is referred to as research undertaken from a *sociocultural* perspective on literacy. New literacies can be studied from a range of research and theoretical orientations (cf. Leu et al. forthcoming). For reasons that will become apparent from our account of "new literacies," however, a sociocultural perspective is especially appropriate and valuable for researching new literacies.

A Sociocultural Approach to Literacies

Understanding literacies from a sociocultural perspective means that reading and writing can only be understood in the contexts of social, cultural, political, economic, historical practices to which they are integral, of which they are a part. This view lies at the heart of what Gee (1996) calls the "new" literacy studies, or socioliteracy studies (see also Hull and Schultz 2001, Knobel 1999, Lankshear 1997, Street 1984, 1995). The relationship between human practice and the production, distribution, exchange, refinement, negotiation and contestation of meanings is a key idea here. Human practices are meaningful ways of doing things or getting things done (Scribner and Cole 1981; also Franklin 1990, Hull and Schultz 2001). There is no practice without meaning, just as there is no meaning outside of practice. Within contexts of human practice, language (words, literacy, texts) gives meaning to contexts and, dialectically, contexts give meaning to language. Hence, there is no reading or writing in any meaningful sense of each term outside social practices.

If we see literacy as "simply reading and writing"—whether in the sense of encoding and decoding print, as a tool, a set of skills, or a technology, or as some kind of psychological process—we cannot make sense of our literacy experience. Reading (or writing) is always reading something in particular with understanding. Different kinds of text require "somewhat different backgrounds and somewhat different skills" if they are to be read (i.e., read *meaningfully*). Moreover, particular texts can be read in different ways, contingent upon different people's experiences of practices in which these texts occur. A Christian Fundamentalist, for example, will read texts from the Bible in radically different ways from, say, a liberation theology priest. They will make different meanings from specific texts, interact with these texts differently, put them to different "uses" (e.g., to justify or affirm different courses of action to be taken in the world), and so on.

Learning to read and write particular kinds of texts in particular ways presupposes immersion in social practices where participants "not only read texts of this type in this way but also talk about such texts in certain ways, hold certain attitudes and values about them, and socially interact over them in certain ways" (Gee, Hull and Lankshear 1996, 3). Different histories of "literate immersion" yield different forms of reading and writing as practice. The texts we read and write—any and all texts we read and write; even the most arid (and otherwise meaningless) drill and skill, remedial session "readings"—are integral elements of "lived, talked, enacted, value-and-belief-laden practices" engaged in under specific conditions, at specific times and in specific places (ibid.). Consequently, it is impossible to abstract or decontextualize "literacy bits" from their larger embedded practices and for them still to mean what they do in fact mean experientially. Furthermore, and obviously, there is no one singular phenomenon that is *literacy*. Rather, there are as many literacies as there are "social practices and conceptions of reading and writing" (Street 1984, 1).

Sociocultural Definitions of "Literacies"

Sociocultural definitions of literacy, then, have to make sense of reading, writing and meaning-making as integral elements of social practices. One such definition is provided by Gee (1996), who defines literacy in relation to Discourses. Discourses are socially recognized ways of using language (reading, writing, speaking, listening), gestures and other semiotics (images, sounds, graphics, signs, codes), as well as ways of thinking, believing, feeling, valuing, acting/doing and interacting in relation to people and things, such that we can be identified and recognized as being a member of a socially meaningful group, or as playing a socially meaningful role (cf., Gee 1991, 1996, 1998). To be in, or part of, a Discourse means that others can recognise us as being a "this" or a "that" (a pupil, mother, priest, footballer, mechanic), or a particular "version" of a this or a that (a reluctant pupil, a doting mother, a radical priest, an untrained but expert mechanic) by virtue of how we are using language, believing, feeling, acting, dressing, doing, and so on. Language is a dimension of Discourse, but only one dimension, and Gee uses discourse (with a small "d") to mark this relationship. As historical "productions," Discourses change over time, but at any given point are sufficiently "defined" for us to tell when people are in them.

Gee distinguishes our primary Discourse from our various secondary Discourses. Our primary Discourse is how we learn to do and be (including speaking and expressing) within our family (or face to face intimate) group during our early life. It (we each have only one primary Discourse, although there are many different primary Discourses) comprises our first notions of who "people like us" are, and what "people like us" do, think, value, and so on. Our secondary Discourses (and we each have many of these, although they differ from person to person) are those we are recruited to through participation in outside groups and institutions, such as schools, clubs, workplaces, churches, political organizations, and so on. These all draw upon and extend our resources from our primary Discourse, and may be "nearer to" or "further away from" our primary Discourse. The further away a secondary Discourse is from our primary Discourse and our other secondary Discourses—as in the case of children from marginal social groups who struggle to get a handle on the culture of school classrooms—the more we have to "stretch" our discursive resources to "perform" within that Discourse. Often in such cases we simply are unable to operate the Discourse at the level of fluent performance.

Gee holds that any socially useful definition of literacy must build on the notion of Discourse and the distinction between primary and secondary Discourses. In part this is because the context of all language use is some specific social practice or other, which is always part of some Discourse or other. Gee defines literacy "as mastery (or, fluent performance) of a secondary Discourse" (Gee 1996). Hence, to be literate means being able to handle all aspects of competent performance of the Discourse, including the literacy bits: that is, to be able to handle the various human and non-human elements of "coordinations" (Gee 1997, Latour 1987, Knorr Cetina 1992) effected by Discourses. To play a role, be a particular identity, etc., is a matter of both "getting coordinated" as an element in a Discourse, and of coordinating other elements. Language/literacy is a crucial element of discursive "coordinating," but it is only one aspect, and the other elements need to be "in sync" for fluent performance—literacy—to be realised.

In similar vein we have recently defined literacies as "socially recognized ways of generating, communicating and negotiating meaningful content through the medium of encoded texts within contexts of participation in Discourses (or, as members of Discourses)" (Lankshear and Knobel 2006, 64). Identifying literacies as *social practices* is necessarily to see them as involving socially recognized ways of doing things. Scribner and Cole (1981, 236) claim that "social practice" always refers "to socially developed and patterned ways of using technology and knowledge to accomplish tasks." They describe literacy in terms of "socially organized practices [that] make use of a symbol system and a technology for producing and disseminating it" (1981, 236). Literacy, then, is not a matter of knowing how to read and write a particular kind of script. Rather, it is a matter of "applying this knowledge for specific purposes in specific contexts of use" (ibid.). This means that literacy is really like a family of practices—literacies—that includes such "socially evolved and patterned activities" as letter writing, keeping records and inventories, keeping a diary, writing memos, posting announcements, and so on (ibid.). More recently Brian Street (2001, 11) has defined literacy practices as "particular ways of thinking about and doing reading and writing in cultural contexts."

Literacies call us to generate and communicate meanings and to invite others to make meaning from our texts in turn. This, however, can only be done by having something to make meaning *from*—namely, a kind of content that is carried as "potential" by the text and that is actualized through interaction with the text by its recipients. If there is no text there is no literacy, and every text, by definition, bears content. Gunther Kress (2003, 37–38) makes this point in relation to alphabetic writing. He talks of readers doing "semiotic work" when they read a written text. This is "the work of filling the elements of writing with content" (ibid.); that is, the work of making meaning from the writing in the text. Kress argues that meaning involves two kinds of work. One is *articulation*, which is performed in the production of "the outwardly made sign" (e.g., writing). The other is *interpretation*, which involves producing "the inwardly made sign" in reading (see also Gee 2004, Ch. 6).

Our idea of "meaningful content" that is generated and negotiated within literacy practices is, however, wider and looser than many literacy scholars might accept. We think Gee's (1997) Discourse approach to literacies draws attention to the complexity and richness of the relationship between literacies and "ways of being together in the world" (Gee 1997, xv). So, for example, when we look at somebody's weblog we might well find that much of the meaning to be made from the content has to do with who we think the blog writer *is*: what they are like, how they want to think of themselves, and how they want us to think of them. Likewise, a particular text that someone produces might well be best understood as an expression of wanting to feel "connected" or "related" right now. The meaning carried by the content might be much more relational than literal. It might be more about expressing solidarity or affinity with particular people. Our idea of "meaningful content" is intended to be sufficiently elastic to accommodate these possibilities.

This is an important point when it comes to understanding the internet, online practices and online "content." Almost anything available online becomes a resource for diverse kinds of meaning making. In many cases the meanings that are made will not be intelligible to people at large or, in some cases, to many people at all. Some might be shared only by "insiders" of quite small interest groups or cliques. Consider, for example, the way that eBay has been used to spoof a range of social conventions and to generate diverse kinds of quirky and "nutty" activity. A man auctioned his soul in 2006 and received a cash payment that came with the condition that he would spend 50 hours in church. In another case an individual auctioned a ten-year-old toasted cheese sandwich the owner said had an imprint of the Virgin Mary on it, and that had not gone mouldy or disintegrated since it was made in 1994. Moreover, she said it had brought her luck at a casino. An internet casino purchased the sandwich for $28,000 and planned to take it on tour to raise money for charity. Other sellers responded with Virgin Mary toasted sandwich makers, T-shirts, etc. (see: news.bbc.co.uk/2/hi/americas/4034787.stm). On 5 May 2006, Yahoo! sports pages reported a Kansas City Royals baseball fan of 25 years finally giving up on the club and auctioning his loyalty. The meaning of such actions have little to do with established practices of auctioning, and the interpretation of texts describing the items have little or nothing to do with the literal words per se. People may be prepared to spend money just to be in solidarity with the spoof: to say "I get it," and thereby signal their insiderness with the practice, express solidarity with the seller, or, even, to try and save a soul.

By defining literacies in relation to "encoded texts" we mean texts that have been rendered in a form that allows them to be retrieved, worked with, and made available independently of the physical presence of another person. "Encoded texts" are texts that have been "frozen" or "captured" in ways that free them from their immediate context of production so that they are "transportable." Encoded texts give (semi) permanence, transcendence, and transportability to language that is not available in the immediacy of speech, hand signs, and the like. They can "travel" without requiring particular people to transport them. They can be replicated independently of needing other human beings to host the replication. The particular kinds of codes employed in literacy practices are varied and contingent. Literacies can involve any kind of codification system that "captures" language in the sense we have described. Literacy includes "letteracy" (i.e., within the English language, recognition and manipulation of alphabetic symbols), but in our view goes far beyond this. Someone who "freezes" language as a digitally encoded passage of speech and uploads it to the internet as a podcast is engaging in literacy.

Finally, the point that we always engage in literacy practices as members of some Discourse or other takes us back to Gee's account of literacies outlined above. Humans "do life" as individuals and as members of social and cultural groups—always as what Gee calls "situated selves"—in and through *Discourses*. A person rushing an email message to head office as she hands her boarding pass to the airline attendant at the entrance to the aircraft boarding ramp is recognizable (to others and herself) as a particular kind of person. In this moment she is part of a *coordination* that includes as its elements such things as the person herself, some way of thinking and feeling (maximizing time to get more done), rules (the phone must be switched off after leaving the gate), institutions (airports and air travel, the company she works for), tools (a phone, a network), accessories (a briefcase and compact travel bag), clothes (a suit, perhaps), language (facility with emailing concisely and accurately), and so on. These various elements all get and are got "in sync" (Gee 1997). The various elements simultaneously coordinate the others and are coordinated by them (institutional requirements and timetables prompt the particular use of the phone during the last seconds before boarding; the email message makes a demand back on someone in the company; the meeting ahead has influenced choice of clothes—smart but comfortable; etc.). This "in sync-ness" tells us who and what that person is (like, a business executive in the middle of a three-city day). As Gee puts it: "Within such coordinations we humans become *recognizable* to ourselves and to others and *recognize* ourselves, other people, and things as meaningful in distinctive ways" (1997, xiv).

As constitutive elements of participation in or membership of a Discourse, literacies always involve much more than simply producing and negotiating texts per se. They are contexts and pretexts for enacting and refining memberships of Discourses that include such dimensions as feeding back, providing support, sharing knowledge and expertise, explaining rules, sharing jokes, commiserating, doing one's job, expressing opinions, showing solidarity, enacting an affinity (Gee 2004) and so on. Hence, our claim that literacies are "socially recognized ways of generating, communicating and negotiating meaningful content through the medium of encoded texts within contexts of participating in Discourses (or, as members of Discourses)" (Lankshear and Knobel 2006, 64). As such, blogging, fanfic writing, manga producing, meme-ing, photoshopping, anime music video (AMV) practices, podcasting, vodcasting, and gaming are *literacies*, along with letter writing, keeping a diary, maintaining records, running a paper-based zine, reading literary novels and wordless picture books, reading graphic novels and comics, note-making during conference presentations or lectures, and reading bus timetables.

When Are Literacies "New"?

The question of what constitutes "new" literacies is interesting, and different views exist. Our view (see Lankshear and Knobel 2006) is that new literacies have what we call new "technical stuff" and new "ethos stuff." We distinguish two categories of "new" literacies, which we refer to as paradigm cases of new literacies and peripheral cases of new literacies, respectively. The new literacies sampled in this book are all examples of what we regard as paradigm cases.

Paradigm cases of new literacies have *both* new "technical stuff" (digitality) and new "ethos stuff." Peripheral cases of new literacies have new "ethos stuff" but not new "technical stuff." In other words, if a literacy does not have what we call new ethos stuff we do not regard it as a new literacy, even if it has new technical stuff. Once again, not everyone is going to agree with this view. We adopt it because it is possible to use new technologies (digital electronic technologies) to simply replicate longstanding literacy practices—as we see *ad infinitum* in contemporary classrooms as well as in many workplaces. We think that what is central to new literacies is not the fact that we can now "look up information online" or write essays using a word processor rather than a pen or typewriter, or even that we can mix music with sophisticated software that works on run-of-the-mill computers but, rather, that they mobilize very different kinds of values and priorities and sensibilities than the literacies we are familiar with. The significance of the new technical stuff has mainly to do with how it enables people to build and participate in literacy practices that involve different kinds of values, sensibilities, norms and procedures and so on from those that characterize conventional literacies.

New "Technical Stuff"

For present purposes, most of what is important "new technical stuff" is summarized in Mary Kalantzis' idea that "You click for 'A' and you click for 'red' " (Cope et al. 2005, 200). Basically, programmers write source code that is stored as binary code (combinations of 0s and 1s) which drives different kinds of applications (for text, sound, image, animation, communications functions, etc.) on digital-electronic apparatuses (computers, games hardware, CD and mp3 players, etc.). Someone with access to a fairly standard computer and internet connection, and who has fairly elementary knowledge of standard software applications can create a diverse range of meaningful artifacts using a strictly finite set of physical operations or techniques (keying, clicking, cropping, dragging), in a tiny space, with just one or two (albeit complex) "tools." They can, for example, create a multimodal text and send it to a person, a group, or an entire internet community in next to no time and at next to no cost. The text could be a photoshopped image posted to Flickr.com. It could be an animated Valentine's Day card sent to an intimate friend. It could be a short animated film sequence using toys and objects found at home, complete with an original music soundtrack, attached to a blog post. It could be a slide presentation of images of some event with narrated commentary, or remixed clips from a video game that spoof some aspect of popular culture or that retell some obscure literary work in cartoon animations.

Relatively unsophisticated desktop publishing software can generate text and image effects that the best printers often could not manage under typographic conditions, and "publishing" now is no longer limited to print or images on paper, but can include additional media such as voice recordings, music files, 2D and 3D animation, video, paintshopped images, scanned images of paper-based artworks, etc. Even the concept of "text" as understood in conventional print terms becomes a hazy concept when considering the enormous array of expressive media now available to everyday folk. Diverse practices of "remixing"—where a range of original materials are copied, cut, spliced, edited, reworked, and mixed into a new creation—have become highly popular in part because of the quality of product it is possible for "ordinary people" to achieve.

Machinima animations are a good example of what we mean here. "Machinima" refers to the process by which fans use video game animation "engines" (the code that "drives" or generates all the images in a given video game) and computer-generated imagery (CGI) to render new animated texts on their desktop computers. Until recently such productions required expensive, high-end 3D graphics and animation engines that were usually the preserve of professional animators. Creating machinima involves using tools found within the game engine, like camera angle options, script editors, level editors, and the like, along with resources, such as backgrounds, themes, characters, settings etc. available in the game (see: en.wikipedia.org/wiki/Machinima).

Similarly, music can be sampled and remixed using desktop computers and audio editing software. The term "remix" grew out of the DJ sampling, scratching and mixing scene that began in the late 1970s and early 1980s (although music remixing itself has a long history as a practice; cf., blues music, ska music from Jamaica). Music remixing no longer requires extensive and eclectic vinyl record collections, multiple turntables and bulky and expensive mixing and amplification equipment as it did in the 1970s. Software that comes bundled with most computers allows users to convert music files from a CD into an editable format (e.g., *.wav), edit and splice sections of different songs together and to convert the final music files back into a highly portable format (e.g., *.mp3) and upload them to the internet for others to access or, alternatively, use them as background soundtracks in larger do-it-yourself multimedia projects.

These are some typical examples of the kinds of technological trends and developments we think of as comprising new technical stuff. They represent a

quantum shift beyond typographic means of text production as well as beyond analogue forms of sound and image production. They can be employed to do in new
ways "the same kinds of things we have previously known." Equally, however, they
can be integrated into literacy practices (and other kinds of social practices) that in
some significant sense represent *new* phenomena. The extent to which they are integrated into literacy practices that can be seen as being "new" in a significant sense
will reflect the extent to which these literacy practices involve different kinds of values, emphases, priorities, perspectives, orientations and sensibilities from those
that typify conventional literacy practices that became established during the era of
print and analogue forms of representation and, in some cases, even earlier.

New "Ethos Stuff"

When we say that new literacies involve different "*ethos* stuff" from that which is typically associated with conventional literacies we mean that new literacies are more
"participatory," "collaborative," and "distributed" in nature than conventional literacies.
That is, they are less "published," "individuated," and "author-centric" than conventional literacies. They are also less "expert-dominated" than conventional literacies.
The rules and norms that govern them are more fluid and less abiding than those
we typically associate with established literacies. We understand this difference in
"ethos" between conventional and new literacies in terms of a much larger historical
and social phenomenon that involves a "fracturing of space" accompanied by the
emergence of a new kind of mindset (Lankshear and Bigum 1999, 457).

Contemporary Fracturing of Space

The idea of space having been fractured refers to the emergence of *cyberspace* as a
distinctively new space that co-exists with physical space (Lankshear and Bigum
1999). Cyberspace has not *displaced* physical space, of course, and will not displace
it. Neither, however, can physical space "dismiss" cyberspace. For the majority of
young people in so-called developed countries who are now adolescents, cyberspace
has been integral to their experience of "spatiality" since their early years. In these
same countries an entire generation has grown up in a world saturated by digital
electronic technologies, many of which are linked via cyberspace to form an enormous network. Co-existence is the destiny of physical space and cyberspace. Neither
is about to go away.

The idea that this fracturing of space has been accompanied by the emergence
and evolution of a new mindset is evident in the difference between people who
approach the contemporary world through two different lenses. The first is what

we call a "physical-industrial" mindset. The second is what we call a "cyberspatial-postindustrial" mindset. The "ethos stuff" of new literacies reflects the second mindset. As we will see, much of this ethos is encapsulated in talk which has emerged recently around the concept of Web 2.0.

Mindsets

The first mindset assumes that the contemporary world is essentially the way it has been throughout the modern-industrial period, only now it has been technologized in a new and very sophisticated way. To all intents and purposes, however, the world on which these new technologies are brought to bear is more or less the same economic, cultural, social world that has evolved throughout the modern era, where things got done by means of routines that were predicated on longstanding assumptions about bodies, materials, property and forms of ownership, industrial techniques and principles, physical texts, face to face dealings (and physical proxies for them), and so on.

The second mindset assumes that the contemporary world is different in important ways from how it was even 30 years ago, and that this difference is growing. Much of this change is related to the development of new internetworked technologies and new ways of doing things and new ways of being that are enabled by these technologies. More and more the world is being changed as a result of people exploring hunches and "visions" of what might be possible given the potential of digital technologies and electronic networks. The world is being changed in some quite fundamental ways as a result of people imagining and exploring new ways of doing things and new ways of being that are made possible by new tools and techniques, rather than using new technologies to do familiar things in more "technologized" ways (first mindset).

Some important differences between the mindsets can be dimensionalized along lines presented in Table 1.1 on p. 11. This is a heuristic device that somewhat polarizes the mindsets. Things are obviously more complex than a simple table can capture. And other people are likely to emphasize alternative dimensions of difference than the ones highlighted here. Nonetheless, the dimensions addressed here will be sufficient to convey our view of the new "ethos stuff" we believe characterizes new literacies.

At an early point in the development of the internet as a mass phenomenon John Perry Barlow (in interview with Tunbridge 1995) distinguished between what he saw as the different paradigms of *value* operating in physical space and cyberspace respectively. In physical space, says Barlow, controlled economics increases value by regulating scarcity. To take the case of diamonds, the value of diamonds is not a function of their degree of rarity or actual scarceness but, rather, of the fact that a single corporation owns most of them and, hence, can regulate or control their

TABLE 1.1. Some dimensions of variation between the mindsets

Mindset 1	Mindset 2
The world basically operates on physical/material and industrial principles and logics. The world is "centered" and hierarchical.	The world increasingly operates on non-material (e.g., cyberspatial) and post-industrial principles and logics. The world is "decentered" and "flat."

• Value is a function of scarcity
• Production is based on an "industrial" model
  • Products are material artifacts and commodities
  • Production is based on infrastructure and production units and centers (e.g., a firm or company)
  • Tools are mainly production tools
• The individual person is the unit of production, competence, intelligence
• Expertise and authority are "located" in individuals and institutions
• Space is enclosed and purpose specific
• Social relations of "bookspace" prevail; a stable "textual order"
	• Value is a function of dispersion
	• A "post-industrial" view of production
	  • Products as enabling services
	  • A focus on leverage and non-finite participation
	  • Tools are increasingly tools of mediation and relationship technologies
	• The focus is increasingly on "collectives" as the unit of production, competence, intelligence
	• Expertise and authority are distributed and collective; hybrid experts
	• Space is open, continuous and fluid
	• Social relations of emerging "digital media space" are increasingly visible; texts in change

scarcity. Within this paradigm, scarcity has value. Schools, for example, have traditionally operated to regulate scarcity of credentialed achievement, including allocations of literacy "success." This has maintained scarce "supply" and, to that extent, high value for those achievements that are suitably credentialed. In the economy of cyberspace, however, the opposite holds. Barlow argues that with information it is familiarity, not scarcity that has value. With information, however,

> it's dispersion that has the value, and [information's] not a commodity, it's a relationship and as in any relationship, the more that's going back and forth the higher the value of the relationship (in Tunbridge 1995, 5).

The implication here is that people who bring a scarcity model of value with them to cyberspace will act in ways that diminish rather than expand its potential. For example, applying certain kinds of copyright and permissions restrictions to the use of information may constrain the dispersal of that information in ways that undermine its capacity to provide a basis for *relationship*. This will, in turn, undermine the potential of that information to work as a catalyst for generating creative and productive conversations, the development of fruitful ideas, the emergence of effective networks, and so on (cf., Lessig 2004). The kind of value Barlow sees as appropriate to cyberspace has to do with maximizing relationships, conversations, networks and dispersal. Hence, to bring a model of value that "belongs" to a different kind of space is inappropriate and creates an impediment to actualizing the new space.

The emphasis on relationship and its connection to information—indeed, the *significance* of information in terms of relationship—is further developed by Michael Schrage's (2001) argument that it makes more sense in the current conjuncture to talk of a relationship revolution than an information revolution. Schrage argues that viewing the computing and communications technologies of the internet through an information lens is "dangerously myopic." The value of the internet and the web is not to be found in "bits and bytes and bandwidth." In a celebrated comment, Schrage claims that to say the internet "is about 'information' is a bit like saying that 'cooking' is about oven temperatures, it's technically accurate but fundamentally untrue" (Schrage 2001, no page). The internet and other digital technologies have certainly "transformed the world of information into readily manipulable bits and bytes" (ibid.). At the same time, "the genuine significance of these technologies isn't rooted in the information they process and store." Rather, the greatest impact they have had and will continue to have, "is on relationships between people and between organizations." Schrage argues,

> The so-called "information revolution" itself is actually, and more accurately, a "relationship revolution." Anyone trying to get a handle on the dazzling technologies of today and the impact they'll have tomorrow, would be well advised to re-orient their worldview around relationships (2001, no page; original emphasis).

The points made by Barlow and Schrage translate into elements of an ethos associated with the second mindset and that can be seen "writ large" in diverse emerging online literacies. Two stand out in particular. One might be described as the "will" of information to be "free," in the sense of "free" elucidated by Lawrence Lessig (2004) in his book, *Free Culture*. This is the idea that cultural creation requires the freedom and capacity of ordinary people to draw on elements of prior cultural production to use as raw materials for further creative work. This does not mean pirating, and it does not mean copying without citation. What it does mean, however, is that people should be free to take (with appropriate recognition) "bits" of cultural production that are in circulation and use them to create new ideas, concepts, artifacts and statements, without having to seek permission to re-use, or to be hit with a writ for using particular animation or music sequences as components in "remixes" (Lankshear and Knobel 2006, Ch. 4) that make something significantly new out of the remixed components.

The contemporary explosion of remix practices in fan fiction, Anime-Music-Video production, music, cosplay, photoshopping images and the like, bespeaks mass popular participation in expressing this will of information to be free. Lessig (2005) is correct when he states that at a general level all of culture is remix, and all of culture is fundamentally dependent on information being free in the relevant sense. At the same time, he is also correct in identifying the special and *new* way in which young people particularly are exercising in very conscious ways the will to freedom on the part of cultural information. Contemporary practices of remix vary in significant ways from, say, academic scholarly models of remix where, in addition to putting cultural components together in a new mix the scholar was expected to tweak theory, critique the original components, and so on. This relates to a second point.

This second point is the way in which information is mobilized for, or made into the medium of, *relatedness* through participation in online affinity spaces (Gee 2004, Black 2005a, Davies 2006, Stone Ch. 3, this volume). Much of the point behind remix practices, for example, is to be and feel connected to other people and to celebrate a fandom: to participate in an affinity, to make shared meanings, to brighten the day, share a laugh, share one's passion for a product or a character, and so on. Conventional practices analogous to cultural remix, such as academic research and scholarship, include such values and orientations at their best, but typically embrace "higher callings" like pursuit of truth, advancement of knowledge, contribution to modernist progress, and furthering the field.

In such ways we can begin to relate the "newness" of new literacies to a distinctive kind of "ethos stuff" that is reaching a scale hitherto unprecedented, and turning the consumption of popular culture into active *production*: the production of consumption (cf., Squire forthcoming, Steinkuehler forthcoming). Beyond this, of course, we can recognise diverse "new" literacies built around mobilizing information creation and exchange for relatedness purposes: chat, IM, multiplayer online gaming of all kinds from role playing to first person shooter, blogging, photo sharing, among many others.

Before turning to those aspects of ethos associated with the second mindset that are encapsulated by talk of Web 2.0, and that in our view constitute "new" in a significant sense, we will briefly address those dimensions of Table 1.1 pertaining to different dimensions of space: as in "bookspace" and "workspace."

The dominance of the book as the text paradigm, social relations of control associated with "bookspace," and a discernible textual "order" are integral to the first mindset. During the age of print the book comprised the text paradigm. It shaped conceptions of layout, it was the pinnacle of textual authority, and it played a central role in organizing practices and routines in major social institutions. The book mediated social relations of control and power, as between author and readers, authorial voice as the voice of expert and authority, teacher/expert and student/learner, priest/minister and congregation, and so on. Textual forms and formats were relatively stable and were "policed" to ensure conformity. Certain genres of texts were privileged over others and seen as appropriate within particular (institutional) settings—e.g., school classrooms—whereas others were regarded as more marginal and not appropriate.

Books exerted great influence on institutional space, architecture and furniture, as well as on norms for conduct within particular spaces.

The book in no way comprises the text paradigm in the emerging digital media space. Indeed, there is *no* text paradigm. Text types are subject to wholesale experimentation, hybridization, and rule breaking. Conventional social relations associated with roles of author/authority and expert have broken down radically under the move from "publishing" to participation, from centralized authority to mass collaboration, and so on. The organization of space, architecture and furniture, and control of movement associated with bookspace has become a curious aberration under the sign of new media. While people who grew up under the hegemony of the book and a stable "generic order" may ponder whether it is "proper" to write this kind of way in a blog, or to focus on this kind of theme, digital insiders seem much less preoccupied by such concerns. This is not to say there are no norms in the new space, for there are. They are, however, less fixed, more fluid, and less policed, controlled and defined by "centralized" authorities and experts. The sheer proliferation of textual types and spaces means there is always somewhere to "go" where one's "ways" will be acceptable, where there will be freedom to engage them, and where traditional emphases on "credibility" are utterly subordinated to the pursuit of relationships and the celebration of sociality.

Similarly, the new ethos stuff associated with the second mindset seriously disrupts authorial social relations. This can be illustrated nicely by game "modding," which involves the use of a video game's image and strategy engines to create fan-driven "modifications" to or extensions of the game itself. These modifications remain "true" to the game's "universe" (i.e., how characters can move, act, solve problems and what kinds of challenges are put in place, etc. within the world of the game), but add, say, a new mini-adventure or quest for characters to complete. Such additions may expand a level by adding new skills or qualities to the game, or create an entirely new level for players to complete that adds a layer of difficulty or complexity to the game (cf., Squire forthcoming, Steinkuehler forthcoming).

A quite different ethos is equally evident within the second mindset in relation to conceiving, negotiating, and enacting workspace. From the standpoint of the first mindset, space is typically thought of as enclosed, as having borders. In the educational context, learning space is bordered by the classroom walls, lesson space by the hour or 40-minute time signal, and curriculum and timetable space by the grid of subjects to be covered and the time and physical space allocations assigned to them. Tasks tend to be singular and defined or assessed at a given point in time, and learners are expected to be on task, which often means all students on the same task at the same time. Being not on that task is seen as being disengaged from learning.

Learners who have grown up on the inside of a cyberspatial mindset often see things very differently and approach them very differently. The presumption that one will be working on one task at a time or in one "place" at a time when engaged in learning (or, for that matter, in entertainment or recreation) is foreign to many who approach and respond to their world from the second mindset. Multitasking has become ubiquitous among digital youth. Moreover, the multitasking mode is not seen simply some casual kind of modus operandi confined to interactions with one's closest friends—as when chatting, roleplaying, updating a weblog, IM-ing, etc. simultaneously (Thomas forthcoming; Lankshear and Knobel 2006, Ch. 2). Rather, it is widely seen as a way of operating that applies generally in everyday life at home, at school and at play.

Kevin Leander and colleagues (Leander and Frank 2006; Leander and Lovvorn 2006; Ch. 2 this volume) observed students who were in wireless classrooms spending considerable time engaged simultaneously in multiple "self-selected purposes" during lessons. These included gaming, shopping, and downloading music, as well as more to be expected activities like emailing, chatting, instant messaging, and browsing and updating weblogs. They did this while staying in touch with what was going on in class. Some of the students who engaged most in pursuing self-selected purposes during class time did not believe they were learning less than they otherwise would as a result of this. Even when they were "drifting" on their screens they demonstrably participated as much if not more in class discussions than their "on task" peers. Two of the students observed by Leander and colleagues claimed that being able to go to other places during time in class when they already knew about the matters under discussion alleviated boredom. Their capacity for multitasking seemingly allowed them to maintain one eye on the class task while going about other business.

This is not to imply that people operating from the second mindset cannot and do not compartmentalize time and space and/or dedicate long stretches of time within a particular space to a single task or purpose—for clearly they do. It is, however, to say that a lot of contemporary literacy activity *is* conceived and undertaken "on the fly" and simultaneously with other practices. New literacies spaces are often fluid, continuous and open. Online and offline lives and "literacyscapes" (Leander 2003) merge and augment, and researchers are constantly seeking new methods and means for "traveling" with these traveling literacies (Leander forthcoming).

Web 2.0

As we have noted, however, much of what we regard as the new kind of "ethos stuff" that characterizes "new" literacies is crystallized in current talk of "Web 1.0" and "Web 2.0" as different sets of design patterns and business models in software development, and in concrete examples of how the distinction plays out in real life cases and practices.

Tim O'Reilly (2005) traces the origins of the distinction between Web 1.0 and Web 2.0 to discussions at a conference following the 2001 dot.com crash. It was observed that major companies to survive the crash shared features in common. Discussants assigned examples of internet applications and approaches to Web 1.0 or Web 2.0 respectively and explained their allocations (see Figure 1.1). Some examples likely to be familiar to readers were assigned as follows.

O'Reilly observes that examples in the Web 1.0 column comprise products, artifacts or commodities produced from a source and made available to internet users. Britannica Online is an internet product subscribers can access for a fee. Ofoto began as a front for Kodak to sell digital photo processing online to users who could post digital photos on the Ofoto server to share with friends. Ofoto's gallery space was an enticement to buy a product rendered by a supplier. O'Reilly notes that even the free web browser offered by Netscape was an artifact—a "piece" of software in the form of a desktop application—released from time to time as updated versions to be downloaded and installed on one's computer. It was the centerpiece of Netscape's strategy to create a "webtop" that would "push" information from various providers at consumers, and, in doing so, to "use their dominance in the browser market to establish a market [among information providers] for high-priced server products" (O'Reilly 2005, no page).

The point here is not about *commercial* product delivery so much as the fact that what users receive are readymade artifacts or commodities. O'Reilly speaks here of "packaged software." In Web 1.0 the "webtop" as a platform or user interface still largely emulates the desktop, with producers and consumers engaged in creating and consuming applications and informational *artifacts*. Users are not positioned as controllers of their own data. What one "gets" on a website is what web publishers put there. The logic is of use rather than participation; of reception and/or consumption

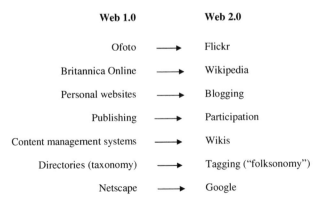

Figure 1.1. Examples of Web 1.0 or Web 2.0 internet applications and approaches *(adapted from O'Reilly 2005, no page)*

rather than interactivity and agency. Directories and the taxonomies they are based upon or "enact" are developed at a "center" and are made available for users in the form that their creators have designed. They get used because they are presumed to be "authoritative" and to reflect "expertise" and "experience" and "wisdom" possessed by their designers.

While this oversimplifies things somewhat, there is enough here that is familiar to readers for making a link to the first mindset. The first generation of the Web has much in common with an "industrial" approach to material productive activity. Companies and developers worked to produce artifacts for consumption. There was a strong divide between producer and consumer. Products were developed by finite experts whose reputed credibility and expertise underpinned take up of their products. Britannica Online stacked up the same authority and expertise—individuals reputed to be experts on their topic and recruited by the company on that basis— as the paper version of yore. Netscape browser development proceeded along similar lines to those of Microsoft, even though the browser constituted free software. Production drew on company infrastructure and labor, albeit highly dispersed rather than bound to a single physical site.

The picture is very different with Web 2.0. Part of the difference concerns *the kind of products* characteristic of Web 2.0. Unlike the "industrial" artifactual nature of Web 1.0 products, Web 2.0 is defined by a "post-industrial" worldview focused much more on "services" and "enabling" than on production and sale of material artifacts for private consumption. Production is based on "leverage," "collective participation," "collaboration" and distributed expertise and intelligence, much more than on manufacture of finished commodities by designated individuals and workteams operating in official production zones and/or drawing on concentrated expertise and intelligence within a shared physical setting.

The free, collaboratively produced online encyclopedia, Wikipedia.org, provides a good example of collaborative writing that leverages collective intelligence for knowledge production in the public domain. Whereas an "official" encyclopedia is produced on the principle of recognized experts being contracted to write entries on designated topics, and the collected entries being formally published by a company, Wikipedia entries are written by anyone who wants to contribute their knowledge and understanding and are edited by anyone else who thinks they can improve on what is already there. Wikipedia provides a short policy statement and a minimal set of guidelines to guide participants in their writing and editing. It is, then, an encyclopedia created by *participation* rather than via publishing. It "embraces the power of the web to harness collective intelligence" (O'Reilly 2005, no page).

Various commentators associate Wikipedia with the open source software adage coined by Eric Raymond that "with enough eyeballs all bugs [or glitches] are shallow" (ibid.). In the context of software code this means the more that people with some knowledge of programming—they needn't be *experts* and most of them aren't—apply that knowledge in the act of peering at code, the more likely and easy it is that "bugs" in programs will be identified and fixed. It is also more likely that many small contributions will be made (not simply bug elimination) that positively *enhance* the elegance and functionality of the program. In the context of Wikipedia we can see these two sides to harnessing collective intelligence. One side enhances the quality of what is already there by adding cumulative positive improvements (i.e., 40 million edits were clocked by the site early in 2006). The other side maintains quality by removing value-subtracting material, whether malicious or simply low quality fare (i.e., "noise"). We might say that Wikipedia employs an "open source epistemology." It encourages free and open participation and trusts to the enterprise as a whole functioning as a self-correcting system. While identifiable people are responsible for beginning and overseeing the initiative, the content is generated by anyone willing to contribute. The idea is that as more and more users read and edit entries online, the more the content will improve. At the same time, ideally, the content will reflect multiple perspectives, excesses and blindspots will be edited out, and by countless incremental steps the resource will become increasingly user friendly, useful, reliable, accountable and refined.

Trust is a key operating principle. The ethos is to reach out to all of the Web for input, through limitless participation, rather than the more traditional belief that expertise is limited and scarce, and that the right to speak truths is conferred on the "properly credentialed." The idea is *not* that anyone's opinion is as good as anybody else's but, rather, that anyone's opinion may stand until it is overwritten by someone who believes they have a better line, and that the right to exercise this belief is not constrained. This, then, is collaborative writing supported by the "technical stuff" of a "wiki" platform or some other kind of collaborative writing software like Writely.com (or similar). It builds on distributed expertise and decenters authorship. In terms of ethos it celebrates inclusion (everyone in), mass participation, distributed expertise, valid and rewardable roles for all who pitch in. It reaches out to all the web, regardless of distinction.

Other literacy practices—like fan fiction, fan manga and anime, and online gaming—reflect Wikipedia's commitment to inclusion, collaboration, and participation, while going somewhat further in explicating what counts as successful performance and providing guidelines for participants. Gee (2004) and others (e.g., Black 2005a, 2005b, Ch. 6 in this volume, Lankshear and Knobel 2006, Ch. 3) describe how participants in various online affinity spaces share their expertise, make as explicit as possible the norms and criteria for success in the enterprise, and actively provide online real time support for novices and, indeed, participants at all levels of proficiency. These range from statements about how to develop plausible characters and plots in fan fiction, to elaborate walkthroughs for games produced for the sheer love of the practice and shared with all online. The practice is marked by generosity and a sense that the more who participate the richer the experience. In terms of "ethos," the ontology of literacies like blogging, writing fan fiction and collaborating in Wikipedia celebrate free support and advice, building the practice, collective benefit, cooperation before competition, everyone a winner rather than a zero-sum game, and transparent rules and procedures.

The final aspect to be considered here of the new kind of ethos we associate with the second mindset, and that we believe defines the heart of new literacies, is the practice of user annotations to help categorize and manage information within a field of endeavour. We will focus here on the recent mass uptake of "tagging" to generate what are called "folksonomies," using the highly popular photograph sharing service Flickr.com as an illustrative example.

Tagging has generated a "bottom up" approach to providing metadata for classifying online content to enable searching, popularly known as "folksonomy." The principle involved is simple. Flickr is a service that allows people to post photographs to the web after they have signed up for an account. For each photograph or set of photographs account holders upload to their site they can add a number of "tags." These are words they think describe their photo—such as, "Mexico," "hamburger," or "spooky"—and that would lead other people who key the word(s) into the Flickr search engine to their photos (and there are a range of options that determine who a person permits to view their photos). Account holders can also invite or accept other people to be on their list of contacts. Contacts can then add tags to the photos posted by those people who have accepted them as contacts. The account holder, however, has the right to edit tags—their own and/or those added by contacts—as they wish. The millions of photos publicly available on Flickr become a searchable database of photos. Tags provide a basis for patterns of user interests to emerge in ways that enable communities of interest to build and for relationships to develop among members who share common interests, tastes, etc. They have enabled different interest groups to coalesce around shared image projects (e.g., the Tell a Story in Five Frames group, the Secret Life of Toys group).

The concept of "folksonomy" was developed in juxtaposition to "taxonomy." Taxonomies are centralized, official, expert-based or top-down classification management systems. The operating principle of taxonomies is that people who presume— or are presumed—to understand a domain of phenomena determine how the individual components of that domain shall be organized in order to make a shared sense or meaning of the domain. The Dewey library classification system is a taxonomy of types of texts, according to which a given book is assigned a number on the basis of the kind of book it is deemed to be and where it fits into the system. By contrast, a folksonomy is a "popular," non-expert, bottom-up classification management system, developed on the basis of how "authors" (e.g., of photos) decide they want their works to be described or "catalogued." Interestingly, O'Reilly (2005, no page) notes how Amazon.com's use of user annotations and other user inputs has led to it becoming the pre-eminent source of bibliographic data, outstripping (even) Bowker's *Books in Print*—previously the pre-eminent source and, indeed, the source for Amazon's original database (cf., Lankshear and Knobel 2006, Ch. 2). O'Reilly says that Amazon

> relentlessly enhanced the data, adding publisher-supplied data such as cover images, table of contents, index, and sample material. Even more importantly, they harnessed their users to annotate the data, such that after ten years, Amazon, not Bowker, is the primary source for bibliographic data on books, a reference source for scholars and librarians as well as consumers . . . Amazon "embraced and extended" their data suppliers (O'Reilly 2005, no page).

One interesting consequence of folksonomic organization is that the tags people choose say something about *them* as well as about the tagged object. When a user finds a photo they would not have expected to fall under a particular tag they might think the tagger's approach to classification is sufficiently interesting to delve further into it; for example, as a pursuit of "the idiosyncratic," or the "quirky," or "of someone who might think a bit like me." The scope for participants to speak their own meanings, find collaborators who share these meanings, and build relationships based on shared perspectives opens up possibilities that are foreclosed by centralized and authoritative regimes that circumscribe norms of correctness, legitimacy or propriety.

The "New" as Historical

What we call "new ethos stuff," then, comprises the spirit of Web 2.0 values and priorities like inclusion—reaching out to the long tail of the Web (Shirky 2003)—active collaboration and participation, leveraging collective intelligence via practices like eliciting user annotations, distributing and wilfully sharing expertise, decentering authorship, mobilizing information for relatedness, hybridization, and the like. This is profoundly different "stuff"—a different essence—from that which constitutes the paradigm literacies of bookspace. We see this as an historical trend. It may even be an "epochal" trend in Freire's sense of the word (1972), if we think of postmodernity as marking an epochal shift from modernity, and if we see the second mindset as an aspect of the postmodern spirit.

This has some noteworthy corollaries, of which we will mention just two here. First, it means that what is "new" is not fleeting. The epochal themes (Freire 1972), if such they are, of the second mindset will take some time to work themselves out; to be fulfilled and, in turn, to be transcended. Hence, if we link the concept of "new" literacies to this new ethos stuff—as we are suggesting we should—then it follows that "new literacies" should not be seen in terms of fleeting instances, such that email is already an "old" new literacy. Rather, new literacies are as "long" as the "moment" of their juxtaposition with "conventional" literacies may last. This could be some time. The significance of the concept of new literacies is that it invites us to take a long term view, and to develop a sociological imagination (Mills 1959) with respect to literacy, education, identity, and our contemporary location within a much longer history that stretches into the future as well as grows out of the past. To do this well would constitute a valuable contribution to humanizing our collective condition.

A second corollary is that this view of the new ethos stuff of new literacies, as historical rather than fleeting and at the whim of each new technological innovation, assigns the "technical stuff" to its proper place: as more of a "contingent enabler" than a "prime mover" or a "heart of the matter." And if we err on the side of giving the technical stuff too little credit, we think it is better to err this way than to gravitate toward technological determinism. New literacies like fan fiction, manga-anime fan practices, scenario planning, popular music remixing and zine publishing, among others, pre-date their digital electronic internetworked forms—sometimes by decades and, in the case of fan practices, arguably for centuries. The ethos was there—embryonic, perhaps; "waiting" for an enabling technology, undoubtedly. The spread and realization of the new ethos stuff becomes possible with the new technologies, but the ethos stuff itself does not depend upon them. Conversely, new technologies can be taken up without and, indeed, in opposition to the new ethos stuff, as the Web 1.0-Web 2.0 distinction, among other things, reminds us.

New Literacies

Briefly, then, we would argue that the more a literacy practice can be seen to reflect the characteristics of the insider mindset and, in particular, those qualities addressed here currently being associated with the concept of Web 2.0, the more it is entitled to be regarded as a *new* literacy. That is to say, the more a literacy practice privileges participation over publishing, distributed expertise over centralized expertise, collective intelligence over individual possessive intelligence, collaboration over individuated authorship, dispersion over scarcity, sharing over ownership, experimentation over "normalization," innovation and evolution over stability and fixity, creative-innovative rule breaking over generic purity and policing, relationship over information broadcast, and so on, the more we should regard it as a "new" literacy. New technologies enable and enhance these practices, often in ways that are stunning in their sophistication and breathtaking in their scale. Paradigm cases of new literacies are constituted by "new technical stuff" as well as "new ethos stuff."

The literacies addressed in the following chapters are new in the sense of comprising new ethos stuff, and they are paradigmatically new in respect of their technical stuff. In the chapters that follow, Kevin Leander discusses school and new technology use with respect to space-time tensions and competing discourses. Jennifer Stone explores a range of websites integral to a range of cultural affinity spaces popular with adolescents and analyzes the complexity of these texts; in so doing, she challenges deficit claims regarding young people's reading practices. Jessica Hammer addresses the issue of agency and authority for secondary authors in role playing games and offers significant insights into an important set of complex narrative practices. James Paul Gee examines video game playing and learning to develop a concept of "projective stance," whereby the world is seen as something both imposed upon us and as something onto which we can project our own goals, desires and values. Rebecca Black and Angela Thomas respectively address online fan fiction; Rebecca focuses on the fan fiction writing of an English as a Second Language learner and the role of reader reviews in the development of this young woman's online writing. Angela discusses the complex textual worlds and identities of two adolescent authors as they collaboratively produce a range of texts together. Julia Davies and Guy Merchant investigate academic blogging and tackle head-on some of the vexing methodological issues that online research raises for researchers. Michele Knobel and Colin Lankshear discuss a pool of high profile online memes and some of the implications meme-ing practices may have for education. Cynthia Lewis concludes by discussing new literacies as new *practices* emerging in a context of new technologies, forms of communication, and economic flows. Focusing on the dimensions of agency, performativity, and circulation she presents a reflective synthesis of how the book as a whole addresses what writers of new literacies *do* when they write, and highlights the significance of this for education.

As a final note, some of the terms used in this book may be unfamiliar to some readers. In lieu of an unwieldy and quickly out-dated glossary at the end of this collection, the following online services are useful for finding further information about a particular term or topic:

- http://www.google.com
- http://www.wikipedia.org
- http://www.howstuffworks.org

References

Black, R. W. 2005a. Access and affiliation: The literacy and composition practices of English language learners in an online fanfiction community. *Journal of Adolescent & Adult Literacy* 49(2): 118–28.

Black, R. W. 2005b. Online fanfiction: What technology and popular culture can teach us about writing and literacy instruction. *New Horizons for Learning Online Journal* 11(2). Spring. newhorizons.org/strategies/literacy/black.htm (accessed 4 April, 2006).

Cope, B., Kalantzis, M. and Lankshear, C. 2005. A contemporary project: An interview. *E-Learning* 2(2): 192–207. wwwords.co.uk/elea/content/pdfs/2/issue2_2.asp#7 (accessed 3 April, 2006).

Davies, J. 2006. Affinities and beyond. Developing new ways of seeing in online spaces. *E-Learning* 3(2): 217–234. wwwords.co.uk/elea/content/pdfs/3/issue3_2.asp#8 (accessed 10 August, 2006).

Franklin, U. 1990. *The Real World of Technology*. Toronto: House of Anansi.

Freire, P. 1972. *Pedagogy of the Oppressed*. Harmondsworth: Penguin.

Gee, J. P. 1991. What is literacy? In C. Mitchell and K. Weiler (Eds), *Rewriting Literacy: Culture and the Discourse of the Other*. New York: Bergin and Garvey. 159–212.

Gee, J. P. 1996. *Social Linguistics and Literacies: Ideology in Discourses*. 2nd edition. London: Falmer.

Gee, J. 1997. Foreword: A discourse approach to language and literacy. In C. Lankshear, *Changing Literacies*. Buckingham: Open University Press. xiii–xix.

Gee, J. P. 1998. The new literacy studies and the "social turn." Madison: University of Wisconsin-Madison Department of Curriculum and Instruction (mimeo).

Gee, J. 2004. *Situated Language and Learning: A Critique of Traditional Schooling*. London: Routledge.

Gee, J. P., Hull, G. and Lankshear, C. 1996. *The New Work Order: Behind the Language of the New Capitalism*. Boulder, CO: Westview Press.

Hull, G. and Schultz, K. 2001. Literacy and learning out of school: A review of theory and research. *Review of Educational Research* 71(4): 575–611.

Knobel, M. 1999. *Everyday Literacies: Students, Discourses and Social Practice*. New York: Peter Lang.

Knorr Cetina, K. 1992. The couch, the cathedral, and the laboratory: On the relationship between experiment and laboratory in science. In A. Pickering (Ed.), *Science as Practice and Culture*. Chicago: University of Chicago Press.

Kress, G. 2003. *Literacy in the New Media Age*. London: Routledge.

Lankshear, C. 1997. *Changing Literacies*. Buckingham & Philadelphia: Open University Press.

Lankshear, C. and Bigum, C. 1999. Literacies and new technologies in school settings. *Pedagogy, Culture and Society* 7(3): 445–65.

Lankshear, C. and Knobel, M. 2006. *New Literacies: Everyday Practices and Classroom Learning*. 2nd edn. New York: Open University Press.

Latour, B. 1987. *Science in Action*. Cambridge, MA: Harvard University Press.

Leander, K. 2003. Writing travellers' tales on new literacyscapes. *Reading Research Quarterly* 38(3), 392–97.

Leander, K. forthcoming. Toward a connective ethnography of online/offline literacy networks. In D. Leu, J. Coiro, M. Knobel and C. Lankshear (eds.), *A Handbook of New Literacies Research*. Mahwah, NJ: Erlbaum.

Leander, K. and Frank, A. 2006. The aesthetic production and distribution of image/subjects among online youth. *E-Learning* 3(2), 185–206.

Leander, K. and Lovvorn, J. 2006. Literacy networks: Following the circulation of texts, bodies, and objects in the schooling and online gaming of one youth. *Cognition & Instruction* 24(3), 291–340.

Lessig, L. 2004. *Free Culture: How Big Media Uses Technology and the Law to Lock Down Culture and Control Creativity*. New York: Penguin.

Lessig, L. 2005. Creative commons. Paper presented at the 2005 Annual ITU Conference, "Creative Dialogues." Oslo, Network for IT-Research and Competence in Education (ITU), University of Oslo.

Leu, D., Coiro, J., Knobel, M., and Lankshear, C. Forthcoming. *A Handbook of New Literacies Research.* Mahwah, NJ: Erlbaum.

Mills, C. Wright 1959. *The Sociological Imagination.* New York: Oxford University Press.

O'Reilly, T. 2005. What is Web 2.0?: Design patterns and business models for the next generation of software. oreillynet.com/pub/a/oreilly/tim/news/2005/09/30/what-is-web-20.html (accessed 4 April, 2006).

Schrage, M. 2001. The relationship revolution. seedwiki.com/wiki/Yi-Tan/TheRelationship Revolution.htm?wikipageversionid=417577&edit=yes&i=87 (accessed 4 April, 2006).

Scribner, S. and Cole, M. 1981. *The Psychology of Literacy.* Cambridge, MA: Harvard University Press.

Shirky, C. 2003. Power laws, weblogs and inequality. shirky.com/writings/powerlaw_ weblog.html (accessed 7 March, 2006).

Squire, K. Forthcoming. Videogames literacy. In D. Leu, J. Coiro, M. Knobel and C. Lankshear (eds.), *A Handbook of New Literacies Research.* Mahwah, NJ: Erlbaum.

Steinkuehler, C. Forthcoming. Cognition and literacy in Massively Multiplayer Online Games. In D. Leu, J. Coiro, M. Knobel and C. Lankshear (eds.), *A Handbook of New Literacies Research.* Mahwah, NJ: Erlbaum.

Street, B. 1984. *Literacy in Theory and Practice.* Cambridge: Cambridge University Press.

Street, B. 1995. *Social Literacies: Critical Approaches to Literacy in Development, Ethnography and Education.* London: Longman.

Street, B. 2001. Introduction, in B. Street (Ed.), *Literacy and Development: Ethnographic Perspectives.* London: Routledge.

Thomas, A. Forthcoming. Community, culture and citizenship in cyberspace. In D. Leu, J. Coiro, M. Knobel and C. Lankshear (eds.), *A Handbook of New Literacies Research.* Mahwah, NJ: Erlbaum.

Tunbridge, N. 1995. The cyberspace cowboy. *Australian Personal Computer.* December. 2–4.

CHAPTER TWO

"You Won't Be Needing Your Laptops Today": Wired Bodies in the Wireless Classroom

KEVIN M. LEANDER

Introduction

Ever since it had implemented its wireless laptop program three years previously, Ridgeview Academy struggled with a number of contradictions between traditional schooling and ubiquitous internet access. As one teacher put it, "You're kind of opening Pandora's box [the internet] and trying to just kind of stick it in a different box [the school]." Even as Ridgeview had heavily invested in providing internet access to its single gender (female) student body, it has also structured, over three years' time, an array of implicit and explicit means of closing this access. In short, Ridgeview Academy was a contradiction of social spaces: on the one hand it presented itself and technically structured itself to be an "open" wired social space for 21st century girls, while on the other hand, official school practices and discourses domesticated, or pedagogized (Street and Street 1991) potential openings of space-time provided by the wireless network. In official school practice, the wireless network was "rewired" or closed off and anchored in ways that reproduced traditional school space-time.

This chapter, then, begins with a puzzle. Suppose we imagine a school where access to computing and the internet is not a problem? Say, for instance, a private school for girls in grades 5–12, where parents buy new laptops for their daughters, who then carry them from class to class and home at night? What if this school had a wireless network installed throughout all of the buildings on its 38-acre campus? What might happen to schooling as we know it?

Technology Refusal

In an important article on the failure of most technological innovations to change the culture of schooling, now dated by over a decade, Hodas (1993) examines how technologies are value-laden, as is schooling itself, which is also a type of technology. Hodas argues that the mismatch between school values and technology values explains a great deal about why school practices are seemingly so intransigent. While critics of schools might conceive of them as failing or floundering in their relationship to technology, Hodas reminds us that schools, as institutions, are "doing exactly the jobs they were set up to do and have been refined over generations to perform." Even when new technological tools are introduced into this flow of practice and valuing, these tools fail to change what Hodas calls the "look-and-feel" of schooling, marked as it is by the "conservation and transmission of pre-existing, pre-defined categories of knowledge and being" (Hodas 1993, no page).

Hodas' (1993) argument is primarily sociological, considering schooled practice as institutional practice and examining something of the working conditions, career paths, and culture of teaching. The argument is also partially historical. Drawing from Cohen (1987), for example, Hodas argues that school structure and teaching practice has remained substantially unchanged for seven hundred years. He also cites Cuban (1986) to argue that new developments in information and entertainment technologies, as they move into the popular realm (e.g., radio, film, television, computers), bring with them a popular hope that they will "bring the classroom out of the dark ages and into the modern world" (Hodas 1993, no page).

In this chapter, I follow the impulse of Hodas' insight to consider how technologies are essentially social, and thus serve to constitute particular values, ideologies, preferred practices, power relations, social relations, and modes of learning. Likewise, schooling may be seen as a (heavily institutionalized) technology, and "refusal" or acceptance of technology in school must be understood as a relational construct—as some potentially frictional or smooth movement along the interstice of new tech/school-as-tech. However, I would also like to push beyond the sociological constructs that Hodas is drawing on, including institutional reproduction, school-as-factory, historical inertia, institutional self-preservation, and institutional irrationality. Sociologically and culturally, I argue that we need to consider a very basic dimension of school in order to understand its relation to technology: the production and organization of school space and time. While I posit this dimension as a general construct of interest for thinking about technological integration in schooling, I focus in particular on the relationship between school space-time and space-time as practiced by youth on the internet in their everyday lives. I argue that the challenge of "integrating" the internet into school is not chiefly technical, in the sense of providing tools and tool training, but rather spatial and temporal.

In this vein, Jones (forthcoming) discusses features of the schooling of space-time in his discussion of school-related digital literacies in Hong Kong. Drawing on Hall (1959), Jones contrasts the school's perspective as essentially monochronic (treating time as linear and tangible, and divisible) in contrast to the students' perspectives as essentially polychronic (seeing time as more fluid, layered, and simultaneous). In the monochronic orientation, one action occupies time to the exclusion of all other actions, an approach to activity that would be quite foreign to many cultural contexts, including much of the modern workplace (Gee, Hull and Lankshear 1996), and interestingly, the historical cultural practices of Mayan mothers interacting with their children (Rogoff et al. 1993).

Technologies That Support School Space-time

Hodas (1993) briefly discusses several technologies that appear to be perfectly suited to traditional schooling, including the blackboard, the overhead projector, and the duplicating (photocopy) machine. The primary sources of cultural match that Hodas discusses in most of these cases are that such technologies reduce the physical labor of teachers to communicate written information, and they also enhance the teacher's authoritative position. Rather than imagining the shoring up of authority as an explicit goal of such technologies, however, we might conceive of them as more implicitly involved in the constitution of school space-time. The blackboard and the overhead projector, for instance, gather entire classrooms of students around a common textual surface. The overhead projector has the added affordance of being run in a dimly lit room, so that other possible interactions are muted. Moreover, both blackboards and overhead projectors are used to temporally organize lessons and classroom activities; lessons often move left to right, across a single or multiple blackboards, and some teachers scroll entire sequences of activity (e.g., problem sets) on overhead transparency rolls. The photocopy machine provides for the repetition of a common text across the space of the classroom (or school), and is an important technology for creating lessons and common texts that span years and even decades of pedagogical practice. It is critically important to recognize that each of these technologies is typically controlled by a teacher or teacher assistant, not in an explicit display of power, or even toward that end. Rather, teacher bodies/technologies as ensembles are disciplined and configured to spatio-temporally produce and organize schooling as a particular kind of activity.

Given this background, it may come as no surprise that the most prevalent literacy practices in using the laptops at Ridgeview included the following:

1. Writing process pedagogies
2. Student note-taking
3. An online newsletter for the school community, produced by the central office
4. Distributing assignments and submitting work
5. Keeping absent students up-to-date
6. Quick searches for online information

With the exception of the last two practices, the most common uses of the laptops either did not require a wireless network, or were simply online versions of former print technologies and distributions (e.g., the school newsletter). Julie, one of the teachers, summarized the dominant practices as follows:

Julie:	I mean mostly in English it's still pretty staid, I still . . . I'm sure you know 90% of their work is . . . on a computer . . . is with a word program.
Kevin:	Taking notes?
Julie:	Taking notes, writing assignments, and writing papers. A lot of the stuff that I . . . I can do now though is rely on email to . . . email or our web to post assignments or if they were missing that day it's so much easier now to be able to say, "Boom, here's the worksheet; or here's the assignment sheet or whatever . . ."

At the same time, even though the laptops and network were used to support traditional school practices, these practices themselves were undergoing some internal change at Ridgeview, changes which can be conceived in terms of their spatial and temporal dimensions. For example, with respect to writing process pedagogies, students researched topics on the web in and out of school, and used email to gather information and conduct interviews. The laptops encouraged a constant writing process and the girls quickly moved into a project at whatever stage it was at: brainstorming, information gathering, drafting, revising or editing. The laptops also facilitated feedback as students exchanged drafts with peers and teachers via e-mail and loosened the boundaries of the school day and calendar. For instance, one teacher told students she would be giving them feedback on a project over spring break. Although the process of turning in a final draft of a paper could be chaotic and the laptops appeared to encourage last minute completion, they also seemed to encourage the final moments to become a dynamic space of feedback that was reportedly less present when students arrived in class with print versions of their pieces. In the new temporal arrangement, students enquired of themselves, peers, or the teacher regarding citations, grammatical points, and if enough textual support was present in their text in the final moments prior to online submission.

Discursive Conceptions of (Online and Offline) Social Spaces at Ridgeview

As I examine the case of Ridgeview in detail and attempt to bring a spatial perspective to its technology refusal, I dialectically interpret social space (Leander and Sheehy 2004, Leander 2002, Lefebvre 1991, Soja 1989) across representations (e.g., classroom texts, discourse, official documents concerning the wireless network), material structures (the network itself, classroom spaces), classroom practices (pedagogy as discursive and material practice) and the lived experiences of space-time by the students and teachers. In what follows, I engage two broad approaches on the constitution of social space. I first examine discourses (Fairclough 1995, Gee 1999) of social space, considering discourses (or, Discourses; Gee 1999) as not only ways of using language, but as the ways in which language use is related to thinking, valuing, acting, and identity work of all kinds (Gee 1999, 17). For Lefebvre (1991) and Soja (1989), discourses are a powerful constitution of second space, or conceived space; such conceptions have a hold on how spatiality is lived out, even more so than visible perceptions of space. I attempt to examine these discourses as multiple and conflicting; the first two sets are dramatized as "duels" to suggest how Ridgeview was caught up in a struggle of expansion and contraction. These discourses are primarily investigated by drawing on material from extended (1–2 hour) interviews with the high school principal and four faculty members: Barbara, Fran, and Julie (all of whom teach English) and Bill (who teaches Psychology). Following the discussion of these discourses, I examine specific vignettes of practice in order to consider how conceptions and perceptions of social space come together, and in particular, how the online space was domesticated and closed off at Ridgeview.

Strong Wired Women vs. Vulnerable Girls in Frightening Online Spaces

A first set of dueling discourses involves the school's construction of tech-savvy, strong young women on the one hand, and, on the other hand, the school's construction of them as girls who are vulnerable to all of the dangers on the internet and who need to be protected. The first discourse imagines the internet as a space for experiences that would help these young women compete and succeed in a (male dominated) technology world, whereas the second discourse imagines the internet as a space of stalkers, of uncontrolled behavior, of unknown dangers. The first discourse is constructed on the school's website, which uses technology as an artifact (Hine 2000) for identity construction and recruitment:

> [Ridgeview] is committed to preparing students to be effective users of information and ideas, because a well-rounded education requires preparing students for any type of career they might choose. [Ridgeview] strives to weave technology into everyday activities in the classroom and around the school.

The principal of the high school also constructed this discourse in relation to academic preparation for girls in areas previously dominated by boys:

> If you're going to have an all-girls' school, you need to afford them opportunities that they may not get in a co-ed environment, or may not get as concentrated in a co-ed environment. And so technology, math and science courses, areas that are not traditional to girls . . . that girls traditionally follow, I should say . . . are just, we feel are part of the mission. And they're part of the mission of the Coalition of Girls Schools, too, which is one of our associations, professional associations, is to push math and science. And along with that, technology in girls' curriculum.

In this instance, technology becomes described more as a curricular topic, akin to math and science, rather than as a set of social practices.

Barbara brought the two discourses together around the issues of teachers' and parents' goals. She related technology to the broader project of making the girls "stronger," and as part of developing the "whole student":

> I always have in the back of my mind what's going to help them be stronger. Now whether that's stronger than I was or stronger than they are right this second . . . and again, that's always a kind of intellectual, emotional and spiritual thing that I'm thinking about all the time. That whole student. So I'm always aware of that. And yet I also really want them to think of themselves and really enjoy being women. I don't want them . . . I'm not trying to . . . even though the men at the school sometimes accuse us of this because of some of the texts that we read, no I don't want them to be in that what used to be radical feminist sense of being angry with men. I want them to be able to really be great women and have great lives and get into the best college their parents can afford. Because finally that is our narrower mission. I mean, I think that's the reason most of their parents send them here, other than just to be safe. But we have broader goals for them.

Multiple tensions are apparent in Barbara's response, including the tension between being a "whole student," rather than an unbalanced student, with, for example, intellectual preparation but no emotional or spiritual preparation. Another evident tension involves the idea of being strong versus the idea of being angry with men, or a radical feminist. A final tension in the interview excerpt involves the narrower goal of "getting into the best college their parents can afford" and yet experiencing the broader goals of the faculty, which, presumably, include preparation as a "whole student." Safety is attributed to parent goals, and somewhat associated with the "narrower mission" of parents. Yet, safety was also more generally apparent as part of Barbara's discourse in responding to the internet and its potential threats to girls, many of which were relatively unknown. This discourse was apparent as Barbara described one of her teaching innovations with an internet-based chat room:

> And in fact this year started something that two or three other people picked up in the department and that I plan to pick up next year, which is this on line forum where the kids are . . . they're in their own little chat . . . they have their own little chat room basically. You post questions for them. I mean, it's closed. That's the other thing that's so scary about teaching girls and having them out in cyberspace. But that's a whole other story. But you have to have the proper I.D. to get into this chat room.

While Barbara couldn't think of any direct danger to the girls from being online, she had heard a story of one of the girls who had "gone off to meet someone" once she was in college, and she also recounted a story of a private school in Kentucky, where a friend of hers worked, that had been infected with an internet virus that downloaded porn into its network. The discourse of internet danger appeared, for Barbara, to be a site or node where the parents' narrow goals (of safety, and preparation for the best colleges) came together with the teachers' goals of educating the "whole student," including the student who was savvy about internet safety. Moreover, the idea that the internet was potentially dangerous, even though nothing particularly dangerous had happened to girls they knew, was a common feature of the discourse around internet danger among the faculty.

Other teachers more directly described the actual and potential dangers of internet spaces. Fran, for instance, described certain areas of the internet as containing "frightening places," such as "diary.com." She seemed to have a vague sense of such sites, but considered them as "filled with positive [possibilities] and fraught with some negatives":

> Well, they're sexual; they're inappropriate for people 13 and 14 years old. The language, you would . . . I would not quote to you the language that is on some of the . . . like dear diary or diary.com. I mean, it's blatant misuse of the computer, and one girl was suspended for it. I don't know. They have access to sites. I mean, I don't know how the word spreads.

The internet danger discourse here seems particularly gendered around the idea of protecting girls from sexual knowledge, such as contained also in inappropriate language. Fran also draws generally on policy to support her stance: "It's blatant misuse of the computer." Extending her discussion of this kind of event, Fran framed danger around the issue of development:

> There's a long time between 7th grade and your senior year. And I later learned . . . yeah my source of information is the [high school] girls. They spend a lot of time in [my classroom] . . . that a 7th grader was involved in one of those sorts, one of those sites where you post all sorts of information about what you're doing. And a lot of it has to do with drugs, alcohol and sex.

Here, the issue for Fran was not merely that girls would find their way into such knowledge and interaction (of drugs, alcohol, and sex) but that young girls, who weren't developmentally ready for such information, would encounter it before their time. Fran's discourse, including the use of general problem descriptors such as "drugs, alcohol, and sex," and the way in which she was relying on informants (older girls) to learn of internet dangers, shares with Barbara's discourse the feature that the greatest fears are those that are the most unknown.

One of the events that crystallized the dangers of the internet for the school community at a relatively early period in its development of the laptops program (i.e., in the third year of the program) was one student's Xanga site which was censored by the school. The principal of the high school described this event:

> [The student] was talking to friends outside of school and in school about her teachers and about people in the school, and very vulgar, very . . . in one instance I thought very threatening. And so she was caught and we . . . and now if you'd ask me how she got caught, I can't remember. Anyway, it came to me. I can't remember who brought it to me, but anyway somebody got their hands on it and brought it to me, and she came before the discipline committee and received a five-day out of school suspension, which is pretty devastating. We don't do that much around here. Thank goodness we don't need to. And I think all in all the embarrassment of it and the realization of it made her want to leave the community. And she eventually left. And then . . . so that would be the most egregious thing we've had.

This event framed the discourse of internet danger around the idea that the internet could be used to do dangerous things. In this case, it is the girls themselves, under the influence of the internet, who are potentially dangerous and are putting others in the school community at risk. The idea that "teachers and other people in the school" were represented in the student's blog interactions in "vulgar" and even "threatening" ways was seen as a direct threat to the school as a certain type of community, with an investment in its own image and how this image was protected. The offender's response of "want[ing] to leave the community" is described as a natural outcome of her individual offense of harming the community and its agreed upon values. With respect to social space, this case is particularly noteworthy in that the student was posting to her blog both in and out of school. She was constituting and challenging representations of the school in space where the school had little control. Hence, her danger to the reputation of the school, through representations, was responded to, eventually, by helping to constitute her identity as (spatially) outside that of the school. In this case, relatively isolated, but nonetheless significant in the eyes of the students, faculty, and administration at Ridgeview, the discourse of internet danger became framed as a threat to the school community: students engaging in internet dangers threatened the integrity of the school community. Here, internet danger was supported by institutional discourses of school community, school policy, and school reputation.

Open and Closed Information Spaces

A second set of dueling discourses among the Ridgeview faculty and administration involved, on the one hand, opening up the classroom to a wide range of available information, and on the other hand, reconstructing the classroom as a closed information space. Key in this spatial dilemma are containment and closure as ways of measuring individual knowledge. With ubiquitous online access, the individual can become connected to an unprecedented world of texts. The vision of open information access—seeing the internet as an unlimited digital library—is supported by the discourse of the liberal arts tradition, which was dominant in the school. From this perspective, the internet is the new library at Alexandria, containing all classic and modern works, print and paintings alike. Fran expresses something of this tradition:

> Well [the internet] certainly has enlarged their world within the walls of this school because they can go anywhere or do anything as they're . . . and some of it is terrific. And for example, I had them do broadsides on poets and several of them pulled up art, pieces of art to put . . . that they thought . . . there's a "Starry Night" poem by Ann Sexton, and somebody had on her broadside "Starry Night" by Van Gogh. So that kind of access is fabulous. It breaks down the world, the walls.

In making their broadsides or posters, the students could "go anywhere," with "anywhere" defined as a voyage through the liberal arts where new texts would be found to support canonical texts and authors authorized by the school.

The discourse of bounding the school as a closed information space is constituted and supported in different ways. One relatively simple way is through online/offline distinctions as formed by the faculty, where offline texts are privileged, as in Barbara's remark following:

> You know, at first we had to make them do certain things with technology. For example, in our research that we do . . . used to be the kids automatically went to books and you had to build into the assignment, and you must use at least one online source. Well now it's the opposite. They immediately go to the online sources and you have to say, "You have to look at so many books or printed articles or things like that."

The online/offline distinction functions as the definitive quality of a "source," a binary of two different types of media. Since the students wanted to give online sources primacy, Barbara and other faculty suggested that they now needed to be taught to focus attention on offline print. Another discourse on closing the information space indexed in Barbara's response involves distraction from schooling through too many texts, or too many unauthorized texts. This discourse is connected to how adolescent identity is more generally constructed as easily distracted:

> And you know . . . and teenagers have always been distracted, but it's a difference, I feel, between being distracted by a magazine and being distracted by every magazine ever written. You know . . . and on top of having at their fingertips every magazine ever written, they have every book ever written, every comment on every book ever written, every piece of art, their boyfriend's e-mailing them from [another school]. And it's difficult. And we've got some ways that we're going to try to be able to control that in classroom settings in later years.

The idea of distraction, discussed in the following section, is even more strongly related to the notion of the problem of the internet being a mode for communication (rather than information), which severely disrupts schooled assumptions about containment and surveillance of individual activity in identifiable locales.

The most powerful conflicts with the discourse of an open information space involve, unsurprisingly, testing and writing events imagined as individual performances. Test cheating and writing plagiarism are seen as supported by the internet as an open text space. While these issues can be described as school practices that enter into conflict with new technology practices, a spatial perspective here is instructive in examining the conflicting assumptions and ideologies of school and widespread internet activity spaces. The school test is typically based on the idea of the individual who is isolated from her or his environment, with the "open book" test being an exception to this idea. (Even open book tests are often temporally structured in school such that, while books are available, they are not practically of much use in the given time slot of the test.) The school test is also often structured around the idea that much of what is taught and tested is known information, available in the world in the format in which it was given. With an open information space, the idea of the skill set necessary to succeed changes entirely. In this case, rather than remembering information, locating, and, if necessary, combining and synthesizing information are at stake. The laptops program at Ridgeview brought these two discourses into direct conflict, and with respect to testing, began to close the newer space of open information through the containment of testing, as captured in Fran's remark:

> The downside is that there are things like Sparknotes. We had two girls last year that were doing in-class essays and apparently had Sparknotes up and then minimized and were cutting and pasting to their own essay. Now when I have an in-class essay . . . and

I have them sit on the inside of the circle so I can see all the screens. Next year we have, as a department, agreed that in-class essays will be hand written.

Fran also described how she had begun to rethink how she assigned compositions for the students, given that students could just go online and either order papers from essay mills for "$9.95," or would simply cut and paste from other papers and put a patchwork together of their own. Fran primarily framed this issue as one of moral failure on the part of the students: their lives were simply too busy, and the temptation was too great to cut corners and plagiarize. Thus, the machinery she described putting into place for her own teaching involved more steps on the part of the student to document how information had been accessed and combined:

I have had to redo how I assign papers to avoid, to help them avoid, the temptations of plagiarism. I now, they always do a topic outline in class. They always do their full outline in class. I require that they use citations from the Tennessee Electronic Library. They have to print their article and highlight what they're using. In other words . . . and I develop topics that don't lend themselves to being pumped into the computer.

Again, as in the case of testing, the idea of what it meant to be knowledgeable or to do knowledge work was not challenged. The space of where knowledge was located (in authorized texts and individual memories) and how it was measured (in individual performances) and what it was characterized by (unique voices) was held stable. Indeed, in some ways, the school's response to the open information space became hyper-schooled and closed, where processes that were relatively less visible in early eras of school research (e.g., uses of source material) were now being brought under scrutiny. Barbara explains:

And in fact with our freshmen we've decided we're going to go back to paper note cards that they have to use first. And then we do have an electronic note card program that we teach the kids that is pretty fun. But if they don't have a sort of visual sense of what a note card is and what you're supposed to put on it to start with, it's hard to understand what you're supposed to do with an electronic card except just download information into it.

The Damaged Classroom Interaction Space

In addition to the duels of discourses that positioned the girls online, and with respect to access to texts, a powerful discourse among the faculty regarded the damage to classroom interaction from online activity. This discourse is most strongly associated with how the communication dimension of ICT's (the "C") is downplayed or denied with respect to the information dimension, but as the previous section discussed, the information dimension is not unproblematic for school space either. In this discourse, with respect to communication, the laptops were seen as damaging to classroom interaction in that they distracted girls into forms of communication and activity other than the core communicative activity at hand. Second, beyond their promotion of multi-spatial activity, the laptops were seen as damaging by putting up physical barriers between interlocutors in the classroom.

Prior to considering these activity and physical aspects of the discourse in turn, it seems useful to consider some assumptions common to English and social studies courses, where texts and talk play a central role. At a semi-abstract level, we might describe the flow of texts and talk in many such classes as moving through the following stages:

1. Some common print text is given as "input" (e.g., a poem, an image, an historical description).
2. Oral interpretation by the teacher and students follows, in the form of recitation or discussion.
3. The teacher has full access to this oral interpretation and all participants in it, and a key role in guiding it. The oral interpretation has one common context or "footing" (Goffman 1981).
4. Later, some common print output (e.g., test or composition) is assigned that draws on the input text and the oral interpretation.

The sequence may seem painfully obvious, but these basic assumptions about the constitution of space through texts and talk are important to recognize in considering that it is not only through the common (monospatial) text that wireless practices might challenge these assumptions, but also through the types of literacy practiced, often against the common flows of the classroom.

Following is a re-description of classroom interaction as shaped by wireless online access:

1. A common print text is given as "input" and accompanied by many other uncommon textual inputs that are read simultaneously to it, and against it.
2. Oral interpretation by the teacher and students follow, which is highly mixed with (digital) print interpretations developed by individuals.
3. The teacher has only partial access to the interpretations, many of which extend beyond the classroom space to distal online spaces and persons, taking on multiple footings and emotional "keys" (Goffman 1981). The teacher is one participant in the interaction, but much less central and sometimes at the periphery.
4. Oral (schooled) interaction is seen as something to record in print for further study rather than something to engage in for its own right.
5. Later, a print output, once assigned, can draw on input text, on the print record of schooled interaction, and from a pastiche of online and offline texts.

These contrasting lists begin to suggest how monospatiality is contested through ubiquitous online access, and also through the "hyperliteracy" of online interaction in the classroom. Teachers lament that everyone seems to be writing, but no one talking. The classroom space of common talk around common texts is damaged. For the text-talk-text pedagogue, the classroom becomes asocial, nonsensical. The discussion below suggests more of how this discourse is constituted and sustained.

Distraction. One of the most common complaints about the laptops in the classroom space involved how online interaction distracted the girls into a range of individual activity, most of which involved communication of some type. This type of activity was seen as off-task by teachers, and often framed through the lens of management and discipline, as evident in the high school principal's consideration:

> I'm sure kids order their summer wardrobe off of AOL in their spare time. One of the keys to making a laptop program work is classroom management. And teachers really have to watch what their kids are doing. I think it's a lot of kids who appear to be taking classroom notes, are actually just e-mailing their friends. And it's . . . we call it electronic note passing. It's just a little harder to police . . . But you know, if a teacher can watch a kid, then that really keeps it from getting to the disciplinary level, before it comes before a discipline committee.

Teachers often lamented that just before they could correct a student's behavior, the student would minimize the computer window of the off-task, and thus the procedural display (Bloome, Theodorou and Puro 1989) of "good student" would be maintained.

Julie noted coming to a kind of compromise for herself: if the students appeared to be taking notes and participating at the same time in the common talk of the classroom, then she would back off policing their activity:

> And sometimes if they're taking notes and if I can tell they're on task and they can also look up and you know sort of participate at the same time that's fine. If they don't need it and if they're not taking notes and if I have a suspicion that, you know, what they're looking at instead is, I don't know, some kind of email or you know it's hard to tell sometimes and you don't want to stop in the middle of class and be the laptop police but I'll just tell them, "Put your laptops down we don't need them, let's just talk." So that's what we'll do instead.

This movement to limiting the use of the laptops to only times when they were specifically needed, as deemed by the teachers, was a common response across the classrooms we observed and teachers we interviewed. In interview, Fran frames this response as a return to the "old fashioned class," which seems most appropriate for indexing the reconstitution of classroom space:

Fran: But I don't want to spend my time wandering around the back side of this classroom trying to catch people who are e-mailing. I want to spend my time thinking about what we're talking about and getting them to engage in a conversation. And one of the things I think I have to try . . . now maybe . . . you'll have to ask me next year. I think I've got to limit the use of the computer.

Kevin: To get that attention focused.

Fran: Yeah, and to make it more like the old, an old fashioned class. I've noted to you that I think that first period class is very quiet and not interactive, that I find myself having to survey that class. And a lot of it is they all use their computers. They're all behind those screens.

Fran further described how she felt that the laptop use was responsible for the classroom losing its "unity," "personality," and "spark": ". . . if they're not instant messaging or e-mailing, if they're just staring at the pictures that they've put on their screen, they're not really with you." This experience of being "with" the teacher is central to the discourse of the laptops interfering with the classroom interaction space, as is the idea of "unity." The teachers often described nostalgia for the pre-laptop days, in which interaction was more focused, common conversations richer, and teacher roles within these common conversations were clearer.

Atypically, Barbara departed somewhat from the discourse on distraction and considered how different practices might reframe the use of the laptops in the classroom. In particular, Barbara was impressed with the use of an online forum by one of the young, new science teachers in the school, who would structure online conversations among students prior to their arrival in class. Barbara saw Kristen's ability to create this activity as linked to her generational mindset being closer to that of the students: "I mean . . . for Kristin it's not a problem. For me it's a problem. But she's . . . she's in her 20s, I'm in my 40s. That's the difference." Barbara, however, also asserted the importance of verbally arguing one's ideas in public as central to English education, to the school's broader purposes of educating strong young women, and to their future prospects in college. At the same time, she questioned and challenged how such values might be changing:

You know you have all this clicking sound all over the place in ways that you didn't when people were just taking notes on a piece of notebook paper. I don't know. It changes the dynamic of your classroom. I mean that seems really trivial, but for an English class that's a big deal because so much of what . . . even when we used to talk about part of what we want our students to learn. It's to articulate verbally certain ideas and to be able to have that kind of debate and intellectual debate. And again I think that's important for young women. You've got to be able to have an idea and defend it.

And that's important for all young people, but you know, it becomes particularly important, I think, as we send these girls off into other academic institutions where they're just going to have to hold their own. And maybe they don't need to anymore. I don't know. Maybe I just need to get into a few college classrooms for a while and see what they're asked to do. Maybe it doesn't matter if they articulate it in [an online] forum or if they articulate it verbally.

Physical barriers. Faculty at Ridgeview conceived that the classroom interaction space was damaged not only by the lack of common activity, but also by the physical barriers created by the laptops. In this manner, first space (materially observable) and second space (discursively constituted) (Lefebvre 1991, Soja, 1989) appeared to be coordinated, not in opening up thirdspace, but rather in affirming the loss (and nostalgia) experienced in the classroom space under the reign of the laptops program. Many of the teachers described how their own physical positions were affected, and how they could no longer see students' faces and eyes with the laptops. The essential primacy of physical interaction was very strong in these responses, as reflected by Bill, the psychology teacher:

> Bill: But in terms of . . . I could sit at a student desk with all the other ones and psychologically that's where I like to be. And I think it works better in terms of drawing out discussion. What also is bad, just from a purely physical standpoint, many of the girls can't be seen. Their faces are shielded from peers because they're behind the screen. And I personally have to tell them to lower the screen, or they'll look and they're talking between their screen and their neighbor's screen. I can't always . . . I have to read lips a lot of times and I have to say, lower your laptop, I can't see you. I have to . . . and it just . . .
>
> Kevin: You don't see their mouth and you don't see their eyes.
>
> Bill: Right. It walls them off and I can't . . . if their head is down I don't know if they're working at the . . . I don't know always what is going on. So in that sense I don't like what it's done to that part of the atmosphere in here. It's made it a little less open. Does that make sense?

First, Bill reflects in this segment on his own position vis-à-vis the students: he likes to take a position on the same physical level as the student, but feels this is affected by a physical laptop barrier. This physical barrier also creates a fragmented classroom space where the girls can carry out verbal, offline conversations with peers. Bill also suggests that this physical shield prevents him from monitoring activity-in-common, as we saw with the distraction of online interaction, previously considered. Finally, Bill notes that the physical (and presumably, digital) barriers have made the face-to-face interaction in his class "a little less open." His discourse asserts how closure had been affected by the physical erection of new boundaries.

Likewise, Julie expressed a notion of physical separation similar to that of Bill:

Julie: Right off the bat as soon as we got [the laptops out] I was amazed that day at how much it changed [everything] because immediately those black cases went up, their faces were in the computer and it looked to . . . from my perspective like a classroom full of tombstones . . . it literally deadened the class because everybody was involved, you know, in their individual little program, their individual little projects, you know. There was no interaction.

Kevin: This was supposed to be discussion?

Julie: No, no, no. I was just trying like, oh, they had just gotten their laptops. Let me create, you know whatever we were going to do, let's do this online or whatever and ah and I lost them I just felt like I had no connection with them whatsoever.

Particularly striking in Julie's response is the embedded assumption that even when the teacher and students are not involved in some activity of common interaction, such as classroom discussion, a kind of habitus (Bourdieu 1977) or embodied assumption of being able to see, monitor, and immediately recognize some type of activity in common was at the base of her experience of the class as a space of life. Individual activity online, within the classroom space, with its privileging of face to face, verbal interaction, was experienced by Julie as death, and as a loss of her own personal sense of connection and purpose. Finally, not only did virtually all of the teachers interviewed conceive of the laptops as interfering with the physical space of the classroom by erecting barriers, many of them also commented on how difficult it was for them to attempt to move about the classroom and monitor laptop activity. In classrooms that already felt small, the addition of laptops, cords, power strips, new desk arrangements (to allow for monitoring), computer cases, and books on the floor contributed to teachers' constructions of loss of the classroom space and loss of their mobility within it.

The Schooling of Digital Space at Ridgeview: Vignettes of Practice

The most obvious examples of the bracketing of school space and time that might come to mind for secondary schooling would be the walled divisions of classrooms (and respective student groups) and the separation of learning into 50 or 55 minute periods. Beyond these obvious features of the pedagogization (Street and Street 1991) of space-time, a number of other prominent features of pedagogization were recognizable within the digital literacy practices at Ridgeview:

- Defined plans precede resources and activity; actors know what they need or are seeking in advance.
- Sequential activity is dominant, and everyone follows the same sequential path.
- Asynchronous communication is primary to synchronous communication (e.g., e-mail or web searching is more "schooled" than instant messaging).
- A single space is dominant (and under surveillance) for each task; "task" is mono-spatial and "off-task" is partially defined as departure into another social space.
- Public social spaces, including the internet, must be bracketed for student use; school needs to produce kindergartens of public spaces for students to understand them, learn within them, and be safe within them.
- Material print texts and print spaces (the built environment) are primary and are authorized, while virtual texts are unauthorized and supplemental.
- The internet is primarily tool for information rather than a tool for communication. Information and Communication Technologies (ICT's) are primarily "IT's" in school.

These features of schooling or pedagogizing digital space at Ridgeview, where the thinking, valuing, and identity work of space-time practices becomes evident not only in discourse but also in activity, are briefly captured below in four vignettes of practice. This discussion is not intended as a critique of particular pedagogical practices (in fact, some of the experiments with new online forms of pedagogy were admirable), but more broadly aims to understand how schooling involves the production of space-time that remains invisible until challenged by other spatialities and temporalities, such as those produced by ICTs.

Vignette one: Library research. All of the 9th grade English classes were sent to the library during different class periods to conduct research on a poetry project. The project, assigned over a few weeks, included gathering several poems around a common theme, formal explications of two poems, a foreword, and other work. On the library visit, the teachers and the librarian put a great deal of emphasis on the idea that the girls should privilege the material space of the library over access to texts in virtual space. Directions given by the librarian about resources targeted specific shelves and carts:

> This side of the cart has books for freshmen on it. Check the books here first. Then do a power search of the card catalogue. Check the websites at home on your own time.

The directions to first make use of the material library space may be considered part of a practical consideration of what was being made available only at official times (the school library). However, several well-schooled assumptions about space-time are built into this activity that are made more evident by the eventual responses of the girls. Among them, everyone was directed to follow the same sequential path in searching for information, print texts were primary to digital texts, "checking websites" was associated with home space-time, and the built environment was primary over the virtual. (In this latter regard, it is noteworthy that, while the school is entirely wireless, the girls went to the library to do a search in its online card catalogue.)

The practice of separating and bounding space-time was not limited to making distinctions between the material and virtual worlds, however, but was also evident in boundaries within online space. The school had bracketed its own card catalogue as a primary source on the web and the librarian had also provided a list of key poetry websites, including "Poet's Corner," "Favorite Poem Project," and "Poetry 180." A common assumption in this case was that the school had taken a piece of the web that was prepared and authorized for student engagement—a type of web *kindergarten*. To search the card catalogue and other resources culled by the librarians, the library staff had attempted to teach the girls what they termed a "power search," using particular Boolean operators to find information:

> Barbara: Today you are trying to get the poems you love. What words would you use to do a power search of what's here in the library?

An operating assumption across the teachers and librarian was that the students needed a large degree of guidance directing them toward specific online texts, and that online space needed to be greatly simplified and selected for these explorations. On the other hand, browsing was an encouraged practice among the books. Barbara remarked that she was worried that students would go online and simply end up with "poetry written by some kid in Kansas." (On more than one occasion, Kansas or other Midwestern locations were represented as sources of low quality online texts composed by students.)

Several of the girls' individual practices during this library visit are indicative of the difficulty of structuring and enforcing a single space-time with the wireless network and the developed histories of information searching that the girls brought to the event. As the first girl we observed entered "American Poets" into the search engine Google, a second pulled a book from a library shelf and used the directory Yahoo to verify whether the author was American (a project requirement). A third girl attempted a power search of the online card catalogue on fairy poems, with no results, while a fourth, her partner, searched for fairy poems in Google. A fifth girl had brought a book of poems with her from her friend's locker and browsed through it. Another student spent some of her time looking through books on the cart shelves, while also talking with Barbara about her possible theme. Yet another student used most of the searching time in the library to work on a report for her psychology class, including conducting research online. None of the students that we observed followed the sequential, ordered path across resources and space-time as ordered by the librarian and teachers, and only a minority used "power searching" or the online card catalogue.

Vignette two: Online information and text hunt. A second example makes evident some of the same ways in which online space-time was schooled or pedagogized (Street and Street 1991) within school. Figure 2.1 is a copy of a web-based assignment that the students received from Fran in relation to the text *The Joy Luck Club*. As with the work in the library, the assignment involves a bracketed selection of websites made available from the school's "Webliographer" (moreover, a pre-selection of a few sites is made in this case), and the assignment is structured uniformly and sequentially (note the teacher's recommendation to "check off" steps). Moreover, in this case it is very clear that using the web is of secondary importance to following directions. For instance, step 5 simply involves printing off a compass image, which resulted in the same image being printed by every girl in the class. Concerning this assignment, Fran remarked that she thought that following directions was particularly important for girls to learn, who did not "get as many experiences following directions as boys do," and in particular, directions for technical processes. Boys, for instance, would be more apt to build models from a kit and have such direction reading and following experiences.

Besides Fran's particular discursive construction of what girls are lacking, and what might be necessary to help construct strong girl identities with respect to technology, a striking characteristic of this assignment is the way in which it presents the internet as a strange territory, and positions the girls as tourists in this foreign land. Indeed, like many online assignments at Ridgeview, the assignment reveals more about the teacher's relationship to online spaces than the girls' histories in such spaces.

Vignette three: Discussion Board. On another occasion, also associated with the study of *The Joy Luck Club*, Fran had set up a discussion board for students to post responses to her specific questions about the text. The online discussion was relatively short-lived and appeared in some ways even more formal than did oral classroom discussions. The space-time bracketing of the discussion board had much in common with how web spaces were bracketed in other forays into cyberspace. In this case, the discussion board was set up as part of the school's intranet, separate and not available to others outside of the school. Despite her detailed instructions (steps written on the black board) on how to access the discussion board, the class activity and computers broke down when it was introduced. Only three students in the class appeared to have permission to reply to the postings that Fran had made. The teacher circulated around the room to solve problems, and asked for students who seemed to be having computer problems to take their computers down to the "Lion's Den" (a computer repair center staffed by the school). Three students responded and left the room with their laptops immediately, returning ten minutes later, when a fourth student left.

Joy Luck Club: An investigation of Chinese culture

This assignment is designed to give you a sense of the cultural heritage of the Chinese American. In addition, it will familiarize you with another form of writing. Hopefully you will become a little bit Chinese. This assignment is specifically designed to improve your ability **to read and follow directions;** thus, this will be an **important** part of your grade.

Since the directions are so integral to the assignment, I suggest you begin by printing the directions. They are complicated and involve several steps. Printing them will allow you to reread **when** you need to do so. You might even want to **check off** what you have done.

1. Go to the Webliographer. Put in the following address: www.ocrat.com. Go to "Animated Chinese Characters" in the list of selections to the left. Write the word "east" using the Chinese character on unlined paper of your own. Enrichment: write the name of someone you admire or have a crush on.

2. Go to the Zodiac. First write the date of this year's Chinese New Year. Next, find which animal represents you. You do this by pulling down the menu until you find the year you were born. The year you were born determines the animal that represents you. Record this information. Also record the years and animals which represent the rest of your family and the boy you have a crush on. Write the character which represents your animal.

3. Go to the category "Numbers." Write your age in Chinese characters.

4. Go to "Countries." Write in Chinese the name of a country you would like to visit.

5. Go to "Compass." Print the illustration of the compass.

6. Go to a new site: www.new-year.co.uk/chinese. Send a card to a friend or teacher here at school. Check out the Fortune Cooking sayings. Record three that you like. You will need these for a class activity so choose well.

Figure 2.1. Web-based assignment from Fran's class

Fran instructed the students to write down the web link for the discussion board in their notebooks, and moved on to a different plan of discussing the novel. This planned activity and its breakdown could be analyzed from different angles; my primary interest is in how the breakdown is at least partially created by the attempt to create a separate, well-schooled space for interaction. The discussion board isn't very accessible because it is made to be difficult for those outside of the school to access. But, like a pill bottle, no one can seem to get easily past the child- and adult-proofing placed upon the discussion board. This closure is even more evident by how, ironically, during this event of failed access to a well-schooled web, several students in the class were simultaneously involved in online activity that reached far beyond school space-time: one read others' Xanga entries and composed a new entry on her own blog, another student was playing a computer game, and other girls used instant messaging, all officially unsanctioned school activities that depended upon its wireless network and upon publicly available media spaces.

Vignette four: Testing. Over time, while there were some experiments with new forms of pedagogy that involved new forms of digital literacy practice at Ridgeview, attempts with these new practices, or even passively allowing the laptops to be present, were beginning to be closed off during the period of our study. For example, near the end of the third year of its laptops program, the English department agreed to have students write in-class essay exams by hand rather than with their laptops for the following academic year. This policy was to prevent students from cheating on literature tests by culling information from the internet, a practice that had been only partially contained through the teachers' efforts to survey the offline/online social spaces of student work through panoptic practices (e.g., rearranging the desks in a circle for easy walk-arounds). Rather than challenging the tests themselves, the use of texts that are canonized for school on the internet, or the social-spatial assumptions of knowledge existing "inside" the individual and needing to be assessed, the teachers reproduced classic school space-time and had the students close their laptops.

Reform, Technology, and Social Space

This chapter began with a dilemma: Why might it be that a school that has solved the computer and internet access problem, a school in which online access is nearly ubiquitous, would ultimately find itself refusing technology? Why does school seem so intransigent? By examining discourses and pedagogical practices at this school, I have argued that in order to understand the mismatch of schooling on wireless practices, we need to think more fundamentally, beyond the evidence of apparent social practices, values, institutional reproduction, and historical inertia. We need to think, I have posited, about the schooled organization of space-time. History does not provide its own explanation for refusal, or stasis, or reproduction. Rather, as argued by Soja (Soja, 1996), the social, the historical, and the spatial are tied up in complex dialectical, (or trialectical) relations. Social life is both productive of space and produced within the spatialities that precede it; schooled life is never far from schooled space as it has been historically produced and socially reproduced in everyday practice.

However, both schooling and new technologies are often seen as located within social space rather than productive of it. At Ridgeview, this perspective on technology was most apparent in discussions of how reform might occur. A prominent conception was that curriculum must remain at the center of anything "new," and that new technologies must support goals already in place from the curriculum. The dominance of this conception of technology, curriculum, and reform is apparent across the following interview excerpts:

Fran: I start with the belief that the technology must be an outgrowth of the curriculum and that the curriculum can't be formed to appease the technology. And that has been a difficult thing at this school. We have a very strong technology force that even though . . . that expects you to develop curriculum so you can use the technology, even though they don't see that they're doing that.

Julie: Yeah and all we've gotten, which is great, from the administration is just reassurance, keep doing what you're doing, include them if it works with the curriculum, include it if it enhances the curriculum but not just as busy work or just because they're there.

Barbara: And my own colleagues, I think, would be the place that I'd like to start and really hear what they have to say and what they're doing. You know, I mean . . . I guess what I've tried to do, my two rules of thumb: number one, make sure that whatever I'm doing really does enhance the curriculum rather than just being the tidal wave that washes over it. It's very difficult, though.

Bill: And I felt pressure with kids coming out of our middle school doing a lot of laptop stuff. And then they get to my class and I'm sitting there saying, I don't care if you bring it or not.

The idea that teachers might "keep doing what [they're] doing," and that technology might "enhance" or be an "outgrowth" of the curriculum, is essentially a guarantee that the social space of schooling will be saturated by the relations set forth in current curricular practice, including the dominance of mono-spatial activity, sequential activity, text-talk-text cycles, the school as a safe harbor, and other dimensions of schooled spatiality examined across the course of this chapter. Neither the curriculum nor technology is fully spatialized in this view; technology, in particular, is seen as an add-on, a "tool" to support forms of practice that are well-rehearsed circuits that travel along deep grooves.

A key difficulty, of course, is that "keep doing what you're doing" discourse is not merely about refusal, but about giving reassurances to teachers that change can happen gradually and incrementally. While almost everything (the curriculum and pedagogy) can stay the same, technology can be brought in to "work with" teaching and learning, adjusting here, supporting there. However, when the package of technology brought into school involves ubiquitous wireless computing, this kind of promissory note to teachers is fundamentally unsound and even unethical. Because, even as teachers keep doing what they're doing in well schooled space-time, wired kids like many of the girls at Ridgeview bring the following productions of space-time with them to the classroom, through practices and orientations that we have observed in online activity across school and home contexts (see Table 2.1).

This chart only begins to suggest some key differences among traditionally schooled productions of space-time and those practiced by wired kids. It is not intended as a list or recipe of what school ought to become, but rather as one means of understanding the dilemma of introducing laptops and wireless internet into

TABLE 2.1. Space-time productions

Schooled Productions of Space-time	Productions of Space-time Common to Everyday Online Practices
• Defined plans precede resources and activity; actors know what they need or are seeking in advance. • Sequential activity is dominant, and everyone follows the same sequential path.	• Plans develop within activity; actors seek out materials that they need in the course of acting. • Simultaneous activity is normative. Simultaneity is an orientation toward social practice and not a psychological deficit, overload, or resistance, or something else.
• Asynchronous communication is primary to synchronous communication (e.g., e-mail or web searching is more "schooled" than instant messaging).	• Synchronous communication and simultaneity involves monitoring and responding to fluctuating demands of diverse activities as they emerge over time; attention economy.
• A single space is dominant (and under surveillance) for each task; "task" is mono-spatial and "off-task" is partially defined as departure into another social space. • Public social spaces, including the internet, must be bracketed for student use; school needs to produce kindergartens of public spaces for students to understand them, learn within them, and be safe within them.	• Multiple spaces are the norm of practice; action happens *relationally, across* spaces. • Decision-making regarding trustworthy and safe social spaces is embedded in routine practice. Public-private-institutional boundaries are not fixed.
• Material print texts and print spaces (the built environment) are primary and are authorized, while virtual texts are unauthorized and supplemental.	• Online/offline distinctions concerning textual authority are not strongly held; no material bias and online preference likely.
• The internet is a primarily a tool for information rather than a tool for communication. Information and Communication Technologies (ICT's) are primarily "IT's" in school.	• Communication and information are highly integrated; information and communication flows are co-constituted in practice.

well-schooled space. If the goal of such an introduction is to move beyond the domestication of online space-time—to not experience the meeting of schooling and online technologies as containment and closure—then educators must re-imagine and re-enact the social life of schooling as spatial practice.

References

Bloome, D., Theodorou, E. and Puro, P. 1989. Procedural display. *Curriculum Inquiry* 19(3): 265–91.

Bourdieu, P. 1977. *Outline of a Theory of Practice.* Cambridge: Cambridge University Press.

Cohen, D. 1987. Educational technology, policy, and practice. *Educational Evaluation and Policy Analysis* 9 (Summer): 153–70.

Cuban, L. 1986. *Teachers and Machines: The Classroom Use of Technology Since 1920.* New York: Teachers College Press.

Fairclough, N. 1995. *Critical Discourse Analysis: The Critical Study of Language.* London: Polity.

Gee, J. 1999. *An Introduction to Discourse Analysis: Theory and Method.* London: Routledge.

Gee, J., Hull, G., and Lankshear, C. 1996. *The New Work Order: Behind the Language of the New Capitalism.* Boulder, CO: Westview.

Goffman, E. 1981. *Forms of Talk.* Philadelphia, PA: University of Pennsylvania Press.

Hall, E. 1959. *The Silent Language.* Garden City, NY: Doubleday.

Hine, C. 2000. *Virtual Ethnography.* Thousand Oaks, CA: Sage.

Hodas, S. 1993. Technology refusal and the organizational culture of schools. *Educational Policy Analysis Archives* 1(10). epaa.asu.edu/epaa/v1n10.html (accessed June 5, 2006).

Jones, R. (forthcoming). Sites of engagement as sites of attention: Time, space, and culture in electronic discourse. In S. Norris and R. Jones (Eds), *Discourse in Action: Introducing Mediated Discourse Analysis.* London: Routledge.

Leander, K. 2002. Silencing in classroom interaction: Producing and relating social spaces. *Discourse Processes* 34(2): 193–235.

Leander, K., and Sheehy, M. (Eds). 2004. *Spatializing Literacy Research and Practice.* New York: Peter Lang.

Lefebvre, H. 1991. *The Production of Space* (D. Nicholson-Smith, Trans.). Cambridge, MA: Blackwell.

Rogoff, B., Göncü, A., Mistry, J., Mosier, C., Chavajay, P. and Heath, S. 1993. Guided participation in cultural activity by toddlers and caregivers. *Monographs of the Society for Research in Child Development* 58(8): i, ii, v–vi, 1–179.

Soja, E. 1989. *Postmodern Geographies: The Reassertion of Space in Critical Social Theory.* London: Verso.

Soja, E. 1996. *Thirdspace: Journeys to Los Angeles and Other Real-and-Imagined Places.* Malden, MA: Blackwell.

Street, J. and Street, B. 1991. The schooling of literacy. In D. Barton and R. Ivanic (Eds), *Writing in the Community.* Newbury Park, CA: Sage. 106–31.

CHAPTER THREE

Popular Websites in Adolescents' Out-of-School Lives: Critical Lessons on Literacy

JENNIFER C. STONE

Introduction

I first became interested in popular websites several years ago when I was working as a teacher and curriculum coordinator for an after school program for middle school students of color. I noticed that during time in the computer labs, students were often sneaking peeks at websites. I would see several students huddled around a computer, talking, laughing, reading, and writing, all the while deeply engaged. Then, as adults would walk past, they would quickly close the sites and switch back to the official work of the program.

Later, while teaching a workshop on website design in the same program, I started talking more to young people about these sites. In the workshop, students learned about various genres of websites and constructed their own informational sites. At one point during the workshop, a student who I call Devonte turned to me and stated matter-of-factly that the websites we were making were boring and that the sites he liked were entertainment sites, not informational sites. This spurred a great deal of discussion and debate among the workshop participants about what makes for a good website. One student even raised the possibility that an entertainment site could also be informational, leading Devonte and several others to create such sites for their final projects.

These experiences, along with observing similar events in other settings, piqued my interest, both as a researcher and as a teacher, in what impact popular websites have on young people's literacy learning. I have since started a three-pronged study looking at popular websites, including a survey of young people's favorite websites, a textual analysis of these sites, and case studies of young people using these sites. This chapter focuses on the textual analysis component of the study by examining eight websites that adolescents commonly use outside of school. As I illustrate, these sites—despite popular conceptions that they are degrading literacy—actually engage young people in complex literacy practices that converge with many of the values of school-based literacies. However, these sites also raise several key issues that currently are not being addressed in official literacy learning contexts.

In particular, I examine what literacies popular websites support for young people, how these relate to the literacies valued in school settings, and what issues these literacies raise for literacy curriculum and instruction. As I argue, understandings of students' out-of-school engagement in popular culture and their online literate lives can provide powerful inroads toward creating literacy curricula that are both relevant to young people's lives and that prepare them for the complex, technologically mediated literacy activities that they will face in their future school, work, civic, and personal lives. I am not arguing that these websites necessarily should be brought into schools or that we should encourage youth to use popular websites. Rather, I use them to illustrate the types of sites many youth are drawn to and to unpack how we might use such sites to inform our understandings of literacy teaching and learning.

A Sociocultural Theory of Literacy

This study is grounded in a sociocultural theory of literacy, as articulated by the New Literacy Studies (Gee 1996, Street 1995). From this perspective, literacy practices both shape and are shaped by particular social, cultural, historical, and material contexts (Barton and Hamilton 1998, Street 1995); take place both in and beyond school (Heath 1983, Hull and Schultz 2002); include print-based and digital forms of communication (Kress 2003, Lemke 1998); and are implicated in the distribution of cultural capital (Luke 2000, Luke and Freebody 1997).

One of the central contributions of sociocultural approaches to literacy has been the recognition of the relationship between texts and the contexts in which they are produced and used. From this perspective, literacy practices are deeply interrelated with broader social relationships, cultural traditions, economic changes, material conditions, and ideological values. As Heath's (1983) work illustrated and was later expanded on by Street (1995), something as mundane as bedtime story reading involves a range of interactions that includes, and extends beyond, the text itself. Similarly, popular websites are nested within a broader array of social interactions and relationships. As illustrated by the opening examples from the after school program in which I worked, students' uses of websites are both enabled and constrained by the contexts in which they are used. For instance, the secretive uses of sites with peers occurs in relation to both the unofficial peer networks that support young people in locating interesting sites and creating dialogues about their content while simultaneously the use of these sites was limited by the official expectations of the after-school program. Similarly, Devonte's observation that informational sites are "boring" and the students' subsequent negotiation for a place for entertainment sites that are both entertaining and informative, illustrates how they were negotiating a hybrid space between their official and unofficial worlds.

Along with an interest in the relationship between text and context, a sociocultural theory of literacy recognizes that literacy occurs across many contexts, both in and beyond school. This turn towards studying "local" and "everyday" literacies has problematized the primacy of school-based notions of literacy (Hull and Schultz 2002). As Street (1995) argues, basing our understandings of literacy on those practices valued in school alone provides a narrow and problematic theoretical foundation for understanding literacy. This is echoed in the range of sociocultural studies of literacy in non-school contexts, including those focused on family and community (Barton and Hamilton 1998, Heath 1983, Taylor 1983), extracurricular and after-school programs (Heath and McLaughlin 1993, Hull and Schultz 2001, Mahiri 1994, Stone 2005), peer groups (Finders 1997, Knobel 1999, Moje 2000), and workplaces (Gee, Hull and Lankshear 1996). In addition to an interest in out-of-school literacies, scholars from this tradition also examine the intersections of unofficial and official literacies in school spaces (Dyson 1997, Finders 1997, Gomez, Stone and Hobbel 2004, Lankshear and Knobel 2003). Each of these studies, along with many others, traces the complex intersections of literacies valued in school with those, such as popular and media literacies, that are often devalued in school. These insights render texts and textual practices, such as those surrounding popular websites, visible and viable subjects for research. Whereas a focus on only official literacy practices would have framed the students' engagement with popular websites during the after school program as a distraction, recognizing the importance and value of these literacy practices allows educators to explore them as viable sources of literacy learning.

One aspect of literacy that has been highlighted in several studies of students' "unofficial" literacies is the range of modalities that students engage in when producing and consuming texts (e.g., Lankshear and Knobel 2003, Moje 2000). These studies demonstrate that a view of literacy that merely addresses the print-based aspects of texts fails to capture the complexity of literacy. Rather than solely looking at print forms of communication, several sociocultural literacy scholars have argued that we must account for other semiotic systems as well (Kress and van Leeuwen 1996, Lemke 1998). The overwhelming focus of literacy theory and pedagogy on the primacy of print over other modes has left literacy scholars and educators hard-pressed. Theorizing utterances, whether written, spoken, or otherwise rendered, in terms of their multimodality is especially important as we move into a "new communicative order" (Kress and van Leeuwen 1996, Lankshear and Knobel 1997) where nonlinguistic modes, particularly the visual, are gaining dominance. This is particularly pressing when considering websites. To ignore the role of modes such as images, movement, sound, and layout would be to ignore central systems of meaning for these sites.

Finally, this strand of sociocultural literacy studies examines how schools are implicated in the maintenance, evaluation, and distribution of cultural capital associated with textual resources and literacy practices (Luke 1994). This perspective is concerned with how texts and contexts participate in power relations, how narrow views of literacy have served to marginalize students from particular populations, and how some students' out-of-school lives are valued problematically over others. These insights have been used to engage in a social critique through research and pedagogy (Cope and Kalantzis 2000, Luke 1994). As Street (1995) points out, literacy practices are "ideological" rather than "autonomous." That is, they are never neutral even though, like school-based literacies, they may seem to be "disinterested." Rather, literacy practices involve taking on and enacting worldviews that value specific ways of being, knowing, acting, and using language and other semiotic systems. Therefore, it is crucial to attend to the ways in which literacy education is caught up in creating, perpetuating, and possibly changing power relationships. This concern with power and access is of central importance when considering popular websites. By framing popular websites, and similar literacy practices, as outside of the realm of school, these literacies are unevenly distributed. Moreover, this uneven distribution occurs largely along lines of social class. That is, by focusing on a limited view of literacy that excludes digital literacies such as those of popular websites, schools serve to create larger social divisions rather than equalizing access.

Research on Websites in Literacy Education

Within the field of literacy education, there are two primary strands of research and other work (e.g., commentary, curriculum materials) about websites. The first focuses on websites as part of official educational contexts. The second examines websites used outside of school. There is currently little conversation or interplay between these two bodies of work. In response, this project seeks to create a dialogue between the in- and out-of-school understandings of websites and literacy.

A good amount of research and curriculum development has been conducted about using websites in official educational contexts. This work examines websites as tools for supporting existing literacy and other content area curricula. In particular, this body of work addresses three primary aspects of literacy. First, it focuses almost exclusively on the importance of teaching young people how to find and evaluate information (Eisenberg and Berkowitz 2003, Leu 2005). Second, some scholars have examined how the cognitive reading strategies used for traditional school-based texts can be applied to websites, as well as what new strategies may be called for when reading hyperlinked websites (Coiro 2003, Schmar-Dobler 2003). Third, some of this work examines how to use websites and other electronic texts and text practices to support struggling readers (Coiro 2003, Johnson and Hegarty 2003).

However, this body of work has paid little attention to several important areas. Beyond evaluating truthfulness, little attention is paid to developing young peoples' critical readings of websites. Also, these studies tend not to look beyond the scope of what schools are already doing. They tend to support traditional notions of literacy rather than looking at how literacy is changing and, therefore, how literacy education must change. Finally, no specific attention is given to popular websites that young people use for unofficial purposes. This is not to say that it is bad to look at how websites can be used to support existing literacy instruction, or that information finding is not valuable, but rather to point out that these are not enough to prepare a literate citizenry for today's and tomorrow's world.

A parallel but very different body of research has examined websites in out-of-school contexts, primarily coming out of researchers influenced by the New Literacy Studies. This scholarship explores popular, everyday, and out-of-school uses of websites. It examines websites as vehicles for participating in what Gee (2000/2001) calls "affinity groups"—globally distributed, temporary groups who affiliate with each other around a central topic or cause, but who may share little else in common. Much of this work focuses on interactive websites such as chat rooms, fan fiction, and blogs (e.g., Black 2005, Lam 2004, Guzzetti and Gamboa 2005). As a whole, this work underscores how online texts differ from the traditional texts valued in school.

While this body of work has contributed a great deal to understanding young people's out-of-school literate lives, there are some important limitations. They tend to look deeply at individual sites that are part of a single affinity group. As is true in much of the work from the New Literacy Studies tradition, they tend not to deal in depth with how these sites support school-based literacies. However, as Hull and Schultz (2001) point out, it is imperative to start applying the insights of such literacies to educational contexts.

The project discussed in this chapter seeks to build on both of these bodies of work on in- and out-of-school uses of websites to look at how popular websites support many of the literacy practices we value in school, as well as how these sites raise some unique challenges that currently are not being addressed in educational contexts.

A Framework for Analyzing Popular Websites

To address this gap, this analysis examines a sample of websites popular among middle and high school aged students. Over the past several years, I have collected a wide range of websites recommended by young people that they frequently use outside of school. I call these websites "popular" not because of the number of young people who use them (although many of them have millions of fans), but rather because of how they are used in unofficial spaces for unofficial purposes (Alvermann 2003), and therefore are often situated in opposition to the "official" work of schools. For this analysis, I selected eight of these sites, four which are popular among boys and four which are popular among girls. Unlike much of the work that has been done on popular websites, I focus on "traditional" websites, where the content is primarily created and/or mediated by a single entity, although there are usually some interactive aspects to all of these sites. I chose to do so because most of the sites that young people have shown me fit this mold. The websites analyzed include:

- Stickdeath, a subversive site that depicts stick figures engaging in lewd and violent activities
- ArcadePod, a data-base of free, online games
- Cash Money Records, a hiphop record label with information, songs, and images of their major artists
- Gamespot's site for Grand Theft Auto: San Andreas, a site for information about a popular video game
- MTV, the official site for Music Television, a cable television station
- Alicia Keys Unplugged, a site sponsored by this popular musical artist's record label
- Castle-in-the-Sky Sailor Moon, a fan site about the anime series *Sailor Moon*
- Seventeen Magazine, the online companion to the teen girl magazine of the same name

As is evident from this list, the sites included in this analysis represent a variety of affinity groups, ranging from games to music to anime. Likewise, they include sites recommended by youth from a range of cultural and socioeconomic backgrounds. In selecting these sites, I over sampled for sites recommended by students of color and lower socioeconomic class backgrounds—many of whom were seen in school as struggling readers—since the research literature contains few accounts of the online interests of these groups of young people.

These websites are analyzed drawing from work in critical discourse analysis and semiotics (Fairclough 1995, Gee 1999, Kress 2000, Kress and van Leeuwen 1996). This analytic perspective is interested in how multimodal aspects of sites (print, images, movement, sound, etc.) encode values and ideological stances of the websites and their participation in relationships of power. From this perspective, the creation and use of texts is socially situated. Thus, to understand texts is to understand how aspects such as grammar and layout serve to locate them within particular circumstances, to relate them to similar texts used in similar contexts, to position writers in relation to others, and to take action in the world.

Within the larger project, I am developing a framework for analyzing websites that examines four primary areas: (1) relationships assumed between users and others, (2) connections to other texts and contexts, (3) moral orientations, and (4) valued discourse practices. For the analysis reported here, I focused on the second and fourth dimensions of this framework. In particular, I examine five aspects of the websites including the use of genre, sentence length/complexity, vocabulary, modalities, and intertextuality. I conducted two levels of analysis for each of the sites. The broader level of analysis focused on each of the sites as a whole. The closer level of analysis focused on just the homepage and two comparable content pages from each site. (See the appendix to this chapter for a more detailed description of each site and the content pages used in this analysis). Using these analyses, I demonstrate that there are many aspects of these sites that complement school-based literacy instruction. I also point out key ways in which many educators may not be capitalizing on the literacies found in—and required by—websites popular with young people.

Genre, Syntax, and Vocabulary

One aspect of the websites that I examined was what primary genres of writing and other forms of representation they include. As Table 3.1 illustrates, these sites incorporate a wide variety of genres. Indeed, one site potentially engages users in multiple forms of narrative, exposition, and argumentation. Many of these genres overlap with types of reading and writing found in secondary classrooms—such as biographies, news articles, critical reviews, personal narratives, and summaries.

In many cases these websites include extended segments of text (often accompanied by images and audio as well), as with the biography of the rap artist, Baby, from Cash Money Records (to see the Baby biography, go to http://www.cash money-records.com/main.asp, click on "The Artists," then on "Baby"). The biography begins, "When Brian 'Baby' Williams hit the music industry in 1997, neither the critics, fans, nor Baby himself ever imagined that the rap industry would have allowed him and the Cash Money Millionaires to play a significant role in the

TABLE 3.1. Genres incorporated in popular websites

Website	Genres
Stickdeath	Narratives, Satires, Arguments, Commentaries, Descriptions, Arcade games
ArcadePod	Reviews, Description, Narrative, Ratings, Arcade games
Cash Money	Biographies, News articles, Historical accounts, Songs, Music Videos, Discographies, Galleries, Arcade games
Gamespot: GTA San Andreas	Reviews, News articles, Galleries, Instructions, Ratings
MTV	News articles, Reviews, Interviews, Question and answer (Q&A) section or page, Summaries, Narratives, Schedules, Biographies
Alicia Keys	Biographies, Journal, Q&A, Songs, News articles, Galleries
Sailor Moon	Summaries, Narratives, Descriptions, Instructions, Biographies, Q&A, Comparison
Seventeen	Quizzes, Polls, Ratings, Summaries, Instructions

signature sound that is now known as the Dirty South." This segment continues in a seven-paragraph biography of Baby's life and his musical career. As you can see from the introductory sentence, these sites also contain complex sentence structures and vocabulary, as well.

Indeed, each of the content pages of the sites included complex syntactical structures. To get a sense of sentence complexity across the sites, I compared the range of sentence lengths and average sentence lengths for a comparable excerpt from each site. As illustrated in Table 3.2, the sites include a wide range of sentence lengths and most of the sites contain quite lengthy sentences (some as long as 50+ words!). For example, the introductory sentence to the Baby biography cited above contains 49 words and has a complex clausal structure—including multiple dependent clauses, compound subjects, and various verb structures—that is grammatically correct by school-based standards. It is not a run-on sentence (which is often what people claim such sites include), but a well-crafted, sophisticated, grammatically sound sentence.

In addition to complex sentence structures, all of the websites included high level vocabulary. Table 3.3 includes examples of complex vocabulary from the content pages that were examined. As is clear from this list of vocabulary, the words used in these sites are not simple; indeed, each of the sites draws from a wide range of specialized and high-utility vocabulary words. For instance, in the Baby biography, readers have to deal with words such as "significant," "entrepreneur," "amassed," and "empire." Keep in mind that this site was recommended to me by Devonte and several of his peers who were considered to be "poor readers" in school—yet those same children would spend hours pouring over this and other websites, figuring out how to deal with complicated vocabulary and syntactical structures along the way.

TABLE 3.2. Sentence lengths in popular websites

Website/Excerpt	Range of Sentence Length	Average Sentence Length
Stickdeath (Hatemail)	3–26 words	17 words
ArcadePod (N Game)	4–27	17
Cash Money (Baby biography)	19–49	34
Gamespot—GTA: San Andreas (Review)	4–31	16
MTV (Madonna article)	5–37	20
Alicia Keys (Biography)	13–33	26
Sailor Moon (History)	13–28	17
Seventeen (Hairstyle ideas)	5–25	13

TABLE 3.3. Complex vocabulary in popular websites

Website/Excerpt	Examples of Complex Vocabulary
Stickdeath (PTC article)	Distributed, hilarious, distinguishing, advised, interactive, dismemberment
ArcadePod (N Game Description)	Dexterity, metabolism, unquenchable, propensity
Cash Money (Baby biography)	Significant, amassed, entrepreneur, empire
GTA: San Andreas (Game review)	Considerably, predecessor, extensive, stylistic
MTV (Madonna interview/news article)	Self-referential, diatribe, paramount, segued, seamlessly
Alicia Keys (Biography)	Prodigy, amidst, dominance, coupling, penning
Sailor Moon (Inside joke list)	Transliteration, menacing, subliminal, parody
Seventeen (Holiday quiz)	Etiquette, gesture, citing

This disconnect between the reading performance of young people in school and online is perhaps even more striking when the language of the websites is compared with that commonly found in textbooks. Since many of the websites contain biographies, I compared the Baby biography to the biographies Devonte and his peers are asked to read in school. *The American Nation* (Davidson, Castillo and Stoff 2000), a textbook commonly used in middle school social studies classes, includes a number of biographies. Each of the biographies in the text is quite short, usually only one paragraph compared to the extended seven-paragraph biography found on the Cash Money Records site. For example, the biography of César Chávez reads,

> The son of a migrant farm worker, César Chávez attended more than 30 elementary schools. In 1965, he organized the United Farm Workers among California farm workers. He used nationwide boycotts of grapes, wine, and lettuce to pressure California growers into raising wages and improving working conditions. (p. 820)

The entire César Chávez biography is 47 words compared to the 49-word introductory sentence for the Baby biography. Like the other biographies found throughout the textbook, the structure of each sentence in the César Chávez biography is quite simple, mainly including only one or two clauses, uncomplicated subjects, and simple verbs. The vocabulary is relatively functional, with a few key content terms included, such as "migrant" and "boycott."

Yet, the same young people who are willing to struggle through the Baby biography, and similar texts found in popular websites, are viewed as poor readers when asked to read simple texts such as the César Chávez biography in school. This raises serious questions about the kinds of texts we ask young people to read in school and the importance of more complex texts found in popular websites for their literacy development. Although some studies of youths' online reading practices show that students do not actually read them word-by-word (Leu, 2005), in my observations of Devonte and his peers, they often read extended tracts of text like the Baby biography word-by-word once they found something in which they were particularly interested. This challenges the popularly held belief that young people just jump around online and never "really" read anything extended. In fact, this comparison illustrates that young people actually are more likely to have access to complex texts—in terms of length, syntax, and vocabulary—online than they are in their classrooms.

Multimodality and Intertextuality

An analysis of popular websites' use of genre, syntax, and vocabulary illustrates how these sites support many of the values of school-based literacy instruction. In addition, I also investigated a few qualities of the websites that often are not addressed in any depth in educational contexts; the qualities of particular interest in the present discussion include multimodality and intertextuality

Like all texts, websites are multimodal, meaning that they draw upon multiple systems of representation that include but exceed print. As illustrated in Table 3.4, most of the sites included some combination of text, images, movement, and

TABLE 3.4. Modalities used in popular websites

Website	Print	Images	Movement	Audio
Stickdeath	X	X	X	X
ArcadePod	X	X	X	X
Cash Money	X	X	X	X
Gamespot: GTA San Andreas	X	X	X	X
MTV	X	X	X	X
Alicia Keys	X	X	X	X
Sailor Moon	X	X		
Seventeen	X	X		

auditory modalities. For instance, the Baby biography includes an image of the artist, extended text, music playing in the background, as well as easy access to other images, audio, and video clips of him and other artists' performances of their music. A reader of this text not only needs to navigate multiple genres, complex vocabulary, and sophisticated syntactical structures, but must make meaning using images, sound, movement, and juxtapositions between these modes, as well.

Through the heavy use of multiple modes, the sites set up highly intertextual networks, meaning that they were deeply connected to other texts and contexts, including other media, events, and websites. Table 3.5 includes examples of inter-textual connections made within these sites. For instance, on the Baby biography page, a number of references are made to events in the history of hiphop music and the Cash Money record label, other artists, and songs. Indeed, to comprehend the Baby biography, readers must not only make sense of the text itself, but must also traverse a range of references to other texts including events in the record label's history (i.e., the history of rebuilding Cash Money Records); styles of music (e.g., "Dirty South" and "rap conversationalist"), other artists (e.g., Toni Braxton and P. Diddy); and his songs and albums (e.g., his newest album, *Birdman*). Such relationships are not carried through text alone, but also in other modes used by the website. For example, a picture of Baby is included next to his biography, in which he has a shaved head and is wearing large jewelry and a football jersey. These style choices index an aesthetic that goes hand in hand with hiphop music, thus situating Baby further as an insider to hiphop culture. Likewise, in the songs that readers can listen to while reading the biography, there are a number of similar references in the lyrics as well as in the musical style used by Baby and his collaborators.

Additionally, readers can follow a number of hyperlinks to find out about other artists, the record label, watch videos, listen to music, and talk to other fans.

TABLE 3.5. Intertextual connections in popular websites

Website	Intertextual Connections
Stickdeath	Popular culture (television shows and music), media events (Iraq war), PTC newsletter
ArcadePod	Ninja philosophy/culture, comparisons to other games, free versions of console and arcade games
Cash Money	Songs, albums, individuals, prior events
Gamespot—GTA: San Andreas	GTA IV game, previous GTA games, media controversy over rating, movies that frame the game style
MTV	Musical artists & styles, albums and songs, TV shows, prior events
Alicia Keys	Albums and songs, life story, prior events, other musical artists
Sailor Moon	Television show, multiple versions of SM, Japanese fairy tales, references in the show to popular culture
Seventeen	Products, television shows, trends/fashions

The number of hyperlinks varies as the site is updated, but approximately 30 hyperlinks are available from the Baby biography page alone on a given day (keep in mind that this is one of many pages on the Cash Money Records website). As Burbules (1997) points out, each hyperlink in a website sets up a particular rhetorical relationship between the original page and what it is linking to. For instance, one can link to a discography of Baby's new album, *Birdman*, which includes several songs referenced in the biography. Readers can also find out about similar artists who are sponsored by the Cash Money label as well as about other key players in the Cash Money storyline, several of whom are named in the biography. Additionally, readers can find out about Baby and other Cash Money artists' philanthropic activities, tour dates, and other news.

In other words, readers of the Baby biography must make sense of an endless stream of intertextual references, links, and multimodal configurations in order to make sense of this seemingly bounded text. The Baby biography, like the other web pages examined in this study, engages readers in what Ito (forthcoming) calls a "media mix" where products, storylines, and aesthetics are tied together across a range of virtual and handheld media. Through this text, young readers are being hailed into a well-articulated way of life, complete with a detailed narrative about entrepreneurship and philanthropy, a sense of style, and musical products. Like most of the websites in this study, this site is not merely organized to transmit information, but to sell products through a complex network of intertextual and multimodal relationships.

Discussion

These websites illustrate several key issues for literacy education. First of all, these sites demonstrate the limitation of using websites solely to support existing literacy curricula. While these sites do support many aspects of school based literacy practices, such as particular genres, complex syntax, and high level vocabulary, they also include aspects that exceed what is currently being emphasized in school, such as multimodality and intertextuality. We need to begin seriously addressing these issues both with young people and in teacher education contexts. We can no longer treat reading as being solely about print or about the understanding of individual texts. Rather, we need to address a full range of modalities being used by young people. Likewise, we need to help them understand the ways in which such texts are situated in relation to other texts and contexts.

This analysis also points out the limitation of framing websites solely as sources of information. While certainly many of these sites include sections that are informational, this view renders invisible other aspects of websites, such as the affiliative nature of the texts. By using these websites, young people are engaging in identity building activities and aligning themselves with particular affinity groups. Likewise, some of the websites simply cannot be read as informational texts. For instance if you tried to read Stickdeath.com that way, it would read like a guide to becoming a sociopath! Rather, the site is about social commentary and critique, as well as about pushing the boundaries of freedom of speech.

This analysis also points to the powerful intersections that exist between young people's affinity groups and school-based literacy practices. This intersection is rarely addressed in literacy education beyond vague notions of drawing on students' interests. Affinity groups and related texts are incredibly motivating for engaging young people in reading and writing activities. As I have observed with these and other websites, students who struggle with school-based reading and writing will devote hours to working through complex websites. As scholars like Alvermann (2003) and Lankshear and Knobel (2003) have argued, we cannot merely celebrate these literacies; nor should we destroy the pleasures of popular culture. At the same time, there is certainly a need for schools to start helping students to unpack what these texts do and how they do it.

Finally, this analysis raises the need to begin addressing the convergence of genres, modalities, and intertextuality to promote consumption. In all of these websites, the inclusion of multiple genres, multiple modalities, and references to other texts and contexts are all used to position young people as consumers of particular products, whether it is CDs, TV shows, or makeup. This type of advertising is much more complicated than direct marketing strategies such as 60-second commercials, magazine ads, or even pop-up advertising on websites. Rather, these industries are building entire textual networks around products. More than ever, this points to the need for attention to critical literacy in the classroom—a critical literacy that can deal with the complexities of this type of advertising.

It is not by chance that the very moment that we are seeing a rapid expansion of representational resources and complexity of literacy practices such as those used in popular websites, schools are being forced to adopt increasingly narrow views of what it means to be literate. This institutional action pushes these literacies into unofficial spaces and renders them invisible. Ultimately, it means that some young people gain access to them while others do not. It is time for those of us involved in school-based literacy education to start addressing texts such as popular websites and to understand how they are shaping students' literate lives.

References

Alvermann, D. 2003. Children's everyday literacies: Intersections of popular culture and language arts. *Language Arts* 81(2). 145–54.

Barton, D. and Hamilton, M. 1998. *Local Literacies: Reading and Writing in One Community*. London: Routledge.

Black, R. 2005. Access and affiliation: The literacy and composition practices of English Language Learners in an online fanfiction community. *Journal of Adolescent & Adult Literacy* 49(2): 118–128.

Burbules, N. 1997. Rhetorics of the web: Hyperreading and critical literacy. In I. Snyder (Ed.), *Page to Screen: Taking Literacy into the Electronic Era*. Sydney, NSW: Allen & Unwin.

Coiro, J. 2003. Reading comprehension on the internet: Expanding our understanding of reading comprehension to encompass new literacies. *The Reading Teacher* 56(5): 458–464.

Cope, B. and Kalantzis, M. (Eds.). 2000. *Multiliteracies: Literacy Learning and the Design of Social Futures*. London: Routledge.

Davidson, J., Castillo, P. and Stoff, M. 2000. *The American Nation*. Upper Saddle River, NJ: Prentice Hall.

Dyson, A. 1997. *Writing Superheroes: Contemporary Childhood, Popular Culture, and Classroom Literacy*. New York: Teachers College Press.

Eisenberg, M. and Berkowitz, R. 2003. *The Definitive Big6 Workshop Handbook*. Worthington, OH: Linworth.

Finders, M. 1997. *Just Girls: Hidden Literacies and Life in Junior High*. New York: Teachers College Press.

Fairclough, N. 1995. *Media Discourse*. London: Arnold.

Gee, J. 1996. *Social Linguistics and Literacies: Ideology in Discourses* (2nd ed.). Philadelphia, PA: Falmer Press.

Gee, J. 1999. *An Introduction to Discourse Analysis: Theory and Method*. London: Routledge.

Gee, J. 2000/2001. Identity as an analytic lens for research in education. *Review of Research in Education* 25: 99–125.

Gee, J., Hull, G. and Lankshear, C. 1996. *The New Work Order: Behind the Language of the New Capitalism*. Boulder, CO: Westview Press.

Gomez, M., Stone, J. and Hobbel, N. 2004. Textual tactics of identification. *Anthropology & Education Quarterly* 35(4): 391–410.

Guzzetti, B. and Gamboa, M. 2005. Online journaling: The informal writing of two adolescent girls. *Research in the Teaching of English* 40(2): 168–206.

Heath, S. 1983. *Ways with Words*. New York: Cambridge University Press.

Heath, S. and McLaughlin, M. (Eds). 1993. *Identity and Inner-City Youth: Beyond Ethnicity and Gender*. New York: Teachers College Press.

Hull, G. and Schultz, K. 2001. Literacy and learning out of school: A review of theory and research. *Review of Educational Research* 71(4): 575–611.

Ito, M. (forthcoming). Technologies of the childhood imagination: Yugioh, media mixes, and everyday cultural production. In J. Karaganis and N. Jeremijenko (Eds), Network|Netplay *Structures of Participation in Digital Culture*. Durham, NC: Duke University Press.

Johnson, R. and Hegarty, J. 2003. Websites as education motivators for adults with learning disability. *British Journal of Educational Technology* 34(4): 479–86.

Knobel, M. 1999. *Everyday Literacies: Students, Discourse, and Social Practice*. New York: Peter Lang.

Kress, G. 2000. Multimodality. In B. Cope and M. Kalantzis (Eds), *Multiliteracies: Literacy Learning and the Design of Social Futures*. London: Routledge. 182–202.

Kress, G. 2003. *Literacy in the New Media Age*. London: Routledge.

Kress, G. and van Leeuwen, T. 1996. *Reading Images: The Grammar of Visual Design*. New York: Routledge.

Lam, W. 2004. Second language socialization in bilingual chat room: Global and local considerations. *Language Learning & Technology* 83(3): 44–65.

Lankshear, C. and Knobel, M. 1997. Literacies, texts and difference in the electronic age. In C. Lankshear, *Changing Literacies*. Philadelphia, PA: Open University Press.

Lankshear, C. and Knobel, M. 2003. *New Literacies: Changing Knowledge and Classroom Learning*. Buckingham, UK: Open University Press.

Lemke, J. 1998. Metamedia literacy: Transforming meanings and media. In D. Reinking, M. C. McKenna and L. Labbo (Eds), *Handbook of Literacy and Technology: Transformation in a Post-Typographic World*. Mahwah, NJ: Lawrence Erlbaum Associates. 283–302.

Leu, D. 2005. New literacies, reading research, and the challenges of change: A deictic perspective of our research worlds. Paper presented at the National Research Conference, Miami, FL.

Luke, A. 1994. Genres of power? Literacy education and the production of capital. In R. Hasan and G. Williams (Eds), *Literacy in Society*. London: Longman.

Luke, A. 2000. Critical literacy in Australia: A matter of context and standpoint. *Journal of adolescent and adult literacy*. 43(5): 448–61.

Luke, A. and Freebody, P. 1997. Critical literacy and the questions of normativity: An introduction. In S. Muspratt, A. Luke and P. Freebody (Eds), *Constructing Critical Literacies: Teaching and Learning Textual Practice*. Cresskill, NJ: Hampton. 1–18.

Mahiri, J. 1994. African American males and learning: What discourse in sports offers schooling. *Anthropology and Education Quarterly* 25(3). 364–75.

Moje, E. 2000. "To be part of the story": The literacy practices of gangsta adolescents. *Teachers College Record* 102(3): 651–90.

Schmar-Dobler, E. 2003. Reading on the internet: The link between literacy and technology. *Journal of Adolescent and Adult Literacy* 47(1): 80–5.

Stone, J. 2005. Textual borderlands: Middle school students' recontextualizations in writing children's books. *Language Arts* 83(1): 42–51.

Street, B. 1995. *Social Literacies*. New York: Longman.

Taylor, D. 1983. *Family Literacy*. London: Heinemann.

Appendix A

Website & Description	Content Pages	Description of Content Pages
Stickdeath *http://www.stickdeath.com* This site includes a number of animations and games depicting stick people engaging in lewd and violent activities, along with a number of commentaries and responses defending the site.	Hatemail (get off here!!!)	This part of the site contains hate email and the webmaster's responses. The particular exchange I analyzed ("get off here!!!") involves a parent whose child set Stickdeath as the startup page in her web browser. The parent (mistakenly) blames the webmaster for this.
	SD Dissed by the PTC	This page is a response to a Parent Television Council article critiquing popular websites including Stickdeath. It includes a copy of the original article with commentary written on and around it.
ArcadePod *http://arcadepod.com* This site is a database of free, online games. It includes original games and online versions of console games. In addition to the games themselves, it includes descriptions, ratings, and instructions for each game.	N Game description	This page provides a description and instructions for N Game, an arcade game based on "the way of the ninja."
	ZipZaps Street Rally description	This page includes a description and instructions for *Street Rally*, a car racing game.
Cash Money Records *http://www.cashmoney-records.com* This is the official website of Cash Money Records, a hiphop record label. It includes information, songs, and images of their major artists.	Baby: the #1 Stunna	This page contains a biography, photos, and discography for Brian "Baby" Williams, one of Cash Money's top artists.
	Founding Ballers: How it all went down	This page tells the story of how the record label was formed and its impact on the music industry.
Gamespot's site for Grand Theft Auto: San Andreas *http://www.gamespot.com/ps2/action/gta4/index.html* This site is dedicated to the notorious game, Grand Theft Auto. It includes reviews, news, cheats, guides, images, and videos of the game.	GameSpot Review of GTA: San Andreas	This provides a review of the game, including comparisons to previous GTA games, a description of the game story and play format, and connections to other media.
	"Confirmed: Sex minigame in PS2 San Andreas" T. Thorsen	This news story discusses the controversy over an explicitly sexual minigame that was hidden in the PlayStation2 version of the game.

Website & Description	Content Pages	Description of Content Pages
MTV *http://www.mtv.com* This is the official site for Music Television, a cable television station that broadcasts a number of shows, videos, and news segments directed at young people.	Madonna: Dancing Queen, J. Vineyard Laguna Beach Surf Club	This article discusses Madonna's new album, *Confessions on a Dance Floor*. This part of the site includes information, photos, and videos from the show *Laguna Beach*, a show about the challenges and adventures faced by young people.
Alicia Keys Unplugged *http://www.aliciakeys.net/host. html* This site provides information about the popular R&B artist, Alicia Keys. It includes a biography, her online journal, news, music, and fan discussions.	Biography Journal (October 27, 2005 entry)	This part of the site tells the story of Alicia Keys' life and *musical career*. Here, Alicia Keys writes about her thoughts and experiences as a popular musical artist.
Castle-in-the-Sky Sailor Moon *http://www.geocities.com/Tokyo/5976* This is a fan site for the anime series, *Sailor Moon*, about a regular girl who has superpowers. It includes episode summaries and transcripts; information about the history of the series, the voice actors, and the creator; and fan networks.	About Noako Takeuchi Sailor Moon Inside Joke List	This page includes a biography of Naoko Takeuchi, who wrote the original *Sailor Moon* comic books. This page provides detailed descriptions of inside jokes and inside information found in US/Canadian version of *Sailor Moon*.
Seventeen Magazine *http://www.seventeen.com* This is the online companion to the teen girl magazine *Seventeen*. It includes information about fashion, beauty, celebrities, and health.	Hair Ideas How's your holiday etiquette?	This part of the site includes images and instructions for doing your hair in a variety of contemporary fashions. This is one of a number of online quizzes you can take on the site. It assesses readers' manners in a variety of hypothetical holiday situations, such as gift giving, parties, and meals.

CHAPTER FOUR

Agency and Authority in Role-Playing "Texts"

Jessica Hammer

Introduction

This chapter explores issues of agency and authority from the standpoint of "secondary authors" within role-playing games. While the following account addresses both off-line and on-line forms of role-playing (such as that found in table-top games, live-action role-play, internet relay chat, instant messaging exchanges, forum-based games, and massively multiplayer online role-playing games; for details, see Stenros 2004), the focus is on *technology practices*, in online play and in web-supported offline play alike.

A role-playing game is substantially different from other sorts of narratives. For example, it is systemic, improvisational, and collaborative—to the point where even some expert participants insist that role-playing games are not stories (Costikyan 1994; see also comments reported in Thomas, this volume). A "new literacies" approach suggests, however, that it is nonetheless worth examining these texts from a literacy (and literary) perspective (Lankshear and Knobel 2003, New London Group 1996) and asking, for example: What does it mean to be part of a community of practice in role-playing? How can one learn to "read" and "write" role-playing games? In this collaborative process, how do role-playing groups construct agency and authority practices?

This chapter begins by explaining the methodology of the study reported here, which is an empirical investigation of secondary authorship. It then develops some core concepts underlying the theory of agency and authority in role-playing, such as the notion of "primary," "secondary" and "tertiary" authors in role-playing, and how to recognize role-playing across many different formats and domains. Finally, the material from the study is explored in the context of the concepts of authority and agency, with particular attention paid to how participant activities are changed both by the nature of role-playing and by the online practices surrounding role-playing itself.

Methodology

The research reported here looks specifically at the difficulties that secondary authors in role-playing games face when providing agency and establishing authority within the narrative, the game system, and its social context. "Secondary authors" are authors who construct specific fictional situations within a pre-established imaginary world. (More detailed discussion of secondary authors, and why their challenges with regards to authority and agency are particularly difficult, comes later in this chapter.)

The study investigates nine secondary authors who use technology and the internet to support their play. All subjects were recruited online. They were chosen on the basis of their current active participation in role-playing, their comfort with technology, and their use of the internet to support their role-playing practice in some way. The subjects self-identified as both narrative and social leaders in their role-playing who played within the framework of some existing game such as *Vampire: the Masquerade* (Rein-Hagen & Achilli 1998) or *World of Warcraft* (Vivendi Universal 2004). All but one also identified themselves as players in some role-playing game, in addition to their secondary-author role.

Many different styles of role-playing were represented among the group: table-top role-plays, live action role-playing (LARP), internet relay chat (IRC), forum-based role-plays, massively multiplayer online role-playing games (MMORPGs), and role-plays using Livejournal weblogs. Collectively, participants described experiences with playing more than fifteen different specific games, from a home-made system to *Vampire: the Masquerade* (Rein-Hagen and Achilli 1998), to a *Buffy the Vampire Slayer* game (Carella 2002), through to *Everquest* (Sony Online Entertainment 1999), and beyond. These games represented a wide spectrum of role-playing culture.

Interviews with all subjects were scheduled by email and conducted by Instant Messenger. Interviews lasted between ninety minutes and two hours. At the beginning of the interview, subjects were asked to move to a quiet, distraction-free environment and close all other windows on their computer, to increase the odds that full attention was given to the interview. Subjects were also informed about consent issues.

After consent and some basic biographical information had been obtained, subjects were asked to discuss a number of issues regarding their role-playing practices.

The interview was structured around three concrete topics: (1) how they as gamemasters handled player innovation and unexpected behavior; (2) how they used technology to support their play; and (3) how they learned to succeed as gamemasters and role-players. The themes of agency and authority emerged from participants' responses.

What Is Role-playing?

Definitions of what role-playing is, both within the role-playing community and in academic studies, are both multiple and controversial (e.g., Kornelsen and RPGPundit 2006). A fair practical description might be Mackay's definition of a role-playing game as:

> an *episodic* and *participatory* story-creation system that includes a set of quantified *rules* that assist a group of *players* and a *gamemaster* in determining how their fictional *characters'* spontaneous interactions are resolved (2001, 5; original emphases).

While this definition describes well a wide variety of role-playing experiences, it is undermined by several important new sub-cultures of role-playing, all of which have sprung up online. Massively multi-player online games like *Everquest* (Sony Online Entertainment 1999) and *World of Warcraft* (Vivendi Universal 2004); cutting-edge role-playing games such as *Breaking the Ice* (Boss 2005), *Kazekami Kyoko Kills Kublai Khan* (Walton 2006), and *Dogs in the Vineyard* (Baker 2004a); and online freeform role-playing, like *The Nexus* (2006), provide their own distinctive challenges to Mackay's definition.

Because these role-playing communities are large and/or cutting-edge, it is important to develop an approach that accommodates the wide variety of online role-playing practices and communities. Capturing the essence of role-playing, then, may be better served by trying to describe its qualities rather than its practice. Most role-playing shares three core qualities: narration, improvisation, and collaboration.

Narration

In role-playing, participants describe events or speak dialogue that happens in a shared fiction. While there are game-like elements to many role-playing games, such as dice, cards, or points, every role-playing game incorporates narrative events at its heart. Even the most game-oriented role-playing games use the rules and other game elements to describe or determine what happens in an imaginary world (Wizards of the Coast 2006a). As Bal (1998) might suggest, the text may involve game rules, but the fabula (the imaginary actions which take place in a story, regardless of how they are presented) are still a set of fictional events.

Improvisation

Role-playing is an improvisational activity. Players suggest actions that their characters might take, but those actions are not planned in advance. The narrative events that take place in the game are created during play (Mulvihill and Boyle 1998). While it is possible to prepare some elements of a role-playing game in advance, the details of how the game plays out are always up for negotiation. No one participant can know, at the beginning of the game, exactly how things might turn out.

Collaboration

All participants in a role-playing game have the opportunity to contribute meaningfully to the narrative by interacting with the other players. Every participant is able to describe the actions of some character, or in some other way make their influence known in the fictional world of the game (Mulvihill and Boyle 1998). Not all players have equal roles, but all do and must be able to actively participate in the construction of the fabula, the story and the text (Bal 1998).

Collaboration, improvisation and narration together present us with tools by which to recognize role-playing in all its manifestations—from the *Sunnydale Sock Puppets* (2004), a group which role-plays stories set in the world of *Buffy the Vampire Slayer* online, to traditional table-top games of *Dungeons and Dragons* (Cook, Tweet and Williams 2000b).

It is these elements that pose a particular challenge to traditional literary notions of agency and authority, as we will see below.

Primary, Secondary, and Tertiary Authorship

Role-playing games are authored in complex ways by large groups of people. To understand how agency and authority function in that authorship we must examine the various types of authorship available to participants in role-playing. The use of the term, "authorship," in this context is not intended to refer to "author stance" as put forward by Edwards (2004), but rather, to its original sense of "maker" or "creator." The established game roles of "player" (Mulvihill and Boyle 1998) and "gamemaster" (Cook, Tweet and Williams 2000a) do not accurately describe the complex and shifting nature of authorship in practice, particularly with regard to the "social contract" of the game (Edwards 2004) and other forms of social (rather than narrative) authority.

Instead, analyzing the types of texts that come together in a role-playing game leads us toward the notion of primary, secondary and tertiary texts, with corresponding primary, secondary and tertiary authors. The primary text is that which outlines the rules and setting of the game in general. The secondary text uses this material to create a specific situation. Finally, the tertiary text is created as the characters encounter the situation in play.

The primary author develops a world and a set of rules. This is often referred to as "system" and "setting" (Edwards 2004). "System" enables players to take actions and resolve conflicts in the fictional world of the game, while "setting" tells the players about what that fictional world is like. This material is almost never enough to actually tell a story with. It is general rather than concrete, world-building rather than story-building.

Consider, for example, the game *Shadowrun* (Mulvihill and Boyle 1998), an early classic of the cyberpunk role-playing genre. The game book explains that the world of *Shadowrun* features malevolent mega-corporations, elaborate cyberware, computer-savvy elves, and magic-wielding urban shamans. It also contains rules for fighting, hacking computers, using magic, hiding, lying, and resolving other kinds of narrative conflicts. This information delineates the outlines of the game world, but does not tell a specific story within it.

The secondary author takes the work of the primary author and uses it to construct a specific situation or scenario. If the primary author is the world-builder, the secondary author is the story-builder; they take the general ideas of the world and embody them in the concrete (Borgstrom 2005). The secondary author may use both narrative and social tools to get this job done. For example, determining what game the group is playing would certainly be part of a secondary author's job, as would be creating the specific characters who will appear in the story.

In *Shadowrun* (Mulvihill and Boyle 1998), the secondary author creates a situation that is compatible with the primary text of the game. For example, she might decide on a scenario where the corporation Aztechnology asks the characters to retrieve the kidnapped child of a major executive. Though Aztechnology exists in the primary text, the secondary author instantiates it into a particular situation— i.e., a kidnapping, which was not specifically outlined in the book—as part of her secondary text creation. However, the situation is not complete (or the secondary author could just write a novel set in the game universe—as many people do!). The situation is waiting for characters to enter and bring it to life.

The tertiary authors, then, "write" the text of the game in play. They encounter a concrete scenario which is consistent with the larger world of the game, but ultimately it is their moment-to-moment choices which determine what happens in that scenario. Even in the cases where the outcome is fixed (such as with a pre-generated adventures, or in *Polaris*, Lehman 2005, which always end in tragedy), the ways in which the characters arrive at that outcome cannot be anticipated and are always new. If the primary author creates the sets and costumes, and the secondary author provides the characters and a script outline, the tertiary authors are the ones who bring the story to life.

Consider our hypothetical *Shadowrun* (Mulvihill and Boyle 1998) group: their characters are approached by the Aztechnology representative and offered the job. The characters might accept, or decide to betray their contact, or ask for a price the company isn't willing to pay, or blackmail other characters to help them, or do any number of other things as narrative responses to the concrete situation. Some of those actions may be more fruitful than others, but the characters must play these actions out within the world of the game.

What makes this three-layered author scheme particularly appealing is that it works well even for non-traditional role-playing groups. Consider the *Sunnydale Sock Puppets* (2004), for example. The group uses the *Buffy the Vampire Slayer* television show as their primary text, making Joss Whedon, creator of the series, the primary author for their role-playing. Secondary authorship (i.e., specific plots) is performed by many members of the group, who may also serve as tertiary authors in their own plotlines and in those initiated by other people. While this kind of role-playing lacks clear "players" and "gamemasters," and social organization is spread across multiple participants, the division of authorship is clear both in theory and in actual play.

In fact, this authorship approach works well for most games that present a challenge to the traditional division of roles in role-playing. At any moment, one can consider who is acting as world-builder, who as story-builder, and who as story-player.

Agency and Authority

Agency and authority are concepts used to analyze the social power of texts. When analyzing *role-playing* texts, questions of agency and authority become even more pressing. Because the text is actually produced through collaboration between the three types of authors, social factors between authors must be a major element of how the text is produced and understood. How, then, do the different authors negotiate questions of multiple agency and shared authority?

First, of course, one must understand what is meant by agency and authority in the context of textual analysis. Agency and authority are closely related concepts. "Agency" describes the capabilities one has in terms of taking action within a space of possibility (Anstey 2005); "authority" refers to the ability to enforce and judge the results of those actions. In other words, agency proposes, authority disposes. It is easy to see both within a mutually reinforcing context. However, agency and authority are *neither* identical to one another, nor are they directly opposed. One can have agency without authority, which might be the ability to try many things but without any means to impose one's own will if resisted. One can also have authority without agency, lacking the ability to initiate, but able to decide the results of others' actions. Similarly, neither do agency and authority necessarily vary proportionally (although they often do). An increase in one's capabilities does not necessarily imply an increase in the authority needed to enforce the results, or *vice versa*.

According to its dictionary definition, agency means instrumentality; the ways in which someone is capable of acting within a given context (*Merriam-Webster Collegiate Dictionary* 2003). In a literary context, however, agency can be interpreted in a number of ways. *Textual agency* is how much control one has over the actual text in question, such as the text of the book or the shot sequence of the movie. *Narrative agency* refers to how much control one has over the story (or Bal's *fabula*); this includes both an author's capacity to have their characters act in certain ways within a narrative text, and a reader's capacity to interpret and understand those actions (Anstey 2005). *Psychological agency* describes how much control individuals *feel* that they have (Mateas 2003). Of course, a person's sense of their capacities may not match their actual abilities. Finally, *cultural agency* consists of the degree to which one's agentic behavior is culturally recognized by others.

A role-playing game must address these issues of agency in ways different from how they are addressed in traditional texts. While traditional texts are fixed in form but fluid in interpretation (Rosenblatt 1994), role-playing texts are negotiated during play, and all participants can exercise their agency to shape the way that the story goes. Secondary authors, particularly, have a difficult relationship with agency. Because their job is to make a fictional world concrete enough to tell a particular story in, they must have a significant amount of all four kinds of agency in order to do this effectively. At the same time, they must leave the other participants room to exercise their own agency, or they shut down the possibility of meaningful participation from their collaborators.

Authority, on the other hand, has to do with one's ability and right to enforce, demand and judge (*Merriam-Webster Collegiate Dictionary* 2003). In a literary context, authority can be conceptualized in a number of ways. *Narrative authority* refers to who makes decisions about the way the text or story actually turns out. If there is a conflict between multiple narrative stake-holders, who has the final say? *Psychological authority* has to do with the way that the text establishes its fictional authority over the reader, and the degree to which the reader buys in to the story (Bal 1998). *Cultural authority* describes how much value we assign to the text, and to the notion of the author as the final arbiter of meaning within it (Foucault 1977). And finally, *physical authority* is the authority that a traditional text has simply by being a text, as it is handed down over time and becomes an authoritative resource.

Because of their collaborative nature, role-playing texts must also address authority differently from the ways a traditional text might. Authority is constantly being negotiated among the members of the group as they decide the course of the story. Decisions of both narrative and social significance must be made during play. Secondary authors face the challenge of exercising their authority within the group without, again, removing the possibility of meaningful participation by other group members.

How Agency Changes

From the data collected in the course of the study, it rapidly became clear that the nature of agency changes when it is addressed in the framework of a role-playing game. Agency within the "text" and its narrative become quite complicated when there is no fixed text and no pre-generated narrative. Participants in the game have, at least theoretically, full agency to do anything they like with the game and its outcome. Since the group, together, makes up the story, there are theoretically no limitations to its agency except the ones that they voluntarily accept.

Groups do, however, create powerful limits on the agency they permit members. Most groups limit their agency based on narrative plausibility or genre concerns, which one might call a *fabulaic limit* on agency. Another limit, what one might call the *zero-sum limit*, comes from the nature of collaborative play: any participant must cede at least some agency to other members of the group, or those other members cannot meaningfully participate. Finally, groups tend to agree to respect the work of the primary (and sometimes secondary) authors, which one could call a *canonical limit*. This sort of limit comes from participants' need for structure to support their creative practice (Nickerson 1999), and for ways by which to agree that they are playing the same game. It is not accidental that these three forms of voluntary limits on agency parallel the three types of agency themselves. Fabulaic limits relate to the desire for plausible character agency, zero-sum limits relate to the negotiation of participant agency, and canonical limits relate to the extent of a group's framework agency. However, a fuller discussion of these limits is beyond the scope of the present chapter.

In addition to the types of agency afforded groups of role-players discussed above, there are multiple types of agency that role-players themselves may have, and these types of agency may be handled differently by different players or within different games. Before exploring the concrete ways in which role-players deal with conflicts about and limits upon agency, it is worth defining the types of role-player agency available.

Character Agency   Character agency refers to the agency that characters, not authors, have. This agency exists within the diegetic world of the game; in other words, within the internally consistent imaginary environment that the game presents. Character agency describes the character's abilities in that environment. In establishing what character agency is available to them, role-players may ask themselves: Is my character capable of carrying out the actions he or she intends? Do those actions actually affect the flow of the narrative?

Most role-playing games have rules for deciding whether a character is capable of a particular action. These rules are generally based in qualities or characteristics that the character has, though they can sometimes represent the strength of the author's commitment to or interest in the outcome. When a character attempts an action, the rules determine whether the character succeeds or fails (Baker 2004b). Of course, many groups choose to "fudge" or otherwise modify the rules in order to bring the game into line with their expectations (Rein-Hagen and Achilli 1998). However, the rules still generally describe the *kind* of agency the character has in the world. Characters defined by their strength thus can take action related to being strong; characters defined by their charm will tend to use charm to achieve in-game goals, etc. The character's agency exists partly in his or her description on the character sheet, which might be drawn up by any of the primary, secondary or tertiary authors, depending on the structure of the game.

The degree of power the character has in the diegetic world is another level of agency. That is, just how significant are the character's abilities, compared to the rest of the game world? Consider, for example, the game *Vampire: the Masquerade* (Rein-Hagen and Achilli 1998). In this game, the characters are explicitly at the bottom of the social totem pole. While they have powers beyond those of an ordinary person, their agency within the world of the story is structurally limited. On the other end of the spectrum, the game of *Nobilis* (Borgstrom 2002) casts players in the role of demi-gods, able to change the world with merely a thought. Characters can plausibly defeat armies single-handedly, providing a whole different take on character agency!

Participant Agency   Even if the characters can do nearly anything, that is no guarantee that every author can have things her own way. The kinds of questions to ask in establishing the limits of participant agency include: How much control do authors have over game outcomes? Can authors make their characters succeed, or are those choices narratively neutralized? Who gets to introduce new game elements and new characters?

Participant agency is different from character agency. For example, a character might be very strong and able to overcome every strength-based challenge that arises—but if the game is about social politics, the character may never have a chance to exercise her agency in a meaningful way. Alternately, this same character might succeed in every challenge that she attempts, only to find that those challenges were not relevant to the ultimate outcome of the story. Finally, the character might only be permitted to appear in pre-determined scenes that have a fixed outcome; a practice referred to (and much reviled) as "railroading" (Edwards 2004).

Participants in a game need to know what kind of agency to expect in a game so that they can introduce game elements that will be accepted instead of rejected by the rest of the group (Johnstone 1987). Participants want their ideas to be important to the story, and their actions to be significant in the fiction. Whatever their motivations for play—storytelling, winning the game, simulating reality (Edwards 2001)—few players want their actions ignored.

This is easy enough when everyone agrees on what should happen next, but becomes more difficult when authors have different visions. When one author's exercise of agency impinges on another author's desire, conflict ensues. For example, one author might declare that a character is diving behind a table to hide from the gunfire. Another author might block the action by stating that the table is not thick enough to protect him. Both players are exercising their agency within the fictional world, but the second blocks the participation of the first *as an author*. This becomes even more complex when the authors who come into conflict are at different levels of authorship and authority.

While systems of game authority can resolve these conflicts, some agreement about the limits of participant agency can head many conflicts off at the pass. The need for a shared, working theory of participant agency is clear.

Framework Agency   What if authors don't like the way that the game suggests they share agency? What if authors want to change the rules of the game? What if they want to take out major elements of the setting, or introduce their own ideas into the fiction? Role-players have the ability to change the apparently fixed parts of the games they participate in, such as the rules and the setting created by the primary author. Framework agency refers to how primary authors share agency with these structured elements, and with structural elements that they create themselves such as the "social contract" (Edwards 2004).

For example, when a group gets together for a game, it will generally adopt an existing text by a primary author. This may be a published role-playing game, a book or movie or television show, a homebrew or self-published setting, or something they invent during play. This primary text will strongly limit the kinds of actions that characters can undertake, and the ways in which participants can divide up agency. For example, computers do not exist in the medieval setting of *Ars Magica* (Chart 2004). If one individual tried to introduce such a plot element, the group would reject it due to the setting of the game that they have agreed to play. However, by using their framework agency, the group might agree to ignore the primary author's contribution and allow technology in their particular campaign. Inventing "house rules" (Cook, Tweet and Williams 2000a) also falls into the category of framework agency; groups revise the official rules to best suit their own play.

Similarly, authors can choose to limit agency socially by creating a "social contract" or agreement about how the game will run. At the beginning of the game, players can agree not to incorporate certain plot elements such as, for example, suicide. The group agrees to be bound by the limits that they have imposed on themselves, but these limits may be renegotiated during play, or abandoned altogether if the group chooses to exercise its agency to change this framework.

Character, participant and framework agency are often structured by the primary author. For example, most role-playing books will detail the kinds of capabilities that a character has, and describe what players and gamemasters have control over in the diegetic world. Character agency is generally the most clear, participant agency less so, and framework agency the least clear of all. Despite some games' "Golden Rule" (Rein-Hagen and Achilli 1998) of breaking rules if it creates more fun for the players, few games provide much guidance for how and when to change the social, narrative or mechanical rules of the game itself.

These types of agency must also be agreed on by the group in practice—as even the most detailed role-playing materials cannot provide enough information about agency to handle every situation that comes up in play. Most groups come to an implicit or explicit understanding of agency, whether in terms of what they can do with the rules, as social beings, or within the story. It is these individual understandings of agency, and how they are negotiated during play, that are examined in what follows.

Agency in Practice

Secondary authors, in some ways, face the most difficult problems of negotiated agency. As they instantiate the plot and determine the course of the story they must at the same time respond to the actions of the tertiary authors. A secondary author who cannot adapt to the needs of the tertiary authors is blocking their participation. Likewise, the secondary author must also have some degree of agency, or her own participation becomes less than meaningful. A secondary author who does not share her agency with other participants is doing nothing more than writing a metaphorical novel, but a secondary author with no agency of her own is not even playing the game.

To give a concrete example, consider the case of Liz. Acting as secondary author in her *Hunter: the Reckoning* game (Baugh, Grabowski, McCoy and Stolze 1999), she had prepared a story full of politics and intrigue, where players would portray monster-hunters confronting the morality of their choices and being used by forces beyond their control. Unfortunately, her players had other ideas. Based on character actions during play, she quickly realized that they just wanted to fight zombies, werewolves, and other monsters-of-the-week. As she put it, they "just wanted to kill stuff." This was clearly problematic! Liz had to figure out how to balance her own agency as a secondary author (in this case, her ability as a traditional gamemaster to introduce characters and plot) with the desires of the other participants in the game.

Liz's experience was emblematic of one key question that secondary authors found themselves struggling with: how to deal with conflicts in agency between different authors in the "text." When should they limit the agency of participants? How could they respond to unexpected actions by other participants? What could they do to evoke a sense of agency in other participants, even when they might not actually have much?

The secondary authors in the study sample all sought a middle ground, balancing responsiveness to in-play actions with larger narrative concerns. There was clear and conscious attention paid to managing participants' inner states, their emotional arousal, and their awareness of when control was appropriate and inappropriate. However, these secondary authors were not always successful in their attempts to share agency, as we will see.

Opportunity Some of the secondary authors in the group were highly successful at responding productively to the exercise of participant agency. These secondary authors were able to reframe their actions in light of player actions. Instead of seeing participant agency as a danger to their original ideas, they used the surprising actions of characters and players as inspiration in their own play.

One use of this opportunity was simply to yield a large amount of agency to the players. Mike, for example, began his self-described "best game ever" not knowing what the story was about. As secondary author, he introduced a town covered by an unnatural blackness, and waited to see what the rest of the group would do. After observing the players for three sessions, he developed "the general plan for the campaign." However, even these plans, which were designed after observing the players, were later changed by player action! He had intended for them to save a great golden city he had created—but instead the characters destroyed it, which "completely changed my game." Mike found that his expectations within this game concerning how tertiary authors would behave were regularly confounded, and that it was easier to let them lead and then follow along.

Liz found herself acting along similar lines when her players unexpectedly destroyed her prepared story. She had planned an elaborate storyline based on introducing a vampire-turned-to-good into the group of monster-hunting characters, to provide them with an interesting moral quandary. However, the day before this particular storyline was due to begin within the game, one of the player characters decided to kill the vampire, leaving Liz with no plot. Instead of trying to prevent the player from killing the vampire, she decided to follow up on that action with its logical consequence. She pictured the situation, realized that the police might get involved with an apparent murder, noticed that the vampire-killing character had taken no precautions to avoid capture, and arranged for the character to be arrested. The other characters had to decide if their friend was a murderer, and what the implications of his act were for the group. Without removing the agency of the characters or players, she managed to create an entirely new storyline which still incorporated some of the same moral quandaries she had originally hoped to explore.

Even when the secondary author is also functioning as a tertiary author, carrying out the plot in play, using constraints as opportunities can be a powerful approach. Fran, for example, became friends with another player in *City of Heroes* (NCSoft 2004), and they often played their characters together. When the player died in real life, his friends asked Fran to take over the character as a memorial gesture. She agreed, using her own understandings of what her dead friend would have wanted in choosing her actions. She tried to conform to how he would have played, both as a secondary author (creating plot for the character, such as his planned fall to villain-hood) and as a tertiary author (executing that plot in play). By "playing the character right using the tools available, instead of using my own tools and trying to change the character around them," Fran created a powerful narrative experience for herself and the other players in her community.

Taken together, these responses to opportunity involved a strong abdication of participant agency on the part of the secondary author. All three used situations where other people were expressing their agency, and used that to guide their own participation. They found inspiration in responsiveness rather than in agentic control. The characters were given a large amout of agency, as were tertiary participants, and the framework was designed to reflect that.

Coping   Not all secondary authors are willing (or able!) to see player agency as an opportunity. Even secondary authors who take this attitude may not always want to yield so much agency to players at any given moment. Fortunately, the secondary authors interviewed also had strategies to cope with, rather than exploit, tertiary-author expressions of agency.

One strategy was to manipulate the players into thinking they have more agency than they actually do. Bill, for example, often found himself saying, "Yes, but . . ." He would accept the characters' actions, even when unexpected, but then would use the response to move things back toward his vision of how things should be. When his players decided they wanted to get involved with a nasty interstellar mob-based arms dealer, for example, he threw all kinds of narrative obstacles in their way. He allowed them to go to the meeting, but "tried to break [it] up with fairly serious threats from outside forces," allowed them to get a contract out of the arms dealer but told them it would take their characters days to make sure they weren't being exploited. In short, he used character agency to neutralize participant agency! It is worth noting that eventually he accepted his players' desires for this type of action, and used it as an opportunity as described above, but before deciding to accept it he found many narrative ways to cope.

Robert used a more psychological sort of manipulation, causing the participants to feel that they had more agency than they actually did. When he is concerned about agentic conflict, he asks his players what they hope to have happen as the outcome of a particular scene. This gives Robert the ability to have their expectations either purposely thwarted or actively met, depending on how Robert hopes the scene will turn out. For example, consider a conversation that Robert wants to turn angry. Players going in with an antagonistic attitude can play out the scene as planned. If a player intends to reconcile with his conversation partner, though, Robert can find a detail in the conversation and expand on it, making the conversation angry nonetheless. As Robert puts it, by making the player see the results of their actions in terms of the plan they described, "the player will think that . . . his actions have affected his character's success." Even if the player is confused as to the reasons why the character is angry, he will assume it is the result of character agency rather than the gamemaster exercising his participant agency.

When dealing with her monster-hunting players, Liz tried to cope with their expressions of agency as well. While she, like Bill, eventually yielded to her players' desires (in this case, for lots of action), she "tried to sneak my plot in around the edges where I could." The fights with monsters became central, but she kept her original ideas about plot as secondary storylines, backstory, and the motivations for each fight. The group decided they wanted to kill monsters, and they got their chance—but Liz nonetheless found a way to use their desires to deliver the plot she had in mind.

From this sample, coping mechanisms tend to be a strong assertion of participant agency on the part of the secondary author, but strongly veiled in the illusion of character agency (as in illusionism; see Edwards 2004). The secondary authors were willing to give up some of their own agency, but when it came to quietly advocating their point of view, they did so through concrete elements of the story and through social manipulation of the other group participants.

Alternatives   Some secondary authors, however, found few opportunities to share agency, and were unable to cope with the exercise of other participants' agency. These authors tended to role-play in MMORPGs, and had few ways of exercising their participant agency or of manipulating the framework of the game. Instead, they developed alternatives which relied only on their own internal state and on character agency to make the role-playing work.

Fran, for example, described most of her role-playing in *City of Heroes* (NCSoft 2004) as being highly character-centric. Even when acting as a team leader, she had few ways to manipulate the story without the consent of other participants in the group. For example, her character, Faith, had an ongoing rivalry with one of the other characters in the group. Both players had agreed to this, and Fran was excited about pursuing the relationship. During a particularly difficult fight, Fran decided that

Faith had to go off on her own to try to rescue a hostage. Mid-rescue, her rival tele-ported her back to the rest of the group, scotching her plans. She had few alternatives: stay and fight with the rest of the group, leave entirely, or try to go back to her botched rescue. She had no chance to either compromise or cope: despite Fran's role as a secondary author, she had no more flexibility than her rival's player to control the story. Because the game constrained her actions so tightly to a factual, shared reality, Fran's response was to renegotiate the matter within her own mind. Fran decided to weave this into the ongoing story of Faith's rivalry, but this choice was an acceptance that she had little agency in the ongoing situation because of the design of the game.

Charles had a similar experience, where the role-playing was relegated to his own, personal point of view rather than being carried through in the world of the game. He describes how one of his secondary-author activities is inventing backstory for his own characters and for those of his friends. For example, a friend named an elven character in *World of Warcraft* (Vivendi Universal 2004) "Urk," which sounded like an orcish name to Charles. Charles promptly invented an elaborate backstory for the character, involving orcs adopting the infant elf after his parents had been killed by demons. However, Charles found that "this rarely emerge[d] in the con-text of the game" because he was rarely able to create concrete opportunities where it would come up. Only when other players teased "Urk" about his name did the play-er get a chance to bring up the story in play. Neither Charles nor his friend had much say in the matter at all.

From this particular study population it appears that when secondary authors have little framework or participant agency, they turn to other methods to express their story-building. For this group, it seems that character agency filled in some of the gaps where other sorts of agency had failed.

Generally speaking, traditional role-playing formats were most open to reinterpre-tations of agency, and to the sharing of agency in unexpected ways. While few sec-ondary authors explicitly discussed their attitudes toward framework agency, the very rigid framework of MMORPG play seemed to limit the expression of participant agency. Players could only make and pursue goals within the specific contexts that the rules of the game allowed, instead of being able to use a variety of strategies to renegotiate those pursuits on the fly.

On the other hand, MMORPG role-players seemed to have a better sense of themselves as both secondary and tertiary authors, who could plan concrete events but then also negotiate them during play. These secondary authors described them-selves as shifting back and forth between roles and types of agency much more flu-idly than the traditional role-playing authors did. Perhaps because they had fewer opportunities to control their immediate play environment, they were forced to adopt a more flexible attitude.

How Authority Changes

Authority, too, functions differently in role-playing games than in traditional texts. In traditional texts, the author has the ability to dictate the events of the story, while the reader has some degree of authority over how the text is eventually read and used. In role-playing, however, no single individual has all the authority to make decisions about what happens next in the story. Narratively speaking, authority is constantly shared among game participants in various ways at different moments in play.

Many primary role-playing texts attempt to make clear the way in which authority is split among group members. For example, most role-playing books give the gamemaster the authority to adjudicate rules disputes (Cook, Tweet and Williams 2000a, Rein-Hagen and Achilli 1998). This authority may be more or less complete, ranging from "GM fiat," a term for the absolute right of the gamemaster to do whatever they like (Cook, Tweet and Williams 2000a), to making the "gamemaster" a co-participant who is also bound by clear game rules (Lehman 2005).

Many groups choose not to use a primary author's conception of how authority should be assigned, or they play in environments where there are few traditions about the assignment of authority, such as in freeform online play. Nonetheless, these groups must figure out how conflicts within the game will be resolved. As Freeman (1972) points out, the lack of a formal hierarchy of authority does not mean that there is none, only that the way authority is handled is implicit rather than explicit. No matter what players might prefer, there will always be conflicts (narrative, mechanical, social) within the group. Someone must decide how conflicts are resolved—particularly conflicts about how things enter the shared world of the fiction.

In practice, the negotiation of authority within groups rarely conforms precisely to the notions of a primary author, even if there is one. Groups create their own practices of authority during play. Before turning to actual examples, however, it is worth outlining the types of authority for which participants may be struggling.

Explicit authority   Explicit authority frames concrete agreements about what rights participants have, and what kinds of recourse they have if their rights come into conflict with other participants' rights or desires. Explicit authority is generally attached to a rule or to a role. For example, a player might invoke explicit authority by saying, "That's *my* character, so you can't make her do the chicken dance." The player is claiming both that they have final authority over their own character's actions, and that the group agrees with this assignment of authority.

Game rules and social rules can both serve as means of resolving questions of narrative authority, assuming they are accepted by the group. For example, consider the chicken dance example. The primary author's text might explicitly say that one player cannot interfere directly with another player's character, as many such books do (Baker 2004a). Alternately, it could provide a rule by which one player could cause another's character to chicken-dance by succeeding on a die roll or expending points. However, as in many online games, this could simply be a group social agreement, that one person cannot declare the actions of another person's character—even if the primary text has nothing to say about it. Either way, the participants are agreeing on whether or not the fictional character chicken-dances within the imaginary shared space, based on an explicit agreement on how such decisions are made.

Similarly, both game and social rules can serve as a means of authoritatively resolving social conflicts. For instance, *Vampire: the Masquerade*, features a section on how the gamemaster should use his authority to deal with problem players who disrupt the play environment (Achilli 2000). Adding players to the game is another social area where explicit authority is often used. Many online games have teams of people whose job it is to handle formal applications to the game (Copinggoggles, Indy_Go, Muffinbutt and Villainy 2006). It hardly gets more explicit than that!

Explicit authority almost always implies a player-oriented discourse. Speaking about one's rights to authority within the game means that one is speaking about the game itself and, hence, not within the narrative frame of the game. While it is possible to have explicit discussions about which characters have authority over others (for example, if the players are portraying members of the military where there is a clear command hierarchy), such discussions have nothing to do with the way that players negotiate the sharing of authority. The highest-authority character may be portrayed by a player who rarely succeeds in exploiting his narrative authority, and so the character may have far more authority over the other characters than the player has regarding the other players.

Implicit authority   While explicit authority is based on concrete statements about who has the right to resolve conflicts and how, implicit authority resides in every potentially tense situation that does not openly come to a head. In most games, not every situation that could be resolved by an explicit use of authority is so resolved. (Games that try generally break up quite quickly, as the group degenerates into bickering.) Instead, participants go along with each others' actions until a point comes when they must explicitly resolve the conflicts that have arisen. This willingness to go along reflects an implicit acceptance of the authority of other players to make the statements that they are making.

Vampire: the Masquerade provides a case in point. The game features statistics like Charisma, Manipulation, Performance, Subterfuge and Empathy for each character (Rein-Hagen and Achilli 1998). This explicit framework of rules would support players turning to it every time a character attempts any kind of social action. Nonetheless, most games of *Vampire* do not, in practice, require a roll of the dice each time a character speaks. Participants implicitly agree to the actions of other characters, and call for the authority of the dice to be invoked as a kind of "final arbiter" only when they have some specific reason to do so.

Implicit authority is where real social relations tend to matter more than rules and game roles. Authority that is not explicitly invoked or referred to an outside source will tend to accumulate with the player who has the most real-world social status in the group (Freeman 1972). This is particularly true when it comes to social, out-of-game matters which can often be decided implicitly. For example, the end of a game session often flows smoothly from play into socializing into departure without any formal agreement being made. Players with high social standing in the group may assume much of the implicit authority here.

Imposed authority Both implicit and explicit authority are based on the norms of the group. However, those group norms are often referred to a source outside of the group of people who are playing. Role-playing has an accepted canon of texts and behaviors as much as any other discipline does. Role-players often use these canonical elements to establish or reinforce their authority.

Groups may refer to a role-playing text as a source of authority regarding the rules of the game, the setting of the game, the ways of allocating authority in the group, the limits of agency, or nearly anything else. For example, the game *7th Sea* (Wick 1999) describes how the fictional country of Montaigne falls to revolution. Players might explicitly defer their own authority to the authority of the text in which Montaigne falls, and refuse to change that fact specifically because it is in the book. This sort of authority closely relates to how much participants are willing to play with their agency regarding the framework of the game, and is at some level voluntary. After all, no one is hanging over them to be sure that they obey! The group can choose to ignore the "canon" of the game and decide to have Montaigne destroyed. This choice bears with it less risk than the overthrow of a canonical element in traditional text-based disciplines, because part of the expectation of the role-playing genre is that the final "text" after participation of all three authors will be significantly different from what the primary author created. Ultimately, this authority is not truly *imposed* authority.

However, there may be genuine outside forces which encourage the group to obey the primary author's canon. For example, most major game lines have an official group or groups which are recognized by the company. The RPGA requires gamemasters to take an exam on their knowledge of *Dungeons & Dragons* before they will provide certifications for tournament play (Wizards of the Coast 2006a). White Wolf's Camarilla organization organizes hundreds of games into a consistent universe, but requires participating groups to sign a contract to obey certain rules (Camarilla Development Team 2003). Individual games can choose to ignore the Camarilla or the RPGA, but not if they wish to participate in the society to which these organizations are gatekeepers. The Camarilla and the RPGA have an enormous amount of authority in many individual groups.

Code and technological limitations are another powerful authoritative force that players must negotiate, if they are playing on the computer. In *World of Warcraft* (Vivendi Universal 2004), the character races and classes are defined by the code. No matter how much a player may want to introduce their lizardling archer, the game permits neither lizardlings nor archers. If a participant wants to introduce a high-level character to act as a love interest for another player, they must start at the first level and work their way up to power, just like all the other characters do. The dumb brutality of software forces the player to work around its limits.

Explicit, implicit and imposed authority are only partly within the control of the group. Social factors and software can both limit the ways in which groups are capable of allocating and responding to authority. Different sub-cultures within role-playing have different attitudes toward how authority should be split, and to how much exertion of authority is acceptable before the group should simply break up. Face-to-face role-playing is fast and flexible, but brings players' real-world identities into the negotiation of authority; online play must exist within the constraints of software, but permits players to use their chosen rather than their actual identities in play.

Individual groups divide, accept, and resist authority in specific and highly idiosyncratic ways, even if those ways are also mediated by the game they play, the subculture in which they place themselves, their real-world identities and many other factors. It is these individual responses, and how they work out in practice, that are examined next.

Authority in Practice

Secondary authors face specific challenges when it comes to authority, because they are between a rock and a hard place: the often-canonical text of the primary authors and the in-play immersion of the tertiary authors. They may be given important authoritative tasks such as resolving die rolls, but at the same time they are often perceived as being there solely to provide the service of a good game to the rest of the group (Cook, Tweet and Williams 2000a). When it comes to authority, the role of the secondary author is by no means clear.

Nonetheless, the secondary author is highly involved in the narrative conflicts of the game. Authority is invoked when there is a clash between what different participants in the game want to happen. While at times these conflicts will arise between characters or between tertiary authors, the bulk of most game conflicts relate, in some way, to the specific and concrete story the secondary author has instantiated.

One could argue that creating such conflicts is the secondary author's job. Even if secondary authors are not being directly challenged, they are almost always the official 'gatekeepers' of what enters the fiction of the game, and must exert their authority in this fashion.

The secondary authors in the present study attempted to establish their authority in ways that allowed them to pursue their social or narrative agendas, but without offending the rest of the group. Despite strong drives toward dictatorial power from some of the primary texts used by the group, the secondary authors quietly negotiated shared power, shifting power, and even lack of power without abandoning their role-playing goals.

Tradeoffs   Many of the secondary authors interviewed for this study made specific tradeoffs of authority with other members of the group. They ceded certain kinds of authority to other group members in return for an acknowledgment of their own authority in other domains.

Mike, for example, usually calls himself a "benevolent dictator" when it comes to running a game, with final say over pacing, story specifics, background material and more. However, he has experimented with alternate divisions of authority in a forum-based online game of *Nobilis* (Borgstrom 2002). In this game, he has given authority to the players to write scenes involving his non-player characters, and himself taking the role of "coach and overseer." While he maintains a large degree of authority over how conflicts between characters are resolved and the basic setting of the game, he has given up his authority over almost as much of the secondary author's traditional domain. Players can invent, for example, "the Duchess of Flowers," and Mike cannot refuse.

Anne, on the other hand, takes the approach of giving the players authority in general, but not in terms of specifics. While she does not allow her players to have authority over how to resolve conflicts within the game itself, they do have some degree of authority over what conflicts may arise. She created a survey for her players, asking what they hoped and feared for their characters. With this information about "where they saw the character going in the future, and a sense of their goals," Anne was able to create customized plots for each of the players involved. While the players could not *force* Anne to create such story for them, Anne voluntarily agreed to be bound by their responses to this survey. She yielded some of her authority about plot elements and character conflicts to the players who completed her survey.

Tradeoffs are often explicitly negotiated, as participants agree about which parts of the world are within their authority, contested by others, or outside their authority completely. The starting point for negotiation is usually based in the expectations for the game genre being played. However, secondary authors who are committed to sharing authority can go beyond the obvious categories of whatever game genre they are exploring, as Anne did. *Werewolf: the Apocalypse* (Campbell 2000), the game for which she designed surveys, has a very traditional authority structure. Her approach is nowhere to be found in the game book itself, but nonetheless proved very effective in furthering her game goals.

Consensus   Another approach to authority was not to share it out like pieces of pie but, rather, to try to achieve consensus among the group when possible. When consensus is achieved, authority never has to be invoked—at least in an ideal world. Of course, few role-playing games are ideal situations, but some secondary authors reported trying to make them so.

Karl, for example, described his process of negotiation in the game *Dark Age of Camelot* (Mythic Entertainment 2001). He was leading a small group of characters in "farming"—repetitively killing monsters to acquire gold and gear. During play, he was invited to participate in a large-scale story-oriented raid, helping some of their allies to fight a long-standing enemy guild. Karl points out that "I was group leader . . . the call was mine." Despite this understanding, he nevertheless went out of his way to obtain consent for the change in plan from all members of his group. While he had planned certain game activities for them, he nonetheless felt (and acted) as though he needed their consent to the change.

Anne uses a different method to achieve consensus among her players: she refers much of her authority to the official canon of the games she plays. When she plays in a large group, such as in her LARP, she sticks very closely to the official canon of the game. While she understands that she has the authority to make changes in the world of the game, she does not feel that she can accurately convey those changes to all of the players in a way that would make sense to them. "It's easy to explain your vision . . . when dealing with a small handful of players, as opposed to a big group," she explains. Consensus, for her, is a way of short-circuiting the arguments that would arise when different game participants could have different models of what was going on in the game world.

Consensus is only sometimes acknowledged as a formal strategy for handling authority in role-playing games; more often, division of authority is the standard approach. However, the players interviewed in this study found concrete reasons to work toward consensus, and ways to achieve it to establish their authority. Consensus enabled more extensive use of implicit authority within the framework of imposed authority, and prevented many conflicts that often come with a more explicit approach. Secondary authors who felt that their authority was limited or at risk seemed to find this strategy particularly useful.

Helplessness   Sometimes secondary authors could not obtain the authority they'd hoped for. This was particularly problematic in the MMORPG group included in this study, who often described wanting to have more authority over the game world than the code would permit.

Cassie, for example, described a wedding she had helped plan in the online game *Everquest* (Sony Online Entertainment 1999). The event had taken more than a month to prepare, and the two characters involved were about to be wed—when a group of high level characters showed up, pretending to be pirates, and killed the wedding party and all of the guests. None of the participants, many of whom had functioned as the secondary authors of this event, had any ability to prevent the pirates from destroying the wedding. The authority of the pirates trumped the authority of the wedding participants, because the pirates were higher level (and therefore more powerful) characters. Nor were the wedding participants able to do much to punish the wedding pirates afterwards; the pirates were socially ostracized by the guests and their friends, but there was little else to be done. All they could do was resurrect the dead, move to a safer area, and finish the party; although, as Cassie describes it, "it was a bit more subdued, as it would be in a real wedding if someone had barged in right after the vows."

Cassie's story is particularly interesting, because a number of people had been involved in the secondary authorship of the event and there were a variety of reactions within the group to the pirates' invasion. Some were upset, particularly the groom, who ended up arguing with the pirates by means of in-game chat. Other participants tried to incorporate it into the story of the wedding, developing theories "involving jilted exes, father-in-laws paying the pirates, and a groom desperate to get out of a shotgun wedding." Even though the pirates made the wedding memorable, none of the participants would have chosen to have them there. Their "participation" in the wedding came about only because none of the event organizers had the explicit or implicit authority to stop them.

Subversion   Finally, some secondary authors deliberately subverted the authority structures of the game in which they were playing. They exerted their personal authority to question the notion of structures of authority, where they come from, and how they function.

Charles practices what he calls "playing alone," a form of role-playing where he begins to role-play with people who are not actually interested in playing with him at all. He inserts his character into situations that the other characters are playing out, and insists that his character be included as well. One character of his in an MMORPG, for example, came across two other characters having cyber-sex out loud in a private place. Without actually interrupting their activity, he stood nearby and pretended to have his character peek through a knothole in the wall, watching them. He fully accepted the reality of their fictional story—in a way that, say, the wedding pirates describes earlier did not—and yet by introducing himself into different situations, he quickly upset and angered other players (even when sex wasn't involved). While this could be construed as a form of "griefing" or antagonistic play, it actually subverts the notion of who gets to begin, participate in, and end a role-playing scene.

Robert, on the other hand, prefers to subvert the authority of role-playing canon rather than the individual activities of role-players. He deliberately modifies the canon of his role-playing universe to achieve specific effects. His game is meant to be a "secret history" of the role-playing canon of *Vampire: the Masquerade* (Rein-Hagen and Achilli 1998), telling the truth behind the canon that appears in the game books. In order to convey this sense of not-quite-history to his players, Robert has made significant changes to the canon, such as adding new types of vampires which have been forgotten in the present day. In his hands, canon and its violation provides him with specific narrative effects: the ability to tell a counter-text story to the established game history. His group cedes him the authority to subvert the authority of the supposedly authoritative primary texts of the game.

Generally speaking, traditional role-playing formats showed the clearest divisions of authority, while divisions of authority in MMORPGs and, sometimes, other online formats showed more fluid assignment of authority. While some of this may be due to the tight authoritative framework that code provides to online play, some of this may also be due to the copious print materials that "traditional" role-playing builds on. These role-playing books build a specific, clear picture about how authority should be shared between the secondary and tertiary authors, while reserving the authoritative stance of the primary author for themselves.

Participants who had a clear sense of their own authority were most able to use explicit forms of authority. As authors' actual authority diminished, their willingness to take issues of authority to open conflict also diminished, and they relied more on implicit and imposed authority structures. In general, secondary authors had the most real authority in technology-supported offline play, followed closely by freeform online play, with MMORPG play lagging far behind. The more that code structured the game, the less authoritative secondary authors felt and acted.

Conclusion

Stories have been with us forever, from the first whispered tales around a campfire to the oral epics of the Greeks, from epistolary novels, to hard-boiled noir, to the hypertexts of today. Despite these changes in form, however, issues of agency and authority within narrative have remained constant. Authors have always had to work out their practical and culturally-granted abilities to make stories happen. In our increasingly electronic and web-based world, these practical and culturally-granted abilities are related to possibilities and affordances that have not previously been available.

This study shows how role-playing provides particular challenges to agency and authority—and that the nature of the online practices surrounding different types of role-playing can present or eliminate specific solutions. The tools and technologies of the web shape the stories that take place using them. Not only does the web support and enable this kind of participatory storytelling, providing a many-to-many medium rather than a broadcast one, the specific affordances of different technologies help authors participate in different ways.

When considering agency, for example, one must consider the types of agency available to authors. When character agency is stronger than participant or framework agency, as it is in MMORPGs, the story will center on the body and capabilities of that character. The more available other types of agency, the more that authors will be able to create fabulae that go beyond their own character's skin.

Similarly, role-players proved quite sensitive to the degree and type of authority with which they were invested in a particular game. When their own authority was limited, secondary authors withdrew from explicit authority conflicts. They turned, instead, to strategies which would allow them to rely on implicit or imposed authority, or withdrew from authority-challenging conflicts altogether.

Of course, although it might be convenient to argue that the tools available to secondary authors strongly determine the stories they tell, things are hardly that simple. Story and reader and tools are all mutually reinforcing. Reading theory tells us that the construction of meaning is always an interaction between the reader and the text (Rosenblatt 1994). This is particularly complicated in role-playing, when the readers construct the text at the same time as they are reading it. This text is almost always decentralized over multiple forms of media (books, websites, face-to-face interactions), and includes material created by primary, secondary and tertiary authors. Social relationships among authors are immensely important to play, as are the group's spoken and unspoken goals (Edwards 2004). The effects of technology and online practices are significant, but they do not, in and of themselves, determine what a particular group's experience will be like.

Nonetheless, when designing rules and structures for improvisational, collaborative narratives (whether online or off), it is important to consider the types of authority and agency made available to participants. While the naïve view of role-playing texts might be that they are completely unstructured experiences, authors of role-playing texts do a great deal of social and narrative work to establish their agency and authority. The kinds of tools they have available will shape the types of experiences that *most* groups will have.

Role-playing potentially puts authorship into the hands of millions of people, from ten-year-olds rolling dice around the lunch table to the middle-aged guild leader who participates online via a high-speed internet connection. Understanding and deploying agency and authority in supportive ways can help these people learn to be producers, rather than consumers, of narratives. Role-playing opens texts to a new kind of participation—one that can be either enabled by, or constrained by, the affordances of technology. Let us work to be certain that these authors find their technological tools to be useful ones. Perhaps then every one of these millions of people will have the support they need to tell their own stories.

Acknowledgement

I wish to thank Chuck Kinzer, whose patience, encouragement and thoughtful questions made this chapter possible.

References

Achilli J. 2000. *Vampire Storyteller's Handbook*. Atlanta, GA: White Wolf Publishing, Atlanta, GA.

Anstey, J. 2005. Agency and the emotion machine. *Proceedings of the International Conference on Virtual Storytelling*. Strasbourg, France: Springer-Verlag. ccr.buffalo.edu/anstey/RESUME/pubs/VS05Anstey.pdf (accessed 18 March, 2006).

Baker, D. 2004a. *Dogs in the Vineyard*. Greenfield, MA: Lumpley Games.

Baker, D. 2004b. *Roleplaying Theory, Hardcore*. septemberquestion.org/lumpley/hardcore.html (accessed 14 March, 2006).

Bal, M. 1998. *Narratology: Introduction to the Theory of Narrative*. 2nd edn. Toronto, CAN: University of Toronto Press.

Baugh, B., Grabowski, G., McCoy, A. and Stolze, G. 1999. *Hunter: The Reckoning*. Atlanta, GA: White Wolf Games Studio.

Borgstrom, R. 2002. *Nobilis*. London: Hogshead Publishing.

Borgstrom, R. 2005. Structure and Meaning in Roleplaying Game Design, Final Draft. merin.hitherby.com/archives/000814.html (accessed 8 May, 2006).

Boss, E. (2005). *Breaking the Ice*. Plainfield, MA: Shield and Crescent Press,

Campbell, B. (2000). *Werewolf: The Apocalypse*. 2nd edn. Atlanta, GA: White Wolf Publishing,

Camarilla Development Team 2003. *The Camarilla Membership Handbook*. Atlanta, GA: White Wolf Publishing, Atlanta, GA.

Carella, C. 2002. *Buffy the Vampire Slayer, Core Rulebook*. Albany, NY: Eden Studios.

Chart, D. 2004. *Ars Magica*. 5th edn. Roseville, MN: Atlas Games.

Cook, M., Tweet, J. and Williams, S. 2000a. *Dungeons & Dragons Dungeon Master's Guide*. 3rd edn. Renton, WA: Wizards of the Coast Inc.

Cook, M., Tweet, J. and Williams, S. 2000b. *Dungeons & Dragons Player's Handbook*. 3rd edn. Renton, WA: Wizards of the Coast Inc.

Copinggoggles, Indy_Go, Muffinbutt and Villainy 2006. Milliways application page. community.livejournal.com/milliways_bar/profile#join (accessed 15 May, 2006).

Costikyan, G. 1994. I have no words and I must design. *Interactive Fantasy*1(2). costik.com/ nowords.html (accessed 17 April, 2006).

Edwards, R. 2001. *GNS and Other Matters of Role-Playing Theory.* indie-rpgs.com/articles/ 1/ (accessed 12 December, 2004).

Edwards, R. 2004. *The Provisional Glossary.* indie-rpgs.com/_articles/glossary.html (accessed 15 April, 2006).

Foucault, M. 1977. What Is the Author? In D. Bouchard (Ed.), *Language, Counter-Memory, Practice.* Cornell, NY: Cornell University Press.

Freeman, J. 1972. The tyranny of structurelessness. *Berkeley Journal of Sociology* 17: 151–65.

Johnstone, K. 1987. *Impro: Improvisation and the Theatre.* New York: Routledge.

Kornelsen, L. and RPGPundit 2006. *Pistols at Dawn.* nutkinland.com/forums/showthread. php?t=894 (accessed 18 May, 2006).

Lankshear, C. and Knobel, M. 2003. *New Literacies.* Buckingham, UK: Open University Press.

Lehman, B. 2005. *Polaris.* Arcata, CA: TAO Games.

Mackay, D. 2001. *The Fantasy Role-Playing Game.* London: McFarland & Company.

Mateas, M. 2003. Interaction and Agency. grandtextauto.gatech.edu/2003/08/06/interaction-and-agency (accessed 18 March, 2006).

Merriam-Webster Collegiate Dictionary 2003. 11th edn. Springfield, MA: Merriam-Webster.

Mulvihill, M. and Boyle, R. 1998. *Shadowrun, Third Edition.* Chicago, IL: FASA Corporation.

Mythic Entertainment 2001. *Dark Age of Camelot* (computer game), 1st edn. Fairfax, VA: Mythic Entertainment.

NCSoft. 2004. *City of Heroes* (computer game), 1st edn. Austin, TX: NCSoft.

New London Group. 1996. A pedagogy of multiliteracies: Designing social futures. *Harvard Educational Review* 66(2): 60–91.

Nexus. 2006. *The Nexus Game.* dear_multiverse.livejournal.com (accessed 15 May, 2006).

Nickerson, R. 1999. Enhancing creativity. In R. Sternberg (Ed.), *Handbook of Creativity.* Cambridge, UK: Cambridge University Press. 392–430.

Rein-Hagen, M. and Achilli, J. 1998. *Vampire: The Masquerade.* 3rd edn. Atlanta, GA: White Wolf Publishing.

Rosenblatt, L. 1994. The Transactional Theory of Reading and Writing. In R. Ruddell, M. Ruddell, and H. Singer (Eds), *Theoretical Models and Processes of Reading.* 4th edn. Newark, DE: International Reading Association. 1057–1092.

Sony Online Entertainment. 1999. *Everquest* (computer game), 1st edn. San Diego, CA: Sony.

Stenros, J. 2004. Genre, style, method and focus: Typologies for role-playing games. In M. Montola and J. Stenros Eds, *Beyond Role and Play.* Finland. ropecon.fi/brap/ch15.pdf (accessed 28 April, 2006).

Sunnydale Sock Puppets. 2004. Sunnydale Sock Puppet Game. community.livejournal.com/ sunnydale_socks (accessed 10 March, 2006).

Vivendi Universal. 2004. *World of Warcraft* (computer game), 1st edn. Los Angeles, CA: Vivendi Universal.

Walton, J. 2000. *Kazekami Kyoko Kills Kublai Khan.* thou-and-one.blogspot.com/2006/01/ kazekami-kyoko-kills-kublai-khan.html (accessed 12 April, 2006).

Wick, J. 1999. 7th *Sea Player's Guide*. Ontario, CA: Alderac Entertainment Group.

Wizards of the Coast 2006a. RPGA Welcome Page. wizards.com/default.asp?x=rpga/ gmpro-gram/welcome (accessed 15 May, 2006).

Wizards of the Coast 2006b. What Is D&D? wizards.com/default.asp?x=dnd/whatisdnd (accessed 15 May, 2006).

CHAPTER FIVE

Pleasure, Learning, Video Games, and Life: The Projective Stance

JAMES PAUL GEE

Introduction

The questions I want to take up are these: What is the deep pleasure human beings take from video games? What is the relationship between video games and real life? What do the answers to these questions have to do with learning? By video games I mean the sorts of action-oriented games played on computers and dedicated game platforms (e.g., the *Playstation 2*, the *Xbox*, or the *GameCube*); games like *Half-Life, Deus Ex, Doom III, The Elder Scroll III: Morrowind, Ratchet and Clank, Jade Empire*, or *Rise of Nations*, to name just a few.

I believe that good commercial video games are by no means trivial phenomena. They are deep technologies for recruiting learning as a form of profound pleasure. They have much to tell us about what learning might look like in the future, if and when we decide to give up the old grammars of traditional schooling (Gee 2004).

I also believe that good video games are extensions of life in a quite strict sense, since they recruit and externalize some of the most fundamental features of how human beings orient themselves in and to the real world, especially when they are operating at their best. In this chapter, I will argue that good video games create what I call a "projective stance"—a double-sided stance towards the world (virtual or real) in terms of which we humans see the world simultaneously as a project imposed on us and as a site onto which we can actively project our desires, values, and goals (Gee 2003). I argue, too, that a special category of video games allows players to enact the projective stance of what I will call an "authentic professional" and thereby experience deep expertise of the sort that so often eludes learners in schools.

The Projective Stance

Consider two related claims about playing video games:

1. In a video game, players *inhabit* the goals of a virtual character in a virtual world. The virtual world is designed to be *attuned* to these goals.
2. In a video game, a virtual character *instantiates* the goals of a real-world player. The virtual world is designed to *invite* the real-world player to form certain sorts of goals and not others.

The real interest is in the interaction between these claims. But let's get clear on what they each mean first. We can start with the first claim: In video games, players *inhabit* the goals of a virtual character in a virtual world. The virtual world is designed to be *attuned* to those goals.

In a video game the real-world player gains a *surrogate*; that is, the virtual character the player is playing. By "inhabit" I mean that you, the player, act in the game as if the goals of your surrogate are your goals.

Virtual characters have virtual minds and virtual bodies. They become the player's surrogate mind and body. You may wonder what I mean by the "mind" of a virtual character. What I mean is this: as a player, you must—on the basis of what you learn about the game's story and the game's virtual world—attribute certain mental states (beliefs, values, goals, feelings, attitudes, and so forth) to the virtual character. You must take these to be the character's mental states; you must take them as a basis for explaining the character's actions in the world.

By "attuned" I mean that the virtual character, that character's goals, and the virtual world of the game are designed to *mesh* or fit together in certain ways. The virtual character (in terms of the character's skills and attributes) and the virtual world are built to go together such that the character's goals are easier to reach in certain ways than they are in others.

Let's consider an example. Take the game, *Thief: Deadly Shadows*. In this game, the player plays the master thief, Garrett. In inhabiting Garrett's body (whether playing the game in first person or third person mode), the player inherits specific powers and limitations. In inhabiting Garrett's body, with its powers and limitations, the player also inhabits Garrett's specific goals; goals having to do with stealing, infiltrating, and stealthily removing or sneaking past guards to accomplish specific story-related ends in the game. Given Garrett's powers and limitations, these goals are easier to reach in some ways than others within the specific virtual world of this game.

The virtual world in *Thief*—the world through which you as Garrett move—is a world designed to interact with Garrett's powers and limitations in terms of specific affordances and disaffordances. These affordances and disaffordances do not reside in the world alone, but in the combination of the specific mind/body Garrett brings to that world and the way in which that world encourages or discourages that specific mind/body in terms of possible actions.

It is a world of shadows and hiding places, a world well fit for Garrett's superb (mental and physical) skills at hiding, waiting, watching, and sneaking. It affords hiding and sneaking of all sorts. It is not a world well made for outright confrontations and frontal fights: in this world, Garrett can find no guns or weapons much beyond a small dagger, and the spaces that would allow outright fights with multiple guards are pretty cramped, allowing guards easily to surround Garrett. And, indeed, this is all to the good—it fits well with the mind/body Garrett brings to the game—since Garrett most certainly has grave limitations when it comes to fighting outright in the light. He can shoot an arrow unseen from the shadows or he can sneak past guards, but he's quite weak when he shows himself in the light for open battle. The way the world is made, the way that Garrett's mind/body is made, and how they mesh, has major consequences for the sorts of effective plans and goals (you as) Garrett can make and carry out.

So, we see, that a video game creates a three-way interaction among the virtual character's mind/body, the character's goals, and the design features of the virtual world in terms of affordances for effective action: virtual character ← → goals ← → virtual world.

In a game, the virtual character's powers and limitations mesh with the way in which the game's virtual world is designed in quite specific ways so that the virtual character's goals can be accomplished better in some ways than others. Finding this mesh or fit—"sweet spots" for effective action—is, of course, one of the key skills required in playing a video game. You CAN play *Thief* as an out and out fighting game, eschewing stealth, but you will be fighting the mesh (that discourages such actions) between Garrett's mind/body (your surrogate mind/body) and the virtual world of the game all the way.

So, now, onto the second claim: In video games a virtual character *instantiates* the goals of a real-world player. The virtual world of the game is designed to *invite* the real-world player to form certain sorts of goals and not others.

According to the first claim, in a game like *Thief: Deadly Shadows*, you, the player, see the world from Garrett's perspective and need to find ways to use the mesh ("fit") in the world among Garrett's mind/body, his goals, and the design of the virtual world to carry out *his* goals effectively.

But things work the other way round, as well. Garrett becomes a reservoir that can be filled with *your own* desires, intentions, and goals. By placing your goals within Garrett—by seeing them as Garrett's goals—you can enact your desires in Garrett's virtual world. But note that this is a process that works well only if you carefully consider that mesh ("fit") that exists in the game among Garrett's mind/body, his goals, and the design of the virtual world. This is the only way in which your own goals will be effectively added to Garrett's and accomplished, since the game will resist goals that fall outside this mesh. In this sense, your own personal goals must become Garrett-like goals, goals that flow from his (virtual) mind and body as they are placed in this specific game world.

Let me give an example. At one point in *Thief*, Garrett needs to break into a museum to get an important object. This is Garrett's goal and you need to inhabit him and see the game world from the perspective of his affordances in this particular virtual world if you are to play this part of the game successfully. This is just claim 1.

But let's say that you as a player decide that you want to get through the museum by killing every guard (or, alternatively, by killing no one). This is not a goal that Garrett has in the game. There is no in-game way to decide what his goal would be in this respect. To realize this goal, you have to make it Garrett's in-game goal, treat it just the way you would his own goals, the goals that you are inhabiting (according to claim 1). You must do this, because the world in which Garrett moves allows this goal to be reached in some ways and not others, and it allows it to be reached more easily and effectively (even more elegantly) in some ways than others—this all thanks to the mesh built into the game among Garrett's mind/body, his goals, and the specifics of the virtual world in which he moves (as designed by the game's designers).

So, we can revise our three-way interaction a bit: we can say now that a video game creates a three-way interaction among the virtual character's mind/body (the player's surrogate), the character's goals *and* the player's goals, and the design features of the virtual world in terms of affordances for effective action: virtual character (player's surrogate) ← → character's goals ✚ player's goals ← → virtual world.

So, in playing a game, we players are both imposed upon by the character we play (i.e., we must take on the character's goals) and impose ourselves on that character (i.e., we make the character take on our goals). It is interesting to note that this is a theme Bakhtin (1981, 1986) focuses on for language. He uses the term "centripetal force" for my term "being imposed upon" and the term "centrifugal force" for my term, "impose upon." I think there is good reason for this—this symmetry between games and language—but this is a topic that needs to be taken up in a different place. However, we can certainly note that both language and games are semiotic systems for encoding experience in ways that ready human beings for actions they want or need to take (Gee 2003, 2004).

Garrett is a *project* I inherit from the game's designers, and, thus, in that sense an imposition. I had better understand that project if I am to carry it out well. And to understand it I have to think carefully about the design of the game—the mesh among Garrett, Garrett's goals, and the virtual world.

But Garrett is also a being into whom I *project* my own desires, intentions, and goals, but with careful thought about Garrett as a project—that is, once again, with careful thought about the design of the game. This amounts to saying that both to carry out the Garrett project and to project my desires, intentions, and goals into Garrett, I have to *think like a game designer*. I have to reflect on and "psych out" the design of the game. This dual nature of game characters—that they are projects the player has been handed and beings into which the players project their desires, intentions, and goals—is why I refer to them as *projective beings*, a phrase meant to capture their double-sided nature (Gee 2003).

So what? Who cares that video game characters like Garrett are projective beings? The double-sided projective nature of video game characters is one of the central sources of the profound pleasures video games offer humans. This is so, I claim, because in the real world we humans receive our deepest pleasure—our most profound feelings of mastery and control—when we can successfully take what I will call a *projective stance* to and in the real world. This is when things really "work" for us.

I will describe what I mean by the projective stance in a series of steps. But the first two steps can be taken in either order or carried out simultaneously. So, here is what I mean by "taking a projective stance" to and in the real world: First, we look at the real world, at a given time and place, and see it (i.e., other people and objects in the world) in terms of features or properties that would allow and enhance certain patterns of actions in word or deed. Second, we see that these actions would, in turn, realize the desires, intentions, and goals of a human actor who took on a certain sort of identity or played a certain sort of role (and not others). These two steps amount to seeing, imagining, or construing a fit or mesh among the world (construed in a certain way), a particular type of actor, and specific goals that actor wants to carry out. Third, we then try to become that actor—become that sort of person. We act in word or deed in terms of that identity.

Of course, we humans often form goals first and then turn to the world to realize them, though there are times when the world suggests goals to us that we have not preformulated. If we take step 1 first, we are letting the world suggest vectors of effective action to us. If we take step 2 first, we come to the world with goals and an identity we want to render effective in the world and seek to find the mesh in the world that will make things work out right. In reality, we very often iterate the process—bringing goals to the world, looking for an effective mesh, reconstruing our goals, reconstruing the world, and eventually acting and, if not effective, repairing and acting again. This sort of iterative process is not untypical of video game play, either.

Let me be yet more blunt. What I am suggesting is that when we humans act in the world (in word or deed) we are "virtual characters" (i.e., taking on specific identities such as "tough cop," "sensitive male," "hip young adult," "caring teacher," "savvy consumer," "needy friend," "nationalist African-American," and so on and so forth through an indefinite list) acting in a "virtual world" (i.e., construing the world in certain ways, and not others). Of course, the consequences are usually more clear in the real world than in a game world, but in both cases we seek to see how the situation is "designed" or can be viewed as "designed" to enhance a fit or mesh among ourselves, our goals, and the world.

Earlier, I noted an analogy between Bakhtin's remarks on language and the ideas about games I am trying to develop. Here again, I believe, we see an analogy between language and games. What I have called the projective stance is, I would argue, the basic stance that is foundational to conversation as conversation is described in Conversational Analysis research, though this body of work does not use this term (e.g., Goodwin and Heritage 1990; see also Wieder and Pratt 1990).

We seek to construe the world and form an utterance at a given time and place so that it looks as if the situation invited just that utterance at that time and place. If we are successful, the mesh we construed has now been instantiated and exists and our goal has been realized.

The argument, then, is that video games build on and play with a stance that is the norm for effective physical and social human action in the world. They externalize in images much of what remains "mental" (usually unconsciously imaginative) in the real world when we are operating powerfully and effectively. In video games we play with life as if life were a toy.

The Professional Projective Stance and Ways of Seeing

Video games differ in an important way in terms of how they handle the projective stance. In this respect I want to talk about two different types of games (Gee 2005). The first type of game I will consider is a game like *Castlevania: Symphony of the Night*, one of the classic games in the *Castlevania* series. In this game the player plays Alucard ("Dracula" spelled backwards), the half-human son of Dracula, who enters Dracula's castle to defeat his father.

The skills that Alucard and the player need and use to get through this game are generic action-game skills. Alucard walks, runs, jumps, blocks, and attacks in ways that are typical of a great many video game characters. For instance, Mario, in a game like *Super Mario*, also walks, runs, jumps, and attacks, though in a quite different-looking world. These are the typical action skills that a great many virtual characters have in video games.

When I play *Castlevania* I, like Alucard, call on my rather generic action-gaming skills, skills that I use in one form or another in many other games. I push buttons to make Alucard walk, run, block, or attack. Timing and combining the buttons in certain ways can be important. Like many other video game characters, Alucard can do some special moves when I push two buttons at once. These are the typical action skills that a great many games require real-world players to have.

However, we need to note that Alucard has different game skills than I do. He knows how to move and fight in the game world, while I know how and when to order him to do so. I also control Alucard's timing, though he controls his own execution of his attacks, which he varies depending on the weapon with which I have equipped him. So Alucard and I have different action game skills—different game-relevant action abilities—but we need to combine and coordinate these to play the game well and to succeed at it.

Let's call these game skills, parts of which Alucard has and parts of which I (the player) have and which become a coherent system only when they are combined, "action gaming expertise." Thus, in a game like *Castlevania*, we get something like this: Alucard ← action gaming expertise → me. I place an arrow pointing to both sides to notate that the gaming expertise is parceled out between Alucard and myself, neither of whom has the whole set of abilities needed to play the game.

We can now see how we can get to a very different sort of game than *Castlevania*, if we consider one of Alucard's and my (the player's) limitations in a game like *Castlevania*, however much this limitation is, in fact, part of the beauty of the game. Alucard—like all the heroes in *Castlevania* games—is a vampire hunter. When I play him, I am playing as a vampire hunter. However, even though Alucard is a vampire hunter, he has no distinctive skills associated with this profession. As I have said, he has pretty much the same skills—i.e., running, breaking things, and fighting with enemies—as Mario, and Mario is no vampire hunter. Alucard and Mario move in quite different virtual worlds, but they do lots of the same sorts of things.

As a player of *Castlevania*, I need not develop or use any skills distinctive of a vampire hunter, either. While images from vampire lore are important to the game, and while I may imagine all sorts of things about vampires while playing the game, the game does not demand that I emulate the vampire hunter's professional ways of thinking and acting. To win *Castlevania*, I have to think like a gamer, not like a professional vampire hunter. Now I must admit that I personally have no idea what the professional values, knowledge, and practices of vampire hunters are. And *Castlevania* makes no attempt to emulate these, nor to teach them to players.

Things, however, are different in a game like *Full Spectrum Warrior*, the second type of game I want to discuss [NOTE: I am well aware that this game is ideologically laden. I am well aware that it carries messages, beliefs, and values about war, warfare, terrorism, cultural differences, the U.S. military, and the role of the U.S. and its army in the modern, global world. I myself don't agree with many of these messages, beliefs, and values. But all that needs to be left to the side for now. It is not that these issues are not important. However, right now, our only mission is to understand the game *Full Spectrum Warrior* as an example of a particular type of game. Without such understanding, critique would be superficial at best, in any case].

This game teaches the player how to be, albeit not a professional vampire hunter, but a professional soldier. It demands that the player thinks, values, and acts like one to "win" the game. You cannot bring just your game playing skills—the skills you use in *Castlevania, Super Mario,* or *Sonic Adventure 2 Battle*—to this game. You do need these, but you need another set of skills, as well. And these additional skills are, in fact, a version of the professional practice of modern soldiers, specifically, in this game, the professional skills of a soldier commanding a dismounted light infantry squad composed of two teams.

In *Full Spectrum Warrior*, the player controls two (sometimes three) squads of four soldiers each. The player uses the buttons on the controller to give orders to the soldiers, as well as to consult a GPS device, radio for support, and communicate with command. The Instruction Manual that comes with the game makes it clear from the outset that players must think, act, and value like a professional soldier to play the game successfully:

> You command a dismounted light infantry squad, a highly trained group of soldiers who understand how to operate in a hostile, highly populated environment. Everything about your squad—from the soldiers to its equipment to its tactics—is the result of careful planning and years of experience on the battlefield. Respect that experience, soldier, since it's what will keep your soldiers alive. (p. 2)

We have seen that in *Castlevania*, neither Alucard nor the player incorporates any depth of professional knowledge about vampire hunting into his skill set. However, in *Full Spectrum Warrior* **both** the characters the player manipulates (the soldiers on the squads) and the player him or herself knows (or comes to know) professional military practice. As the manual says, the in-game soldiers "understand how to operate in a hostile, highly populated environment" and the player learns this or fails at the game.

Full Spectrum Warrior is designed in such a way that certain sorts of professional knowledge and certain types of professional skill are built right into the virtual characters, the soldiers (and into the enemies, as well). The game is also designed to teach players some of the attitudes, values, practices, strategies, and skills of a professional officer commanding a squad. For instance, consider what the manual has to say about "Moving Your Soldiers":

> Moving safely in the environment is the most important element of successful command. The soldiers on your teams have been trained in movement formations, so your

role is to select the best position for them on the field. They will automatically move to the formation selected and take up their scanning sectors, each man covering an arc of view. (p.15)

Note, again, the value statement here: "Moving safely in the environment is the most important element of successful command." I guarantee you that, in this game, if you do not live and play by this value, you will not get far in the game. You'll just spend all your time carrying wounded soldiers back to CASEVACs, because of another value the game demands. "The U.S. Army has zero tolerance for causalities!" This value is enforced by the very design of the game, since if even one of your soldiers dies, the game is over and you have lost.

But note also that your soldiers, the virtual characters in the game actually have professional knowledge built into them: "The soldiers on your teams have been trained in movement formations, so your role is to select the best position for them on the field. They will automatically move to the formation selected and take up their scanning sectors, each man covering an arc of view." In turn, the game demands that you, the player, attain such knowledge, as well: "Your role is to select the best position for them on the field."

There are lots of things your soldiers know and lots of things you, the player, need to come to know. However, these are not always the same things. That is, your soldiers know different things than you know, they have mastered different bits of professional military practice than the bits you need to master to play the game. For example, they know how to take a variety of different formations and you need to know when and where to order them into each such formation. You yourself do not need to know how to get into such formations (e.g., in the game you don't place each solider in position—upon command, they assume the formation as a group).

As another example of the way in which knowledge is parceled out between you and your troops in this game, consider ways of moving your soldiers from one position to the next in hostile territory. There two ways to do this, one is called "rushing" and the other is called "bounding":

> The standard press version [i.e., single push of the A button, JPG] of a move order is the Rush. It is the fastest way to move since all four soldiers move toward the destination simultaneously. Well trained U.S. soldiers never fire a weapon without stopping their movement and going sighted (raising the gun to a firing position). In other words, Rushing soldiers never fire while moving, so they will not engage targets until they finish the move and you issue a fore order.

> The hold version [hold the A button down] of a move order is the Bounding Overwatch or Bound. Bounding is the safest way to move when your team is going into unknown territory or moving against one or more enemies that are close together because your soldiers are sighted and return fire as they move.

Issuing a bound order has two steps. First you press and hold the A button while the movement cursor is out to order the bound. This automatically opens the fire sector cursor so you can set the area for your soldiers to cover. Pressing the A button again completes the Bound order.

Once they receive a Bound order, the soldiers will move into position. The first two soldiers will start toward the destination while the rear two soldiers provide cover fire. Once the first two soldiers finish their movement, they cover the rear soldiers' move. When soldiers fire while Bounding, they automatically suppress to keep the target's head down.

Note that Bounding is very unsafe if there are enemies who are too far apart to be in the same fire sector. If you Bound under these circumstances, you are very likely to lose one of your soldiers. (p. 16).

Note, once again, the values: "Well trained U.S. soldiers never fire a weapon without stopping their movement and going sighted (raising the gun to a firing position)." Note, again, as well, the parceled out knowledge. Your soldiers know how to rush and bound (and they will abide by the value of not firing without stopping and going sighted). You need to know when to rush and when to bound and what area to have your bounding soldiers cover (i.e., to be prepared to stop and fire if they see any enemies in the area). Note, too, the strategic knowledge that is needed: "Note that Bounding is very unsafe if there are enemies who are too far apart to be in the same fire sector. If you Bound under these circumstances, you are very likely to lose one of your soldiers."

Of course, most of the knowledge, values, strategies, and skills the player picks up in this game, he or she picks up, not from reading the manual, which is, after all, only a small booklet, but from playing the game. The game has a tutorial, hints, and much in its design that helps players learn the knowledge, values, practices, strategies, and skills necessary to enact professional military knowledge and play the game well.

So, a game like *Full Spectrum Warrior* requires more than generic gamer knowledge and skills; it requires professional knowledge and skills as well. But this professional military knowledge is parceled out, shared between, the virtual characters and the player, each of whom knows some things in common, but different things as well. The technical term for a situation like this, where parts of a coherent knowledge domain (like military knowledge) are parceled out in this way, is to say that the knowledge is *distributed* (Hutchins 1995).

What a game like *Full Spectrum Warrior* adds to the gaming space, something that is not in games like *Castlevania*, is a shared professional role and distributed professional knowledge between the virtual character (or characters) and the real-world player. *Full Spectrum Warrior* allows players to experience *expertise*, to feel like an expert.

We argued above that in a game like *Castlevania* the formula Alucard ← action gaming expertise → player is at work. In such a game, the virtual character and the real-world player share knowledge and skills in respect to gaming. In a game like *Full Spectrum Warrior*, this formula, while still required, is overlaid with an additional one: Soldiers ← military expertise → player. In *Full Spectrum Warrior*, the virtual character(s) and the real-world player share both gaming expertise (as in *Castlevania*) and military expertise, which are, of course, combined and integrated.

I have used words like "professional" and "expert," words that make me uneasy. The word "professional" brings to mind doctors and lawyers and other sorts of people with high status who get paid well for specialist skills. But that is not what I want to mean by the word. What I want to mean by the word "professional" is what I will now call "authentic professionals." Authentic professionals have special knowledge and distinctive values tied to specific skills gained through a good deal of effort and experience. They do what they do because they are committed to an identity in which their skills and the knowledge that generates them are seen as valuable and significant. They don't operate just by well-practiced routines; they can think for themselves and innovate in their domains when they have to (Bereiter and Scardamalia 1993). Finally, authentic professionals welcome challenges at the cutting edge of their expertise. This is the sort of identity one must at least role play in order to play *Full Spectrum Warrior* successfully. Being a professional is a commitment to being in the world in a certain way with a certain style and operating by certain values.

Many video games involve the formula: virtual character(s) ← authentic professional expertise → real-world player. For example, *Thief: Deadly Shadows* involves the professional identity of a master thief. Thieving expertise is distributed among the virtual character (Garrett) and the real-world player. The booklet for *Thief: Deadly Shadows* has this to say about you, the player, and Garrett:

> In *Thief: Deadly Shadows*, you play Garrett, a master thief in a dark, sprawling metropolis known only as the City. Rarely seen and never caught, Garrett works alone in the shadow of night, constantly trolling for information and eyeing his next prize. He can sneak past any guard, pick any lock with ease, and infiltrate the most ingeniously secured residences. (p. 4)

Actually, of course, Garrett cannot do any of these things by himself. He has only part of the requisite knowledge and skills. He can make himself virtually disappear in the dark, blending into the background so thoroughly guards don't see him, even as they walk right past him. But you, the player, must know where and when to hide him and when to emerge from the shadows to strike. Garrett and you share a system of professional knowledge, strategies, and skills, as well as certain values (e.g., both you and Garrett need, in the game, to see artful theft as a value).

There need be no name for the profession that the virtual character and the player share. In the game *The Chronicles of Riddick: Escape from Butcher Bay*, you play

Riddick. Here is what the game's booklet has to say:

> Welcome to Butcher Bay, the toughest triple-max security prison in the universe. Impossible to escape, or so they say. Inside these walls are dank tunnels, dimly lit corridors, and other hazardous areas filled with guards, savage inmates and deadly creatures that prowl the darkness. Chaos, madness, and death lurk around every corner.
>
> Only the cunning will survive. Use your strength to overpower enemies. Use your ability to see through darkness to save you. You are Richard B. Riddick, and only you can break out of this hell. (p. 2)

Riddick has special sight that allows him to see clearly even in the darkest corridor. He is so tough in words and demeanor that he inspires fear in the toughest characters (even a guard in a full robotic mech-suit calls for back up when he confronts Riddick). He can engage in great feats of athleticism in quickly moving around the vents and corridors of the prison. And, like Garrett, he can hide in shadows and attack from the dark. He exemplifies and exudes "attitude." But, you, the player, must supply the specialist tactics and strategies to instantiate Riddick's skills and values, you and Riddick must combine your skills to pull off being a professional hard-ass prison escapee of a quite distinctive sort.

To be Garrett or Riddick requires thought, strategy, decisions, and values. *Thief* requires these precisely because the game demands that the player share an authentic professional identity and skills with a master thief. It demands more: the player must make Garrett an authentic professional thief of his or her own sort. My Garrett, for example, would not kill anyone, except in extreme cases, and loved, at times, to taunt guards by showing himself only to disappear before they could find him. Your Garrett might be different.

By creating a joint authentic professional identity (in terms of knowledge, values, attitudes, practices, strategies, and skills) games like *Full Spectrum Warrior,* *Thief,* and *Riddick* demand that the player *learn to see the world* in a certain way, different for each game. Though set in quite different locales and time periods, the physical worlds of these games are at a general level pretty much the same. Like the real world they are composed of buildings and spaces. But each game, to be played successfully, demands that each of these worlds be looked at in very different ways.

Full Spectrum Warrior requires that you (the Soldiers-you) see the world as routes between cover (e.g., corners, cars, objects, walls, etc.) that will keep you protected from enemy fire. *Thief* requires that you (Garrett-you) see the world in terms of light and dark, in terms of places where you are exposed to view and places where you are hidden from view. *Riddick* requires that you (Riddick-you) see the world also in terms of light and dark (where you can hide and where you can't), though much less so than *Thief,* but also in terms of spaces where you have room for maneuver in all-out physical attacks on your enemies (e.g., you don't want to get backed into a corner).

It is important—and this is something we know from recent research on the mind—that seeing, knowing, and action are deeply inter-connected for human beings (Barsalou 1999a, 1999b, Glenberg 1997, Glenberg and Robertson 1999). Humans, when they are thinking and operating at their best, see the world in terms of affordances for actions they want to take. Thus, we see the world differently as we change our needs and desires for action.

You see the world in *Full Spectrum Warrior* as routes between cover because this prepares you for the actions you need to take, namely attacking without being vulnerable to attack yourself. You see the world of *Thief* in terms of light and dark, illumination and shadows, because this prepares you for the different actions you need to take in this world, namely hiding, sneaking, appearing at just the right moment for a surprise attack, and moving unseen to your goal. So, too, with *Riddick*. And, when you see the world in the right way you have effective knowledge of and for that world—it's the difference between knowing Galileo's Laws of Motion as a set of symbols you can repeat and actually being able to see how they apply to specific situations in the world to accomplish something.

In a good game, players find and act on a near perfect fit or mesh between the virtual character's skills, the real-world player's skills, the way the real-world player sees the virtual world, and the desires, goals, and actions shared out between the virtual character and the real-world player. If a player perversely insists on seeing Garrett's world in the way in which players need to see the world of a first-person shooter like *Max Payne*, for example, Garrett would look and feel like an inept and clumsy character and the player would feel inept, as well. Garrett can run out and directly assault guards with his dagger, but since he can't fly smoothly through the air in slow motion while firing a clip of ammo, as Max Payne can, he is usually cut down quickly. Playing the game this way is a mismatch between Garrett's body (the player's surrogate body in the game) and the ways in which the player needs to see the game's world in preparation for effective, rather than ineffective, action.

What I am saying here is that games like *Full Spectrum Warrior, Thief,* and *Riddick* allow players to take a projective stance to the (virtual) world, but a stance that is rooted in the knowledge, values, and ways of seeing and being in the world of an authentic professional, an "expert." In the real world, if you want, for example, to be a successful physicist, to know as a physicist in ways that are effective for action (problem solving), you must learn to see as a physicist. And this involves seeing the right "meshes" in the world in terms of who you, as an individual, are; who a physicist is; your goals and desires both as an individual and as a physicist; and the properties of the world at a time and place that will effectively allow your actions to enhance those goals and desires. But this is the heart and soul, too, of our second category of games, games like *Full Spectrum Warrior*.

Learning

If we took *Full Spectrum Warrior* as a model for learning, it would violate what both conservatives and liberals think about learning, especially learning in school. It forces the player (learner) to accept (for this time and place) a strong set of values connected to a very specific identity. Indeed, the player must follow military "doctrine" as formulated by the U. S. Army or find some other game to play. This is too constraining for the liberals.

On the other hand, *Full Spectrum Warrior* isn't about facts. There's no textbook on army doctrine. It doesn't teach by skill-and-drill. After the tutorial, which is pretty didactic, there is little explicit instruction. Rather, the player (learner) is immersed in a world of action and learns through experience, though this experience is guided or scaffolded by information the player is given and by the very design of the game itself. Too much freedom here for conservative educators.

As a model of learning, *Full Spectrum Warrior* suggests that freedom requires constraints and that deep thinking requires a framework. Once the player adopts the strong values and identity the game requires, these serve as a perspective and resource from which to make decisions about actions and with which to think and resolve problems. If there is no such perspective, then there is really no basis for making any decision; no decision is really any better than any other. If there is no such perspective, then nothing I think counts as knowledge, because there is no framework within which any thought counts as any better than any other.

It is clear that if someone built a war game incorporating quite different doctrine—that is, requiring quite different values and identity—than *Full Spectrum Warrior*, then decisions and ideas that were right in that game might well be wrong in the other. For example, a doctrine that allowed soldiers to run and shoot at the same time, would lead to different sorts of decisions and different ways of solving problems in some contexts. Of course, the test of which doctrine was better in a given situation would be which one works best in that particular war setting. It is also clear that the absence of any doctrine would leave the player with no basis on which to make decisions, no basis on which to construct knowledge.

It is clear, then, too, that in *Full Spectrum Warrior*, its doctrine—its values and the identity it enforces on the player—is the foundation of the set of actions, decisions, and problem solutions from which the player can choose. Actions, decisions, or problem solutions outside this set are either not allowed by the game or are very unlikely to work. Of course, if there is no such set to choose from—if anything goes—then the learner has no basis on which to choose, and is simply left to an infinity of choices with no good way to tell them apart.

Some liberal education does just this to children. They are immersed in rich activities—for example, doing or talking about science—but with no guidance as to what are good choices, decisions, or problem solutions. The idea is, perhaps, that they will learn by making mistakes, but with so many choices available and so little basis for telling them apart, it is more likely they will go down (however creative) garden paths, wasting their time.

Let me give one concrete example of what I am talking about. Galileo discovered the laws of the pendulum because he knew and applied geometry to the problem—not because he monkeyed around with pendulums or saw a church chandelier swinging as myth has it (Matthews 1994). Yet is common for liberal educators to ask children innocent of geometry or any other such tool to play around with pendulums and discover for themselves the laws by which they work. This is actually a harder problem than the one Galileo confronted—geometry set possible solutions for him and led him to think about pendulums in certain ways and not others. For the children, every possibility is still open and they have no powerful tools that help them approach the problem in more rather than less fruitful ways.

On the other hand, unlike conservative educators, *Full Spectrum Warrior* knows that knowledge—when one is going to engage in something like warfare—is not constituted by how many facts one can recite or how many multiple choice questions one can answer on a standardized test. No, *Full Spectrum Warrior* realizes that true knowledge in a domain (like warfare) is based on one's ability to build simulations ("models") in one's head, based on previous experiences and thoughtful conjecture, that prepare one for future action. It is also based on being able to apply values to determine whether the simulation is a good one and to evaluate its outcome when one has acted on it—values given by the values and identity with which the learner started.

One can have a purely verbal definition of a concept like "work" in physics or "bounding" in military practice. These verbal definitions are pretty useless (other than for passing tests), since they don't help facilitate future action in these domains (Gee 2004). On the other hand, if you can run a simulation in your head of how the word "work" applies to an actual type of situation in such a way that the simulation helps you prepare for action and dialogue in physics, then you really know what the concept means. The same goes for "bounding" in the military domain. Of course, you will run somewhat different simulations for "work" in different contexts and when preparing for different sorts of actions in physics. And, of course, the simulations you build will be partly determined by the wealth of experience you have had in doing and talking about physics.

If liberals often leave children too much to their own devices, conservatives often forestall their opportunities for learning to build good simulations to prepare themselves for fruitful action in a domain (like physics) by immersing them in facts, information, and tests detached from any meaningful contexts of action. Ironically, facts come free if we start from carefully guided experience (as in *Full Spectrum Warrior*) that helps learners build fruitful simulations to prepare for action. Anyone who plays

Full Spectrum Warrior will end up knowing lots of military facts because these facts become necessary tools for building simulations and carrying out actions that the player wants and needs to carry out. The same facts become much harder to learn when detached from such simulations and actions.

Since fruitful thinking involves building simulations in our heads that prepare us for action, thinking is itself somewhat like a video game, given that video games are external simulations. If I have to meet with the boss over a problem, I can prepare myself by imagining (simulating in my mind) possible ways the meeting might go, possible responses and actions on my part, and possible outcomes. I can use such simulations—based, in part, on my earlier experiences in person or through media and, in part, on my own conjectures and imagination—to get ready for action. In action, I evaluate the outcome of my actions and run new simulations to correct for errors or mishaps.

Full Spectrum Warrior allows players to experience military situations in a visual and embodied way. They can then learn to build simulations of these situations in their heads and think about possible actions and outcomes before rushing into action. They can then act in the game, judge the consequences (partly based on the values and identity that military doctrine has given them), and build new, perhaps better, simulations to prepare for better actions. Without doubt the same process would work for learning in other domains, domains, say, such as biology, physics, or social science, the sorts of things we learn in school.

The recipe is simple: Give people well designed visual and embodied experiences of a domain, through simulations or in reality (or both). Help them use these experiences to build simulations in their heads through which they can think about and imaginatively test out future actions and hypotheses. Let them act and experience consequences, but in a protected way when they are learners. Then help them to evaluate their actions and the consequences of their actions (based on the values and identities they have adopted as participants in the domain) in ways that lead them to build better simulations for better future action. Though this could be a recipe for teaching science in a deep way, it is, in *Full Spectrum Warrior*, a recipe for an engaging and fun game. It should be the same in school.

Full Spectrum Warrior also realizes, as we have already seen, that deep learning—real learning—is too hard to do all by oneself. The learner needs powerful tools, like Galileo's geometry. These tools have to incorporate their own skills, knowledge, and perspectives: all of which geometry has with a vengeance—algebra works quite differently, with different in-built skills, knowledge, and perspectives, better than geometry for some things and not others.

We have seen that soldiers in *Full Spectrum Warrior* are smart, they know things. They know different things than the player, things the player doesn't have to know. This lowers the player's learning load. Furthermore, as the player gains knowledge, this knowledge can be integrated with the soldiers' knowledge to create a bigger and more powerful type of knowledge. This allows the player (learner) to do and be much more than he or she could if left all alone to his or her own devices. The actor in *Full Spectrum Warrior* is an integration of the soldiers' knowledge and the player's knowledge. The soldiers are smart tools and knowledge is distributed between them and the player.

But tools aren't any good if they do not fit with the purposes and perspectives of the learner. In *Full Spectrum Warrior* the soldiers not only know important things, they are built to fully share the doctrine—values and identity—by which the player is acting. All tools are value-laden in this way, and *Full Spectrum Warrior*'s soldiers are built with the right values, they fit with the player's emerging intentions built on the player's emerging values and identity (based on the doctrine the game enforces).

Full Spectrum Warrior allows players to integrate their emerging professional military knowledge with the professional knowledge of the soldiers. The player, in this way, is guided into thinking, acting, valuing, and deciding like a professional of a certain sort. The player experiences the feel of expertise even before the player is a real expert or even really expert at the game. This is a beautiful example of an important learning principle virtually ignored in school: performance before competence.

Schools usually insist that learners study hard, become competent (the test shows it!), and then perform (and, yet, research shows they usually can't actually do anything beyond answer test questions). Of course, there is little motivation to study and become competent, when the learner has no real idea of what it feels like to act effectively in a domain or why anyone would want to become competent in the area. Further, all the facts and information the learner is studying would make a lot more sense if the learner had had any opportunities to see how they applied to the world of action and experience. Without that, they are "just words" for the learner.

In *Full Spectrum Warrior*, on the other hand, the player (learner) performs, even when not very competent, aided by the soldier's knowledge, the doctrine the game is enforcing, and the very design of the game world itself. Players feel competent before they are. They know what it means to be competent and why anyone would want to be competent in the domain. They pick up facts, information, skills, tricks of the trade. They enact values and a certain identity. All of sudden—miracle of miracles—they are competent. And, further, they are competent in a sense well beyond just being able to answer test questions. They can act, value, feel, decide, and solve problems like a pro or at least like a novice pro, a pro in the making now. Maybe they will never become a real professional, but they will always know what it was like to act and feel like one in that area.

Learning school things, things like biology, say, could work in just the same way. Strong doctrine, values and identity, smart tools, distributed knowledge, well designed experience, guidance on how to build useful mental models or simulations and on how to evaluate their outcomes, performance before competence, competence that goes beyond verbal definitions and test taking (Shaffer 2004). But, in reality, this is all very rare, indeed, in school, though common in good video games.

Of course, I know that some readers are put off by my military example and still quite disturbed by that strong term "doctrine." Strong doctrine, leading to values and identity, engagement and commitment, real choices from within a reasonable and fruitful set of choices, and ways to evaluate what one has done are necessary for real learning, however much they comport badly with the beliefs of liberal educators. It is a pity, indeed, that we have such good examples of such good learning in the military domain, both in the case of commercial games like *Full Spectrum Warrior* and non-commercial simulations used by the military for training, and not in domains like biology, physics, history, social science, urban planning, ecology, and many other more academic-like domains. It is equally a pity that the military does not have simulations as good as the ones they have for warfare for understanding culture and building peace (or running prisons). But there is no reason in principle why this should be so. It surely is a shame that we live in a society that adopts a deeper theory of learning in its video games and in its training of soldiers than it does in its schools. It is surely also a shame that the military so often succeeds with the very 18-year-olds that the schools have failed with. Whatever one thinks of modern technological warfare in a global world (I don't like it), it is not something that dummies can do.

But, of course, strong doctrine, values, and identity can lead to intolerant ideologues, as well, whether these be soldiers, scientists, or religious fanatics. There is a paradox here, of course: no deep learning without doctrine and doctrine can be dangerous. But this paradox is easy to resolve at the educational level: Be sure that learners have lived and acted in multiple worlds based on different doctrines. Be sure they can compare and contrast and think about the relationships among doctrines. They'll make smart choices, then, I believe, about what ultimately to believe and how ultimately to act.

Some doctrines work better than others for given situations and learners will learn this. Here, again, the video game industry is out ahead: the store shelves are full of different worlds based on different doctrines. *Full Spectrum Warrior* sits alongside *Thief* and *Riddick*. Maybe someday it will sit beside Galileo's world and doctrines, as well.

References

Bakhtin, M. 1981. *The Dialogic Imagination*. Austin, TX: University of Texas Press.
Bakhtin, M. M. 1986. *Speech Genres and Other Late Essays*. Austin, TX: University of Texas Press.

Barsalou, L. 1999a. Language comprehension: Archival memory or preparation for situated action. *Discourse Processes* 28: 61–80.

Barsalou, L. 1999b. Perceptual symbol systems. *Behavioral and Brain Sciences* 22: 577–660.

Bereiter, C. and Scardamalia, M. 1989. *Surpassing Ourselves: An Inquiry into the Nature and Implications of Expertise.* Chicago, IL: Open Court.

Gee, J. P. 2003. *What Video Games Have to Teach Us About Learning and Literacy.* New York: Palgrave/Macmillan.

Gee, J. P. 2004. *Situated Language and Learning: A Critique of Traditional Schooling.* London: Routledge.

Gee, J. P. 2005. *Why Video Games Are Good for your Soul: Pleasure and Learning.* Melbourne, AU: Common Ground.

Glenberg, A. 1997. What is memory for? *Behavioral and Brain Sciences* 20: 1–55.

Glenberg, A. and Robertson, D. 1999. Indexical understanding of instructions. *Discourse Processes* 28: 1–26.

Goodwin, C. and Heritage, J. 1990. Conversation analysis. *Annual Review of Anthropology* 19: 283–307.

Hutchins, E. 1995. *Cognition in the Wild.* Cambridge, MA: MIT Press.

Matthews, M. 1994. *Science Teaching: The Role of History and Philosophy of Science.* London: Routledge.

Shaffer, D. 2004. Pedagogical Praxis: The professions as models for post-industrial education. *Teachers College Record.* 106(7): 1401–1421.

Wieder, D. and Pratt, S. 1990. On being a recognizable Indian among Indians. In D. Carbaugh (Ed.), *Cultural Communication and Intercultural Contact.* Hillsdale, NJ: Lawrence Erlbaum. 45–64.

CHAPTER SIX

Digital Design: English Language Learners and Reader Reviews in Online Fiction

REBECCA W. BLACK

The afternoon's sun was still shinning bright in the clear blue sky. The clouds were dancing in circles as the wind blew gently at them. Sighed Sakura dreamily as she looked up at the clear sky and felt her heart filled with happiness. This was how her new life should've been, filled with joy. Everything looked wonderful and fantastic to Sakura. The flowers smelled lovely. The trees waved their branches as if they were welcoming Sakura's presence. The grasses beside the sidewalk were lash and green. Even the fresh air tasted a little sweet. Sakura was in such good mood and she didn't even care if the people were staring at her oddly. Her heart danced in joy as she continued to walk. She never actually noticed the beauty of Tokyo until now.
(Tanaka Nanako, December 1, 2002)

Introduction

In recent years, new media and information and communication technologies (ICTs) have made it possible for youth to engage with popular culture across diverse terrains in their daily lives. Online fan fiction sites are spaces where school-age fans are using new ICTs to engage, not only with pop culture and media, but also with a broad array of literate activities that are aligned with many school-based literacy practices. Additionally, through such activities, fans are able to draw from a range of cultural and linguistic resources to develop identities as knowledgeable participants and to accrue unofficial forms of cultural capital in such spaces. Fan fiction, as the name suggests, denotes texts written by fans about their favorite media and pop cultural icons. Such texts often extend the plotline of the original series (e.g., characters from *Star Trek* discover a new planet), explore relationships between characters (e.g., Shaggy and Velma from *Scooby Doo* fall in love), and/or expand the timeline of the media by developing prequels and/or sequels of sorts (e.g., a journal detailing the many regrets of Darth Vader before his death); however, these are just a few examples of the many creative contributions such fan texts make to the pop cultural imaginary.

My previous work has explored many of the literacy and social practices taking place in one of the largest online fan fiction archives, Fanfiction.net, illustrating how through composing texts, creating fan sites, and interacting on the site many English Language Learners (ELLs) are able to develop social and intellectual cachet as successful writers and users of English (Black 2005, 2006), and develop skills that are promoted through popular writing pedagogy (Black, in press a). In this chapter, I would like to take a closer look at the sort of feedback one adolescent ELL author receives on Fan fiction.net, and her responses to this feedback, as a means of understanding how readers and this author co-design the writing/reading space through their interactions. In addition, analysis will explore how the online fan fiction site affords both author and readers opportunity to display diverse kinds of expertise that are based both on school-based literacy practices as well as in-depth knowledge in the realm of popular culture.

Theory, Design, and the Fan Fiction Context

Scholarship within the New Literacy Studies (Cope and Kalantzis 2000, Gee 2004, New London Group 1996) has dealt with shifts from what is valued within the Old Capitalist/Industrial "mindset" (Lankshear and Knobel 2003) that centers on the production of material goods, to what is valued within social and work spaces rooted in a mindset "forged in cyberspace" (Lankshear and Knobel 2003, 3). Such shifts have come in tandem with the fast-paced development of new ICTs and a New Capitalist focus on the production and exchange of information rather than commodities (Castells 1996, Gee 2004). Jim Gee (2004) posits that facility with *design* has in large part replaced manufacturing skills within the value system of New Capitalism. According to Gee there are "three types of design that reap large rewards in the New Capitalism: the ability to design new *identities, affinity spaces,* and *networks*" (pg. 97). In this paper I use these three interrelated aspects of design as lenses through which to view the interactions and activities taking place on Fanfiction.net.

Affinity Spaces

In his text, *Situated Language and Learning: A Critique of Traditional Schooling*, Gee (2004) draws on the concept of design to shed light on some forms of pop-culture inspired learning and interaction through his exploration of a video game fan site devoted to *Age of Mythology*. In this work, Gee distinguishes between the well known notion of "communities of practice" (Wenger 1999) in which novices learn through apprenticeship and scaffolding in their interactions with experts (Lave and Wenger, 1991) and an alternative construct for looking at learning; that of *affinity spaces*. In affinity spaces, people interact and relate to each other around a common passion, pro-clivity, or endeavor. So for instance, in Gee's example, members of the affinity space relate to each other in terms of the video game *Age of Mythology*. Whereas in my work, members of the online fan fiction site share a passion for the Japanese Animation (anime) series *Card Captor Sakura*. Gee posits that defining the point of affiliation in this way emphasizes how variables such as race, class, gender, sexuality, ability, and edu-cation level, while certainly not eliminated, are backgrounded to a common taste, shared interest or endeavor. Thus, affinity spaces are unique in that they provide oppor-tunity for individuals who may not share the bonds typically associated with "com-munity" to gather across on- and/or offline common ground. Moreover, on such common ground, the expertise of a thirteen-year-old ELL raised playing video games or watching anime often trumps that of the adults or even the university professors participating in these sites. Additionally, as will be discussed in the following sections, in contrast to communities of practice, within affinity spaces there is a wide range of valued expertise and forms of knowledge. Thus, the roles of "expert" and "novice" are highly variable and contingent on activity and context.

Networks

Designing *networks* is another key aspect of design in the New Capitalism (Kelly cited in Gee, 2004) and our information-oriented society (Castells 1996). As a research context, Fanfiction.net provides clear examples of how youth are learning to use new ICTs to develop "communicational links between people and organiza-tions" as well as between "people and various sorts of tools and technologies" (Gee 2004, 99) in ways that traverse temporal, spatial, and linguistic boundaries. For example, in examining interactions between writers and readers on the site, it is clear that participants must be able to navigate "the multiple linguistic, audio, and sym-bolic visual graphics of hypertext" (Luke 2000, 73) in order to successfully partic-ipate in the social network of this online affinity space. The site and its members use an array of text and symbol-based signs to indicate hyperlinked connections both within Fanfiction.net, and across other pertinent sites, such as fan fiction glossaries, fan fiction writing help sites, members' personal web pages, and official corporate sites that provide information on copyright laws for the various media texts that fans are drawing from, to name just a few. Such connections allow members to draw from knowledge that is distributed across different locations. This distribution of resources is also a defining feature of networked affinity spaces (Gee 2004).

In terms of the design-related skills of leveraging new technologies and learning to communicate within global networks, it is also clear that fans "draw on a range of knowledge about traditional and newly blended genres or representational conventions, cultural and symbolic codes, as well as linguistically coded and software-driven meanings" (Luke 2000, 73). For example, although the fictions are written primarily in English and often represent scenarios from the lives of adolescents living in North America, writers and readers alike incorporate Japanese and Chinese language and cultural symbols into their fictions, thus creating linguistically and culturally hybrid texts (Black 2005). In addition, fan fictions are often hybrid textual forms comprised of combinations of various media and narrative genres, such as a songfiction that combines a narrative storyline using anime characters and the lyrics of a popular song, or a crossover moviefiction that combines the characters of an anime series with the setting or narrative elements of a well known movie. Consequently, readers must understand such hybridity in order to successfully participate and give feedback in the space. In addition, fans are also able to provide links to personal web pages where they create fan texts that incorporate various modes of representation such as audio, images, and sound, thus allowing ELLs (and others) to draw on skills with graphic arts and publishing software to display non-linguistic forms of expertise. Having multiple means of attaining status and displaying expertise is also another defining feature of affinity spaces (Gee 2004).

Identity and Discourse

The notion of identity is crucial, not only to design, but to participation in schools as well as in fandoms. By *identity*, I mean the ability to be recognized as a "kind of person," such as an anime fan, within a given context. From this perspective, individuals have multiple identities that are connected, not to some fixed, internal state of being, but rather, to more flexible patterns of participation in social events (Gee 2001). Gee (2001) posits that in institutions such as schools, certain identities are given power through a process of *authorization* by which authorities and policy-makers are able to draw from various rules, laws, and traditions to "author" positions as well as to "author" the occupants of such positions in terms of the rights and obligations that accompany institutionalized social roles.

Such authorized or *ascribed* identities are clearly present in classrooms where teachers are vested with the role of expert, and students by virtue of tracking, individual or independent education programs (IEPs), and sometimes general supposition, are assigned roles as certain kinds of learners. This sort of ascription of identity becomes problematic when students from non-mainstream backgrounds are expected to occupy roles based on deficit models of cultural and linguistic diversity and differences in learning styles. Moreover, such cultural and cognitive-deficit models connote certain types of identities, behaviors, and abilities, without ample consideration of the role that the classroom and curricular contexts play in our assessments of student actions or in our rubrics for categorizing student identities. Conversely, an interesting aspect of fan fiction sites and many other affinity spaces is the absence of imposed social roles or obligatory knowledge for participants. Thus, Fanfiction.net is a learning environment where new ICTs and the absence of authorized roles for experts and novices afford individuals greater freedom in designing or discursively constructing what Gee calls *achieved* rather than ascribed identities.

According to Gee (2001), in the New Capitalist or "modern" value system of the information age, discourse and dialogue play an important role both in designing identities and in having others recognize such achieved identities within affinity spaces and online environments. Fanfiction.net is a clear example of a site where traditional print-based language, as well as post-typographic forms of text, play crucial roles in defining the affinity space, creating and sustaining social networks, and enacting achieved identities within the site. Gee's (1999) big-D discourse theory and method of analysis differentiates between little-d discourse, which is language in use, and big-D Discourse, which is the compilation of semiotic, material, and expressive resources individuals use to "pull off" certain socially situated identities. Thus, d/Discourse is an apt analytical construct for exploring how an adolescent ELL fan fiction writer uses her mastery of design to discursively construct and sustain an achieved identity as a highly popular author in this space, rather than taking on an ascribed identity as an ELL who struggles with writing in English. Such an approach also facilitates understanding of how this author and her readers, through interaction and negotiation, are able to co-design a social and learning-based space where native and non-native English speakers alike are able to display expertise and build on their different forms of personal, cultural, and linguistic capital.

Methods

In order to contextualize my exploration of the literacy and social practices of Fanfiction.net, I used traditional ethnographic methods such as collecting field notes, artifacts, and conducting interviews over two years of participant observation located in the site itself. The artifacts used as data for this paper come from a case study of a sixteen-year-old native Mandarin Chinese speaker, Tanaka Nanako, who had only been learning English for two and a half years when she first began posting anime-based stories on Fanfiction.net. Nanako is an exceptional case in that she has become an expert in design—more specifically, over time she has become very adept at networking in this space and has developed a considerable group of readers and avid followers to the extent that she now has over 6000 reviews of her 50 plus publicly posted fan fiction texts. This paper focuses on reader feedback for Nanako's fourteen-chapter fan fiction titled *Love Letters*, which has received 1694 reviews (as of May 21, 2005).

Data Analysis

Due to the relatively unexplored nature of interaction in this space, analysis of the data required several different layers of coding and interpretation that are grounded in discourse analytic techniques. Initially, through multiple readings of Nanako's *Love Letters* and 1694 reader reviews, the texts were coded in an inductive fashion—specifically, through these readings I focused on coding for various themes appearing in the chapters and the reviews. In the next stage, I coded 200 reviews by breaking them down into *lines* which are simple sentences or clauses that, much like "idea units" (Gee 1986), are counted as separate lines only when the unit introduces new information. The lines were then grouped into topical segments that are similar to what Gee (1996) refers to as *stanzas* or "sets of lines about a single minimal topic, organized rhythmically and syntactically so as to hang together in a particularly tight way" (p. 94). In the next stage, the data (divided into lines and segments) were compared across reviews in order to identify recurring thematic and structural patterns in reader feedback. Such patterns of interaction then were coded as categories, such as greetings, suggestions for improvement, comparisons to own writing, and listed in a typology of information exchange.

For the purposes of this chapter, I chose texts that were representative of salient types of reader reviews. I also focused on reviews that Nanako explicitly responds to in her Author's Notes, in her fictions, and in a Thank You List for Reviewers that she updates for each chapter in order to gain a greater sense of the negotiation between writer and readers. After revisiting the initial thematic patterns from the typology, I then conducted a closer discourse analytic examination of such texts with the following questions in mind:

- What sort of linguistic "work" are Nanako's texts and the reader reviews doing?
- How and in what ways are these texts representative of successful design in terms of affinity spaces, networks, and identity?
- How and in what ways might Nanako's texts and reader feedback be indexing the author's identity as a successful writer and the readers' identities as

knowledgeable participants, thus helping them all accrue forms of social and intellectual capital in this space?

In answering these questions, I coded data on multiple levels. First, I looked at separate lines in terms of form in order to identify the *mood* of each clause (e.g., indicative, imperative) and the main topic or thematic structure of each clause (Gee 1999, Halliday and Matthiessen 2004). Next, I returned and looked at each line in terms of the sort of *socially situated* identities that were being either enacted, referenced, and/or were relevant to meaningful participation in the social network of this affinity space (Gee 1999). I then turned back to Nanako's texts to see her responses to each of these reviews. This portion of the analysis includes explicit responses made through her communications with readers, as well as implicit responses made through revisions to her fan fiction stories. It seems important to emphasize, however, that the focus of this paper is not on minute discourse analysis of individual texts, but rather is aimed at identifying general "types" of reviews and patterns of interaction between Nanako and her readers in order to better understand the learning, social, and interactive aspects of this hitherto unexplored site.

Designing the Fan Fiction Writing Space

This section uses some of Nanako's introductory and concluding Author's Notes (A/Ns), or messages addressed directly to the audience, to illustrate her facility with design. Specifically, Nanako is quite skilled at using language and discourse to shape her own interactional and learning space in such a way that maximizes opportunities for constructive feedback on her language and writing. She also uses these notes as a means of establishing her social and writing-related resource network by cultivating strong relationships with readers. For instance, she begins and ends each of her chapters with Author's Notes such as the following:

Opening Author's Note

Segment A
L1   Important note: English is my second language
L2   and I only spoken it for 2.5 years.
L3   So please excuse my grammar and spelling mistakes.
L4   I might have some typos in the story,
L5   so hopefully you guys can look over them.
Segment B
L6   A/N: Konnichiwa minna-san!!
L7   I'm back! ^^

L8   Okie, I am trying my best to finish up this story,

L9   but I also have to have time to study for my exams. ><;;;;

Segment C

L10   Anyway, since I did good school,

L11   and remembered everything the teacher asked me to,

L12   I will be able to have more time for updating my crappy stories! ^_____^;;;;

Segment D

L13   Thank you all who reviewed this story,

L14   and this chapter is dedicated to **Sakura Blossomz01, wild-gurl, Sweet^-^Rose, DZ pals, Fire Light** and **Lily-Chan.**

L15   Thank you for adding me to your favorite author list! ^//.//^

L16   THANKS FOR THE GREAT SUPPORT YOU ARE GIVING ME! ^_____^

L17   *Hugs her reviewers*

Segment E

L18   By the way, please pay close attentions to the e-mails in this chapter,

L19   because they are some really important clues.

Segment F

L20   ^_____^ MERRY CHRISTMAS EVERYONE!!

L21   THIS ISH MY PRESENT FOR YOU!!

L22   I HOPE YOU'LL LIKE IT!!! ^_____^. (12/1/02)

And she also ends each chapter with closing Author's Notes such as the following.

Closing Author's Note

Segment A

L1   A/N: ><;;; bad writing . . . .

L2   I'm not a good writer . . . . ><;;;

L3   please review, and tell me what you thinks of this story.

L4   Because if you guys don't like it,

L5   I won't write more . . . .

L6   I always say that ^^;;

Segment B

L7   Review!

L8   And no flames!

L9   Au revoir! (12/01/2002)

In the opening Author's Note, Nanako begins the chapter by identifying herself as an ELL in Line 1 and then, in Lines 3 through 5, asking that readers overlook her typos and grammatical and spelling errors. In Segment E, she also directs the readers' attention to certain aspects of the story, in this case the emails between characters. Such communication is a way for Nanako to play at least a small formative role in how readers approach the text and in what sort of feedback they provide. Also, to this end, in the closing A/N she thanks readers for their support and clearly states "no flames!" in Line 8. According the Fanfiction Glossary (2005, no page) "to 'flame' someone is to viciously insult them or their work in a manner that has little or no redeeming value." In this way, she is setting up a supportive writing environment for herself in which readers respond to the content or meaning-value of her fictions rather than to discrete linguistic conventions. Additionally, in Lines 3 and 7 she solicits reader reviews and, through the crying faces ($><$;;;) and by claiming that she is a "bad writer" in Lines 1 and 2, she implicitly is attempting to elicit positive and supportive feedback on her writing.

Nanako's skill at creating and sustaining social networks is also evidenced by these A/Ns. Overall, the conversational tone of the notes, the smiling and crying faces, and the personal asides, such as thanking and wishing readers a Merry Christmas, establishes a backdrop of social as well as writing-related interaction. Additionally, in Segment D, Line 15 of the opening A/N, she thanks readers for adding her to their "favorites list" which is a function of the site by which members can create hyperlinked lists of preferred stories and authors. Such links make it easier for members with shared interests to find each other and for like-minded readers to find Nanako's fan fictions. She also dedicates each chapter to reviewers who provide what she considers to be especially supportive or helpful feedback, as can be seen in Line 14. Another relatively unique aspect of Nanako's A/Ns is the continuously updated *Thank You List* and a *Favorite Reviewers from the Last Chapter List* that she includes with each chapter. In the lists, she writes personal responses to certain reader reviews, thereby through acknowledgment giving explicit encouragement for the sort of feedback she finds helpful, and by omission implicitly discouraging feedback that she finds offensive or trivial. Furthermore, acknowledgment in the chapter dedications or the lists appears to be a status symbol among Nanako's network of readers, and they openly discuss "making it" to the Thank You or Favorite Reviewer lists in their reviews.

Reader Reviews

In looking at posted feedback, it is clear that readers take Nanako's Author's Notes and personal comments into consideration when reviewing. Moreover, close analysis reveals that readers' appreciation for a story, their criteria for what counts as "good writing," as well as the community's notion of what makes a good fan, do not appear to hinge solely on school-based literacy and grammatical conventions. Instead, appreciation for a text seems to be contingent on other elements such as a particular pop cultural aesthetic, readers' affiliation with the anime characters, the author's ability to create engaging storylines, as well as the author's ability and willingness to network and interact with other fans. In this section, I will discuss four types of reviews that are responsive and/or contribute to Nanako's design of her writing space. These types include: (1) the *OMG Standard*, which is a simple form of positive feedback, (2) *Gentle Critique*, which incorporates positive feedback with general suggestions for improvement, (3) *Focused Critique*, which incorporates positive feedback with specific suggestions for improvement, and (4) *Editorialized Gossip*, which focuses on the anime characters as if they were real life personages. Analysis explores how each of these review formats is in dialogue with some aspect of Nanako's online presentation of self. As such, they contribute to Nanako's achieved identity as an anime expert and as an accomplished fan fiction author, as well as to the design of a supportive, interactive writing space. At the same time, these reviews also provide readers with an opportunity to display valued forms of social and intellectual capital for their online peers.

The OMG Standard

In an email detailing her perspective on reader reviews, Nanako explains that "The really sweet ones are actually the ones that inspire me the most. Everytime i read them, i feel all fuzzy and happy inside. It gives me a purpose, a reason for my writing (other than for my own enjoyment XD)" (October 23, 2005). She goes on to explain that "I find the technical-wise suggestions really useful, because it helps me to improve my writing and keep in mind not to make the same mistakes again" (October 23, 2005). Interestingly enough, the most prevalent review structure, one that I call the *OMG Standard*, is a clear example of readers' "sweet" responsiveness to Nanako's stated needs as a writer. OMG is an acronym for the exclamation, "Oh My God!" that is fairly common in Internet Relay Chat (IRC) and online discourse. Basically, this type of review consists of enthusiastic statements of appreciation for the fiction such as, "OMG! I love this chapter!" Of the two hundred coded review structures, 62 were categorized as *OMG Standard*.

While the structure and surface content of *OMG Standard* reviews may appear simple, when viewed in light of the notion of design and socially situated identities, it is clear that there is a notable measure of social networking and affiliatory work being done simultaneously as readers display forms of pop cultural, personal, and social knowledge through such reviews. Moreover, the prevalence of OMG Standard reviews for Nanako's writing is also in keeping with her request that readers overlook her grammatical and spelling errors, as such reviews do not include criticism, but instead provide positive feedback and often some brief encouraging words about features such as plot and character development. Take the following review as an example.

Segment A
- L1   OMG
- L2   this is so kawaii!!
- L3   lol

Segment B
- L4   i guess I should get to the next chapter then!
- L5   Lil' Keko (7/29/03)

In Lines 1 and 2, the reader, Lil' Keko, demonstrates her knowledge of IRC/Online discourse through her use of the common acronyms, "OMG" and "lol" (laugh out loud), and enacts the identity of a tech-savvy member of online networks. In Line 2, she uses the word *kawaii*, a Japanese term for "cute," which serves to mark her insider status as an anime fan. Moreover, Nanako also uses this term a great deal in her personal communications with readers, so it also marks readers' membership in this fan fiction circle as well. In Line 4 Lil' Keko uses the modal verb *should* and an exclamation to express a strong sense of obligation to continue reading, as she is aware that "being a fan" in this space involves enthusiastically following Nanako's chapters and providing reviews throughout a series of chapters. This in turn provides impetus for the author to keep writing. Additionally, this "short but sweet" review format allows Lil' Keko and other readers to comply with Nanako's end-of-chapter requests that they provide many reviews as motivation for her to continue the series.

Gentle Critique

In this section, I focus on reviews that introduce critique in ways that are accepted by Nanako as an English learning writer. Through the analysis and comparison across reviews, I found that reviews including critique often followed a similar structural format. They included: (1) an introduction, personal greeting, or response to an Author's Note, (2) a positive comment on some aspect of the text, (3) critique, (4) a disclaimer or mitigating statement, (5) a positive comment or encouragement to continue writing, and (6) a closing. For example, in the first review type, that of *Gentle Critique*, the reader begins by explicitly responding to an Author's Note in which Nanako claims that her writing "sucks." The reviewer writes,

Segment A
- L1   I THINK YOUR WRITING IS GREAT!!!!
- L2   don't put yourself down
- L3   PLZ CONTINUE!!!!!!

Segment B

L4   there was just a few convention (grammar, spelling, stuff like that.) mistakes,

L5   but you had your reasons.

Segment C

L6   REMEMBER YOU *ARE* A GREAT WRITER OK?

L7   AND CONTINUE!!! (January 12, 2002)

While the reviewer comments on grammatical and spelling errors in Segment B, she also relegates such conventions to the realm of unimportant "stuff" by giving the topic only two lines that are sandwiched between segments that thematically focus on positive comments and encouragement for the author. Moreover, she uses "caps"—or all capital letters—for her text, which is the online equivalent of yelling or raising one's voice, and multiple exclamation points to highlight the importance of the segments and lines containing positive feedback and encouragement. In contrast, Line 4, the line containing critique, is not even capitalized at the start of the sentence. Moreover, in the concluding clause of Line 5, the conjunction "but" is a cohesive device that indicates how the second clause is to be related to the first in Line 4 (Gee 1999). Specifically, Line 5 renders the "conventions" mentioned in Line 4 unimportant with a mitigating statement acknowledging that Nanako "had [her] reasons" for making errors. Presumably the reader is referring to Nanako's self-identification as an ELL in the Author's Notes.

This sort of thematic structure—positive comment; reference to grammatical and spelling errors with an acknowledgment of the author as an ELL; and then encouragement to continue writing—is quite common in reviews of Nanako's work, as well as within other subsections of Fanfiction.net that are frequented by young writers and readers. In addition, this type of review often includes specific comments on how much the reader enjoyed elements of the story such as engaging plotlines or characterizations that are either congruent with common fan expectations, such as pairing popular couples, or congruent with the anime *canon* (the original media on which the fan fictions are based), such as adhering to original character traits. This type of review demonstrates the level of affiliation readers have with the pop cultural subject matter. It also highlights how in this space, writing is deemed valuable not only by virtue of grammatical and conventional correctness, but also by a shared pop cultural aesthetic related to this anime series. (As an aside, different *canons* within Fanfiction.net have separate sections on the site, and the demographic and interactional patterns in these spaces can vary significantly. For instance, the writing community surrounding the soap opera *Guiding Light* has a much older-in-age fan base that focuses on different aspects of writing than the *Card Captor Sakura* community does).

Focused Critique

Another common type of review, that of *Focused Critique,* is one that follows the same structural format and that also includes "sweetness" as well as specific critique and/or "technical-wise suggestions." The review begins with introductory segments aimed at affiliation with and/or encouragement for the author, then has specific critique sandwiched in the middle, and then includes a disclaimer and/or a conclusion that reaffirms the reader's status as a fan of that particular author.

Segment A
> L1   lol.
> L2   Happy early birthday
> L3   *gives her sugar*

Segment B
> L4   I really love your fic.
> L5   It's so . . . sugary
> L6   lol
> L7   I like sugar . . .

Segment C
> L8   I have a couple of suggestions though.
> L9   One is this: the past and present tense (sp).
> L10   Like "I had this to do still."
> L11   Two is the spelling every here and there.
> L12   and Three, like the wording of some things
> L13   like "And thanks again for cheering me up when I'm losing hopes and upset" in the fic.

Segment D
> L14   Okay. That's all.
> L15   Sorry for wasting your time.

Segment E
> L16   Ja ne
> L17   ~Chas (4/22/02)

In Segment A the reviewer, Chas, begins by explicitly responding to one of Nanako's Author's Notes which stated that it was almost her birthday. Assuming an interactive stance, Chas responds by wishing Nanako a happy birthday and displaying her knowledge of the IRC/online discourse by using the acronym "lol" and an *emote* (expression of emotion, action, gesture enclosed in asterisks) in which she *offers her some sugar*. In Segment B she goes on to provide positive feedback and to engage in playful textual banter that draws from the multiple meanings of the word sugar. This playful, performative aspect of her review is another common element in online fan fiction feedback. While not as pronounced in this particular post, many readers respond to the online, networked nature of the site by providing feedback as if they were interacting with and performing for an audience.

After these positive and socially oriented introductory segments, Chas introduces her critiques of the chapter in Segment C. The critiques each begin with a general statement and then narrow to a specific excerpt taken from Nanako's writing. For instance, in Line 9 the reader makes a general statement about Nanako needing to work on past and present tense. Then, in Line 10 she provides a specific example from Nanako's writing that should have been written in the present tense (i.e., I still have to do this.) in order to be consistent with the rest of the paragraph. In these critiques, the reader draws on and displays knowledge of a school-based form of feedback as she comments on specific conventions and traits of writing such as grammar, spelling, and word choice. However, what I find particularly interesting here is the disclaimer in Segment D, Line 15. Such disclaimers are a common feature of how readers structure critique in this space. Specifically, most critique is prefaced by positive input and then followed by a disclaimer or mitigating statement of some sort. In this case, it is interesting that the reviewer seems to apologize for taking up the author's time with the only feedback rooted in a school-based discourse, when she does not add a similar disclaimer/apology after the social and performative lines in Segments A and B.

The next review is also an example of *Focused Critique* in which a reader recasts one of Nanako's paragraphs. Like the other reviewers, Fire Light structures her critique with positive feedback, gentle criticism, a disclaimer, and encouragement to continue. She chooses to recast a paragraph containing two grammatical errors that are relatively salient in Nanako's work, null subjects and comma splices, both of which would be permissible in Nanako's first language (L1) of Mandarin.

Segment A
L1   Hey!
L2   Great story!
L3   I hope you keep going!

Segment B
L4   I just have a little advice for you..
L5   In this paragraph you put:

A few minutes passed., Sakura walked out of the bathroom with a towel wrapped tightly around her body. Hummed a tune as she walked into her room. Her school uniform was placed on her bed neatly. She then got dressed quickly and made her way towards the kitchen. There, she saw her worst enemy eating a bowl of cereals. She glared at him murderously and went to check the fridge, to get some eggs, to make herself some pancakes for breakfast.

L6   You need to change some things.

L7   Instead, for it to make some sense, you could have put:

A few minutes had passed and Sakura walked out of the bathroom with a towel wrapped tightly around her body. Humming a tune, she walked into her room where her school uniform was placed neatly on her bed. She got dressed quickly and then exited and made her way to the kitchen. There, she saw her worst enemy eating a bowl of cereal. She glared at him murderously and went to check the fridge, to get some eggs, to make herself some pancakes for breakfast.

Segment C

L8   That is just an idea!

L9   But this story is really great,

L10   so continue

L11   onegai?!!!

L12   Fire Light (12/22/02)

It seems important to note here that in spite of Nanako's request that readers "overlook" her grammatical and spelling errors, her readers still introduce constructive criticism when they deem it necessary. However, in their critiques, readers only seem to choose errors that are quite salient in Nanako's work and/or that interfere with their understanding or enjoyment of the text. Most readers are careful to avoid "flaming" the writer and instead work to temper constructive critique with appreciation for other aspects of the writing and encouragement for the author. Moreover, the fact that most *Gentle* and *Focused Critique* reviews contain a disclaimer, such as "That is just an idea!" in Line 8, and end with a signal of affiliation and encouragement such as the Japanese term "onegai" in Line 11 meaning "please" or "I beg of you" to continue, seems to indicate that even when making suggestions, readers honor the author's expertise and authority over the writing.

In spite of her earlier request for readers to overlook errors, in a later Author's Note Nanako writes that "nice criticizes, comments, compliments, and suggestions are welcome" (Chapter 12). Moreover, she explicitly expresses appreciation for this pointed sort of "technical" feedback in her *Thank You List* when she responds to Firelight's review and writes, "Thank you! I will correct my mistakes!^___^ *Hugs Fire Light* And thanks for adding me to your favorite list! ^___^." She also returns to her story and corrects the paragraph per Fire Light's suggestions. Additionally, in subsequent chapters, she omits subjects less and less frequently, which could indicate that Fire Light's recasting, as well as other reviewers' references to this particular feature (See Black, in press a, for another example), made Nanako more aware of it in her writing and enabled her to gain a greater command of that aspect of English sentence structure. In addition, there have been instances where Nanako revised a chapter according to readers' suggestions about the storyline. This suggests a negotiation between the author's authority over her own writing and the readers' enjoyment of the text in this space. It seems important for such a balance to exist when all members of the site are so invested in and affiliate around the subject matter.

It is difficult to untangle what grammatical, syntactical, and pragmatic aspects of Nanako's texts might have changed as a result of focused reader feedback versus those that are a result of her in-school English learning. However, there are several common errors from her earlier texts that readers frequently commented on and pointed out in her writing that are seldom present in her later texts. Such features include null subjects and comma splices in instances that would have been permissible in her first language of Mandarin. Another such feature is quotation marks in the representation of dialogue. Other features that changed, although they were not often commented on by readers, include singular/plural errors, subject/verb agreement, and the use of definite versus indefinite articles. So, while I am unwilling to make any causal claims in terms of writing improvement, it does seem reasonable that receiving a great deal of feedback, engaging in written communication with many native English speakers, and practicing writing on a frequent basis may have contributed a great deal to Nanako's language development.

Editorialized Gossip

The last common review type, *Editorialized Gossip*, is one in which the reader discusses anime characters and their exploits as if they were independent of the fan fiction author's pen. For example, the following reviewer, Spryte Luvver, is reacting to a plot twist in which the anime character, Meiling, comes between a popular couple, Sakura and Syaoran. While the review contains several lines referencing Nanako's writing, the primary thematic topics in Segments A, B, D, and E are anime characters as active, independent participants in the story. Moreover in Line 11, Spryte Luvver actually threatens to "hop into the story and shake some sense" into the character Meiling.

Segment A
    L1   OHMYGOD
    L2   Meiling is such an evil evil evil person!
    L3   Not evil, evil's cool, but CREUL!
Segment B
    L4   She really hates Sakura doesn't she!
    L5   And if she DID love Syaoran,
    L6   she wouldn't put him through so much torture by torturing Sakura like that! Ugh!
Segment C
    L7   But the part where Sakura reads the e-mail from "Little Wolf" is so sad!!

Segment D
L8   Meiling better figure out what IS the right thing,
L9   because if she doesn't,
L10   I'm gonna hop into that story and shake some sense into that girl!!
L11   lol . . .

Segment E
L12   And it's a very good thing that Sakura took note of Syaoran's format to write e-mails,
L13   because otherwise she wouldn't pick up the fact
L14   the [that] MEILING IS AN CRUEL PERSON!

Segment F
L15   You use different languages in just the right places . . .
L16   it makes the story quite complete.

Segment G
L17   But I didn't really like the part where Meiling confesses
L18   because it hinted that Syaoran might have FEELINGS for Meiling . . .
L19   I HOPE NOT!

Segment H
L20   And I hope Syaoran gets Sakura back
L21   because this chapter is really sad,
L22   and I want the last chapter to be happy-go-lucky!!

Segment I
L23   Will the season finale be followed up by a sequel?
L24   I hope! (Spryte Luvver; September 6, 2003)

This sort of "willing suspension of disbelief" is a common feature in this space and further demonstrates the high level of commitment these writers and readers have to the pop cultural subject matter. Moreover, this review provides additional evidence of reader's attempts to negotiate with Nanako about her writing. For example, in Segments G and H the reviewer explicitly comments on plot action and concludes each with a line stating her own wishes for the direction of the next chapter. Then, in Segment I, she expresses the wish that Nanako follow the "season finale" with a "sequel" and in each of these three segments, ends by punctuating her wishes with caps and/or exclamation points.

Another interesting aspect of this review that is quite common with Nanako's readers is how the reviewer expresses appreciation for the multilingual nature of her writing. In fact, Nanako's fictions often incorporate Japanese, which she is learning at school in Canada, and Mandarin Chinese, her L1. In this particular instance, Nanako has used Mandarin Chinese, also the L1 of Meiling and Syaoran, to convey intimacy between the two characters in an emotionally charged portion of the story. The characters Syaoran and Meiling are from Hong Kong, so their L1 is most likely Cantonese rather than Mandarin Chinese. Nanako uses a little artistic license here. Some readers bring this point up, but they still express appreciation for the sentiment created through her use of different languages. Syaoran and Meiling are not the preferred couple pairing, and the reader responds emotionally to the effect that Nanako's use of Chinese has in this particular scene. Specifically, it causes the reader to worry that the preferred couple might be in jeopardy. Thus, rather than being viewed as a deficit or hindrance that interferes with her ability to compose in English, Nanako's L1 is recognized as an additive element that contributes positively to her writing and to her achieved identity as a popular anime fan fiction author.

Implications for Literacy and Language Education

Digital Literacies

Research within the New Literacy Studies, and across other professional and academic domains, has explored broad shifts in our increasingly globalized, networked, and linguistically and culturally diverse society. A common thread across such work is the "new division of labor" between people and computers and the imminent divide between "those who can and those who cannot do valued work in an economy filled with computers" (Levy and Murnane 2004, 2). Another commonality is the growing recognition that traditional forms of literacy, such as print-based reading and writing, are necessary but not sufficient for effective work (Levy and Murnane 2004), leisure (Gee 2004), or academic (Labbo, Reinking and McKenna 1998) participation in an information society (Castells 1996) that depends on meaning making through an array of "texts" including conventional print documents, as well as graphic arts, spoken and embodied language, video, audio, and other forms of online and post-typographic communication (Lankshear and Knobel 2003).

This poses a special problem for ELLs and struggling writers and readers in classrooms when they already are ascribed roles as learners who need to focus *primarily* on learning discrete, technical aspects of print-based reading, writing, and the English language, and are not provided with ample opportunities to "engage in processes of digital composing and reading that will allow them to discover their ideas, to realize communicative goals, and to develop digital fluency" (Labbo, Reinking and McKenna 1998). It seems reasonable then, to look at the initiatives school-age ELL writers and readers are already taking in out-of-school spaces, such as Fanfiction.net, in terms of how they might be developing the crucial design (Gee 2004) and key digital literacy skills (Labbo, Reinking and McKenna 1998) required for full social, civic, and economic participation in New Capitalist workplaces and an information-focused society.

In conclusion then, I would like to return to the three interrelated aspects of design, those of affinity spaces, networks, and identities to discuss what implications research in fan fiction sites might have for literacy and language education in the future.

Affinity Spaces, Networks, and Learning How to Learn

Labbo, Reinking and McKenna (1998) argue that educators need to view the computer as a tool that can augment thought and "create opportunities for students to digitally encounter, discover, and articulate their thoughts through digital composing and problem solving" (p. 278) even while engaged in the pursuit of other goals. Fanfiction.net provides a clear example of an affinity space in which members are using digital literacy skills to discover, discuss, and solve writing and reading-related problems, while at the same time pursuing the goals of developing social networks and affiliating with other fans. This is evident in how Nanako learns to leverage the networked technology and the computer-mediated forms of communication available on Fanfiction.net to design an effective learning environment that meets her needs as an ELL and enables her to achieve the online identity of a successful writer. The affordances of online communication allow her to publicly present her writing as a means of discovering and problem solving English language-related issues, while at the same time displaying her expert knowledge as a multilingual speaker and as a fan.

Because there is a wide range of expertise and forms of knowledge that are valued in affinity spaces, and because there is an absence of authorized roles and imposed forms of knowledge, Nanako and her readers are able to maintain confidence while at the same time acting as learners in varying capacities. Writers and readers in this space are also able to draw from various networks of information that are dispersed across people (reviewers, co-writers, fan fiction consultants), tools (spellcheckers, thesauruses), other media, and websites (writing help sites, fan sites). This distributed type of knowledge is also a defining feature of affinity spaces. Thus, in terms of literacy education, Fanfiction.net could provide one exemplar for a classroom learning environment where the emphasis, rather than being focused on *propositional* knowledge that primarily involves the learning of content area facts and figures, is instead moving toward *procedural* knowledge that involves the acquisition of skills and strategies for how to learn and continue learning (Lankshear and Knobel 2003) via networks, distributed funds of knowledge, and computers. This procedural knowledge, also described as "expert thinking" and "complex communication" (Levy and Murnane 2004); the "ability to be a lifelong learner" and "learning in social contexts" (Labbo, Reinking and McKenna 1998); and "progressive, communal knowledge building" (Scardamalia and Bereiter 1994), is also identified as a key aspect of being digitally literate in a society where resources are increasingly dispersed across computer and internet networks.

Popular Culture, Identity, and Critical Media Literacy

Another set of implications for literacy education relates to the pop cultural subject matter that provides a nexus of affiliation for Fanfiction.net. Work within language and literacy studies has begun to emphasize the import of popular culture for students in providing metaphors for the construction of cultural models (Tobin 2000, Zuengler 2003), narratives for interpreting and structuring experience (Alvermann, Moon and Hagood 1999; see also, Thomas, this volume), and semiotic resources for developing social identities through writing (Black 2005, Dyson 1997, Jenkins 2004, Lam 2000, Lam in press, Newkirk 2000; see also, Thomas, this volume). In addition, the preceding analyses reveal how popular culture is an integral component of social affiliations and a springboard for meaningful interactions around language, writing, and literacy on Fanfiction.net. Nanako is able to leverage her knowledge of anime culture to practice conventional and pragmatic aspects of English, experiment with different genres of writing, and gain a great deal of discourse or communicative competence in the fan fiction register through her written exchanges with other fans. Readers are able to draw from their knowledge of grammatical and syntactical aspects of English and school-based forms of peer-feedback, as well as their knowledge of anime, to display forms of expertise and to practice and share specialist forms of language (Gee 2004) with Nanako. Such activities also enable them to build on their achieved identities as conversant anime fans.

The essential implication here is that substantive literacy instruction does not need to focus on learning as an elite and solitary enterprise centered on authorized interpretations of canonical texts (Newkirk 2000). Instead, print literacy can be made "more attractive and possible by being imbedded in systems that are, at least initially, more attractive to the learner" (Newkirk 2000, 297). Such systems might include social scaffolds such as collaborative writing through networks or multimodal writing through digital literacy and online authoring software. Or, such systems might include a range of student-selected pop cultural and current event-related topics in which all students, including ELLs, have a frame of reference and/or a measure of expertise. Choosing such topics can provide a departure point for authentic communication as students use and develop literacy skills to discuss and debate topics and display various forms of expertise in areas that are meaningful and relevant to their achieved identities and social worlds.

Conclusion

In closing, I am not suggesting that educators adopt popular culture and fan fiction wholesale into their curriculum, as this would certainly diminish its popularity with students. Nonetheless, I do think there is a vital need for educators to critically engage with and develop activities around media and popular culture that are central to students' lives. Research in fan fiction sites has the potential to expand our understandings of how new generations of learners are using digital as well as print-based literacies to play agentive roles in designing and negotiating learning spaces, creating and sustaining social networks, and enacting achieved identities as engaged, competent, and literate members of a writing community. Moreover, as Lankshear and Knobel (2003) point out, with the advent of new ICTs and the widespread movement toward globalization, there perhaps have been profound changes, not only in the world of literacies *to be known* but also in *how to know* the literacies of the world. Thus, as literacy educators and researchers, at minimum, we ought to take note of these changes, and optimally, to learn from these changes and integrate them into our understandings of literacy instruction in schools.

References

Alvermann, D., Moon, J. and Hagood, M. 1999. *Popular Culture in the Classroom: Teaching and Researching Critical Media Literacy*. Newark, DE: International Reading Association.

Black, R. W. 2005. Access and affiliation: The literacy and composition practices of English language learners in an online fanfiction community. *Journal of Adolescent & Adult Literacy* 49(2): 118–128.

Black, R. W. 2006. Language, literacy, and culture in online fanfiction. *E-learning* 3(2): 170–84.

Black, R. W. In press a. Convergence and divergence: Online fanfiction communites and literacy pedagogy. To appear in Z. Bekerman, N. Burbules, and H. Giroux (Eds), *Mirror Images: Popular Culture and Education*. Boulder, CO: Rowman & Littlefield Publishing Co.

Black, R. W. In press b. Just don't call them cartoons: The new literacy spaces of anime, manga, and fanfiction. To appear in D. Leu, J. Coiro, M. Knobel and C. Lankshear (Eds), *Handbook of Research on New Literacies*. Mahwah, NJ: Erlbaum.

Castells, M. 1996. *The Rise of the Network Society. The Information Age: Economy, Society and Culture*, Vol. 1. Malden, MA: Blackwell Publishers.

Cope, B. and Kalantzis, M. (Eds) 2000. *Multiliteracies: Literacy Learning and the Design of Social Futures*. London: Routledge.

Dyson, A. 1997. *Writing Superheroes: Contemporary Childhood, Popular Culture, and Classroom Literacy*. New York: Teachers College Press.

Fanfiction Glossary 2005. *Flame*. http://www.subreality.com/glossary/terms.htm#F (accessed 1 May 2005).

Gee, J. 1986. Units in the production of narrative discourse. *Discourse Processes* 9: 391–422.

Gee, J. 1996. *Social Linguistics and Literacies*. London: Taylor & Francis.

Gee, J. 1999. *An Introduction to Discourse Analysis*. London: Routledge.

Gee, J. 2001. Identity as an analytic lens for research in education. In W. G. Secada (Ed.) *Review of Research in Education*. Washington, D.C.: American Educational Research Association. 99–126.

Gee, J. 2004. *Situated Language and Learning: A Critique of Traditional Schooling*. New York: Routledge.

Halliday, M. and Matthiessen, C. 2004. *An Introduction to Functional Grammar*. London: Hodder Arnold.

Jenkins, H. 2004. Why Heather can write. *Technology Review*. technologyreview.com/articles/04/02/wo_jenkins020604.asp?p=1 (accessed 28 September, 2005).

Labbo, L., Reinking, D., and McKenna, M. 1998. Technology and literacy education in the next century: Exploring the connection between work and schooling. *Peabody Journal of Education* 73(3&4): 273–89.

Lam, W. S. E. 2000. Literacy and the design of the self: A case study of a teenager writing on the internet. *TESOL Quarterly* 34: 457–82.

Lam, W. S. E. In press. Re-envisioning language, literacy, and the immigrant subject in new mediascapes. *Pedagogies: An International Journal*.

Lankshear, C., and Knobel, M. 2003. *New Literacies: Changing Knowledge and Classroom Learning*. Philadelphia, PA: Open University Press.

Lave, J. and Wenger, E. 1991. *Situated Learning: Legitimate Peripheral Participation*. Cambridge: Cambridge University Press.

Levy, F. and Murnane, R. 2004. *The New Division of Labor: How Computers Are Creating the Next Job Market*. New York: Sage University Press.

Luke, C. 2000. Cyber-schooling and technological change. In B. Cope and M. Kalantzis (Eds), *Multiliteracies: Literacy Learning and the Design of Social Futures*. London: Routledge. 69–91.

New London Group 1996. A pedagogy of multiliteracies: Designing social futures. *Harvard Educational Review* 66: 60–92.

Newkirk, T. 2000. Misreading masculinity: Speculations on the great gender gap in writing. *Language Arts* 77(4): 294–300.

Scardamalia, M. and Bereiter, C. 1994. Computer support for knowledge-building communities. *Journal of the Learning Sciences* 3(3): 265–83.

Tobin, J. 2000. *Good Guys Don't Wear Hats: Children's Talk about the Media*. New York: Teachers College Press.

Wenger, E. 1999. *Communities of Practice: Learning, Meaning and Identity*. Cambridge, UK: Cambridge University Press.

Zuengler, J. 2003. Jackie Chan drinks Mountain Dew: Constructing cultural models of citizenship. In L. Harklau and J. Zuengler (Eds), Special Issue on "Popular Culture and Classroom Language Learning," *Linguistics and Education* 14(3–4): 277–304.

CHAPTER SEVEN

Blurring and Breaking through the Boundaries of Narrative, Literacy, and Identity in Adolescent Fan Fiction

Angela Thomas

Introduction: Understanding Fan Fiction

The origins of fan fiction can be traced back to the 1930s pulp magazine, *Fanzines*, and enjoyed a surge in the late 1960s with the popularity of *Star Trek* (Jenkins 1992). Since then, according to Black (2004), fan fiction is ". . . an element of popular culture that is ever growing in popularity as new technologies enable native and non-native speaking fans from all over the globe to meet online to share, critique, and build upon each other's fictions" (no page). Borrowing settings, plots, characters and ideas from all forms of media and popular culture, fans weave together new tales, sometimes within the accepted canon (the real works from which they are borrowing), sometimes blending several ideas from different sources together in a type of fiction called "Crossovers" (e.g., *Star Wars* meets Tolkien's Middle Earth), and sometimes imagining new possibilities for additional characters, different histories or different settings that build on existing stories, called "Alternative Universe" fiction.

With the flourishing of fan sites online in general, the number of fan fiction sites has become prolific with many thousands of sites dedicated to fan fiction writing and borrowing from such diverse sources as *Harry Potter*, anime cartoons and *Lord of the Rings* (to name just a few). Academic attention is now being focused on fan fiction, or "fanfic," with Henry Jenkins leading some of the foremost debate about its value for the development of children's writing. His observation that, ". . . not everything that kids learn from popular culture is bad for them: some of the best writing instruction takes place outside the classroom" (Jenkins 2004, no page), sparked a furor in the U.S., and an internet buzz of memetic proportion on websites all over. Jenkins observed that through posting fan fiction online and receiving critical feedback from peers, many young people, particularly female adolescents, were gaining considerable insight into the writing process.

Another of Jenkins's claims was that the fans should be considered active designers and transformers of content whereby they draw upon the canon, or literate texts that are available resources and then manipulate them and integrate them with their own resources, knowledge, backgrounds and identities to construct something new. In further explicating some of the literacy skills developed by fanfic writers, Lewis (2004) discusses the value of pop culture in providing a rich scaffold for children's writing. She claims,

> What fan fiction offers to these young writers is a great, existing storyline; interesting, three-dimensional characters that have already been developed; and a wealth of back story to both pull from and write about. The inexperienced author doesn't have to spend all his or her time developing something original, but instead can focus on the actual skill of writing. It allows young authors to practice their craft without expending huge amounts of time and energy developing something "original." As they build their "writing muscles," their writing improves and they tend to stray farther and farther from the source material (Lewis 2004, 3).

If we accept these two ideas we can re-conceptualize an image of young fanfic writers *without* the stigma associated with Jenkins's use of de Certeau's term "poacher" (Jenkins 1992) and, instead, *with* the notion that they are active manipulators and designers of original texts, using given cultural artifacts as a scaffold and launching point from which to develop considerable and worthwhile originality. In this chapter I focus particularly on fan fiction created in online spaces, with an emphasis on the social and discursive literacy practices in which young people are immersed.

Education scholars including, Cope and Kalantzis (2000), Kress (2003), Luke (1997), and Snyder (2002), have suggested that online literacies form new hybrid textualities and possibly even new genres worthy of further analysis and discussion. Luke (1997, 25), for example, argues that e-literacies have created new forms of literary practice, and states, "blended vocabularies and reading-writing practices require new multi-modal and multi-media literacies . . . new textual forms of conversational turn-taking . . . [and] new writing and communication strategies." At this stage, relatively few scholars are investigating such hybrid forms of textualities. What I am proposing to do in this chapter, then, is to closely interrogate one form of e-literacy: the construction of fan fiction.

Blurring Boundaries: Narrative

This chapter focuses on a case study of two adolescent females: Tiana, aged 14 years, and Jandalf, aged 17 years, friends who met online and who have been collaboratively creating fan fiction for over a year. Tiana and Jandalf were both part of a larger ethnographic study of children's construction of literacy and identity in online communities that I had been conducting online for more than 4 years at the time. This chapter focuses on just these two girls in order to explore the possibilities and potentials of fan fiction.

Both avid writers of fan fiction for some years, Tiana and Jandalf decided to explore the possibilities of co-writing a piece. In speaking of the benefits of co-writing, Jandalf stated:

Oh . . . where do I start . . . (grins) Tiana and I, while being eerily similar in many ways, definitely have our differing strengths. It's such a joy to me to put them together into one big piece because, in this way, we're able to contribute so much more than we could alone. She's good at looking into people's heads, and I love the dialogue and interaction parts, and you know what they say about two heads being four times as good as one . . .

Tiana responded similarly, stating:

By working together in conjunction with someone who writes three times better than I do when it comes to dialogue—though I am probably better at view points—we balance each other out, and contract our individual skills. My spelling, for one thing, has improved, as has my grammar. A lot. I mean, a few months ago I would've spelt grammar as grammer and not known it was wrong . . . heh. But we contrast with our writing skills, and by that, make each other stronger. By focusing on strengthening another's weak points, you begin to allow yourself to write deeper in on your own weaknesses, and strengthen yourself in those points. I think that, in a sense, she has become a Master, at least for some things like this—though I learn through osmosis . . . heh heh. But allowing yourself to see your weaknesses through another's eyes can strengthen your stronger points. I'll always prefer co-authoring fan fictions now.

Tiana and Jandalf engage in a range of literacy practices in the process of creating a piece of fan fiction. To describe this process, Tiana outlined the following:

The process we work through to create our fan fiction, is to first role-play the narrative out using Yahoo Instant Messenger. We go on Yahoo, sometimes spend about

5 minutes talking about where the plot is going, and then just write. If there's any confusion, the narrators step in, or we use OOC (out of character) chatter to help out. But we rarely think about what we're doing, we just write like heck, and get as much done as we can in a short time. When we get big plot bunnies [i.e., narrative plotline ideas], sometimes we email each other about them though. Usually though we just improvise . . . yeah . . . that's about it. We write so much better when we don't think about what's going on.

The fanfiction is then written out by me. I save all the RPG [Role-Playing Game] chats, and rewrite them from their script format into a fan fiction that is more like standard narrative form.

I was intrigued by this process. I have observed role-playing communities, and fan fiction communities, but had not seen any young people who were crossing over from one practice into another. Tiana and Jandalf seemed to be pushing the limits and blurring the boundaries in a number of ways, including blurring understandings about narrative as a distinct form, blurring the boundaries of reality and fantasy and challenging all notions of what it might mean to be literate in the digital age.

When Tiana first sent me a transcript of the role-playing she and Jandalf were engaged in I found it rather difficult to comprehend. Below is an example:

Audreidi:	Auddie: Uh . . . well, there seems to be a connection between us as well. From what, exactly, I'm not sure.
EowynSkywalker:	((Auddie will know, of course . . . later . . .))
Audreidi:	((yes . . .))
EowynSkywalker:	Tiana: And I don't know either. But if my suspicious are correct, you won't have long to figure it out.
Audreidi:	((you mean about the not-yet twins?))
EowynSkywalker:	((Ummm . . . that, and she'll know that Tiana's doomed. Snicker.))
EowynSkywalker:	((and she might understand Shadow's motives . . .))
Audreidi:	Auddie:What do you mean? We're going to take numerous hyperspace trips, aren't we? We've got time. Maybe not all the time in the galaxy, but we've time enough.
Audreidi:	((she already knows about Jandalf's twins thru the bond.))
EowynSkywalker:	Tiana: No . . . not all the time in the galaxy. I don't know . . . . seven months, maybe . . .
EowynSkywalker:	((yes . . . but does she know what's happening to Tiana and Shadow?))
Audreidi:	Auddie: Seven months? You have a lot of explaining to do.
Audreidi:	((not in exact detail, she doesn't. Heh heh.))

EowynSkywalker:	Tiana: Seven months is the longest it'll take to destroy this plot bunny.
EowynSkywalker:	((she will. Tiana's going to tell her.))
Audreidi:	Auddie: Well.
EowynSkywalker:	Tiana: If I'm correct, I'm bound to this plot bunny . . . through . . . something. I don't know . . . I just . . . have a really bad feeling about this.
Audreidi:	Auddie: That makes two of us. Or more.
EowynSkywalker:	Tiana: I'd think so, yes
Audreidi:	Auddie: Jandalf's been extremely concerned about you lately.
EowynSkywalker:	Tiana: I know. I've felt it through the training bond.
Audreidi:	Auddie: That and she's probably told you about it. I'd like to know what's going on, if it isn't too much trouble. About Shadow, I mean. And you.
EowynSkywalker:	Tiana: I don't know everything yet . . . I have a feeling that later, I'll know . . . and later you'll probably be even more worried. Shadow is me, you know . . . but different. She has her own motives.
Audreidi:	Auddie: Motives, eh?
EowynSkywalker:	Tiana: She has reason to want me dead.

In this example Jandalf is writing as Audreidi/Auddie and Tiana is writing as EowynSkywalker/Tiana. When role-playing the girls share numerous secondary characters in addition to their central characters. They have developed an intricate plotline in which both Tiana and Jandalf have alternate identities in a shadowed world which runs parallel to their existing world (like the movie *Sliding Doors*), and Tiana in her existing world is a Padawan (like Annakin Skywalker, she is training to be a Jedi knight) but this is in constant tension with a dark side of her personality which takes on a physical form and is named Shadow. Tiana is struggling not to turn to the dark side (like Darth Vader) and let Shadow overpower her, since if that occurred, Tiana, the Jedi side of her, would die. As they role-play, the out-of-character (OOC) prompts to each other, denoted by the lines of text inside double parentheses, serve to maintain the integrity of the ideas they have had to date and drive the narrative forward in a consistent and coherent manner. Role-playing several times a week over an entire year in a multiplicity of roles, it would be easy to fall out of character or stumble awkwardly over plot details, so the OOC talk is imperative. Additionally, it is clear that Tiana has a sense of where she wants to drive the plot, as evident in her comment, "She will . . . Tiana's going to tell her," so the OOC talk also serves as a narrative device to drive the plot forward.

In the chat interface, Instant Messenger, transcripts of chat can be logged and saved as text files. Tiana uses their chat transcripts as the source for creating the fan fiction. Keeping true to the dialogue, she inserts the contextual cues, setting, and paralinguistic cues of character behavior to transform the role-play into narrative form. In transforming the above role-play, for example, into a piece of fan fiction, Tiana wrote the following:

Confused, Audreidi looked at her closely. "Well, there seems to be a connection between us as well. From what, exactly, I'm not sure."

"And I don't know either," Tiana admitted. "But if my suspicions are correct, you won't have long to figure it out."

There was a connection to the two of them, which existed for one reason—in this mirror world, there was exactly two things that were not mirrored: Tiana and Audreidi.

"What do you mean?" Audreidi asked. "We're going to take numerous hyperspace trips, aren't we? We've got time. Maybe not all the time in the galaxy, but we've got time enough . . ." Hanging at the end of that was one thing. Don't we?

Tiana shook her head, her eyes falling into a strange shadow. "No . . . not all the time in the galaxy. Seven months, maybe . . ."

Audreidi grabbed Tiana's arm. "Seven months? You have a lot of explaining to do."

"Seven months is the longest time it will take to unwravel this plot bunny, and fix this paradox we're caught up in—and creating," Tiana said, quietly. "If I'm correct . . . I'm . . . bound to this time's plot . . . in a manner . . . through . . . Shadow . . . something I don't know. I just have a really, really bad feeling about this."

"That makes two of us. Or more." Audreidi let go of Tiana to observe the girl's reactions.

"I'd think so, yes," Tiana said, still soft, and her tone not her own.

Audreidi narrowed her eyes. "Jandalf's been extremely concerned about you lately."

"I know. I've felt that much through the training bond," Tiana said, dryly, but yet with a deep desperation in her voice.

Audreidi smiled faintly. "That, and she's probably told you about it."

"Well, that too."

Audreidi's eyes were sharp. "I'd like to know what's going on, if it isn't too much trouble. About Shadow, I mean. And you."

Tiana smirked. "How can anyone explain Shadow? You'll never know her until you meet her—and even then, she'll confuse you. I don't know everything yet . . . later, I know I'll know . . . and later, you'll probably be even more confused. Shadow is me, you know . . . but different. She has her own motives." Again, she decided to leave things out—such as that the two of them could not co-exist without destroying the other, and by Jandalf turning Shadow back, Tiana would have to fall. Or something deeper . . .

"Motives, eh?"

Tiana smiled distantly, her face twisting into a wry parody of Shadow's then. "She has reason to want me dead."

In this transformation, Tiana has added narrative voice to the dialogue, which alerts the reader to the character's thoughts and struggles. Here, it is Audreidi who is struggling with confusion and insecurity because of Tiana's strange behavior. Tiana has added the lines "Confused, Audreidi looked at her closely" to foreground and thematize the state of Audreidi's feelings. Adding the word "closely" acts as a modal resource to indicate to the reader the precise manner of Audreidi's actions. Later, the line: "Hanging at the end of that was one thing. Don't we?" offers us an insight into the insecurities experienced by Audreidi, as she worries about her relationship with Tiana. This insecurity is a result of Tiana's earlier admission about her suspicions related to time. The words "hanging at the end" and "Don't we?" have a poignant sense to them, foreshadowing a sense of doom in the narrative that was not obvious from the dialogue alone in the role-playing transcript.

Similarly, in the fan fiction version, readers are given a much better insight into the internal battle Tiana is undergoing as she struggles with the self that is Shadow. In the fan fiction, Tiana has added in words such as "a voice not her own," and "her face twisting in a wry parody of Shadow's." She also speaks "dryly" and "smirks," causing Audreidi to "narrow her eyes," "smile faintly" and have "sharp eyes." The adjectives and adverbs used to describe the characters' actions act as interpersonal resources to illuminate for the reader each character's state of mind.

It is necessary to step back and consider the process of both text construction and text transformation here. I asked Tiana to explain this to me. She responded at length, writing:

> the last scene I did was the "death" segment . . . a month back? . . . something like that. Which, I must say, was the most intensive scene we've ever role-played, to the point of being nerve racking to my real self, who was crying through some of it, and making everyone in the house make odd faces at her. Hey, I couldn't help being in character . . .

> It was hard to transcribe that scene, being as I wasn't just in character for Tiana, but I had to slip somewhat into Audreidi at the beginning. It's an easy process to basically do it—I open up two windows in notepad, and make them half the size of the screen. One I open the [chat transcript] archive into, and the other I use to transcribe. Then it's fairly simple—I recopy the dialogue and narrator-script over, but in proper formatting. (Which is why I complain when Jandalf never does any narrator comments, or character emotions in brackets, and why I always do them. Well, a lot of the time.)

Once I get the basic scene down, I go back over it, and edit it, adding in detail, editing a bit of the dialogue—sometimes I remove whole pieces that don't make any sense or add anything to the plotline. Jandalf actually asked me to add in a line once or twice.

It's similar to the Rping [role-playing] in that I don't think once I'm into the process. Sometimes I'll pull back, and think over it. *Okay, would so and so ever even think of saying that, considering what happened in a later scene?! Of COURSE NOT, GIRL! Okay, edit away . . .*

I force myself to learn to write relatively in character merely for the sake of godmodding some scenes to fit in later on. I . . . go through a scene as each [of the] characters . . . to learn how the other's mind's work. When transcribing the dialogue, you sort of have to, because I have to write thoughts, actions, and describe all of the little things of those likes. It's rather annoying . . . Jandalf comments that I pay attention to all the details that seem unimportant, but for my half of this, I HAVE TO!

When I transcribe over, I sort of become two people—Tiana and a narrator. I make myself see things from the third person POV [point of view], while still writing as my characters, in a sense. . . . That's how I do it, anyhow. See the characters as I see my own world. Heck, it IS my own world.

The intensity of emotion Tiana speaks of when discussing her role-playing reveals her depth of investment in her writing. She feels and identifies so much with her character that her body experiences genuine pain over the tragedies that are written into the plot.

The "godmodding" Tiana referred to is critical to maintaining consistency. Tiana edits illogical lines that do not cohere with the plot and inserts other lines to foreshadow what she knows will later become important to the narrative. Similarly, Tiana's comments reveal her meta-fictive awareness during the role-playing stage, indicating that she always inserts narrator comments or character emotions in brackets because she knows they will play an important role in helping her with transforming the role-play transcript into the fan fiction text.

There are considerable contrasts between the role play text and the fan fiction text. I will focus further on this to describe the genre of each.

Bhatia (1999) claims that although the scope and sequence of any genre have core and necessary linguistic features, expert writers of this text enjoy experimenting beyond a mere prescriptive formula of what needs to be included, and playfully modify genres to fulfil their individual and specific purposes. He asserts:

Practising a genre is almost like playing a game, with its own rules and conventions. Established genre participants, both writers and readers, are like skilled players, who succeed by their manipulation and exploitation of, rather than a strict compliance with, the rules of the game. . . . It is not simply a matter of learning the language, or even learning the rules of the game, it is more like acquiring the rules of the game in order to be able to exploit and manipulate them to fulfil professional and disciplinary purposes (Bhatia 1999, 25–26).

The earlier description of the process used by Tiana and Jandalf to jointly construct fan fiction is clearly a playful manipulation of everything they have learned about the fantasy genre, coupled with their exploitations of the affordances of technology. Furthermore, they have mastered a range of literary techniques in their writing, drawing upon intertextual references from literature, media and personal experiences to create their intricately woven narratives.

In fact, the complex process through which Jandalf and Tiana's fanfic is mediated raises questions about the nature of narrative. According to Barthes (1966), narratives are universal in the human condition, informing our very understanding of life itself. He claimed:

> The narratives of the world are numberless. Narrative is first and foremost a prodigious variety of genres, themselves distributed amongst different substances—as though any material were fit to receive man's stories. Able to be carried by articulated language, spoken or written, fixed or moving images, gestures, and the ordered mixture of all these substances; narrative is present in myth, legend, fable, tale, novella, epic, history, tragedy, drama, comedy, mime, painting . . . stained glass windows, cinema, comics, news items, conversation. Moreover, under this almost infinite diversity of forms, narrative is present in every age, in every place, in every society; it begins with the very history of mankind and there is nowhere nor has there been a people without narrative. . . . It is simply there, like life itself (Barthes 1966, cited in Sontag 1982, 251–252)

In examining the range of discursive practices in which Tiana and Jandalf are engaged, we can argue that they all work synergistically to form the narrative. The role-playing, the out-of-character discussions occurring synchronously within the role-playing, the character journals, the artwork, the careful plotting out of story-lines, the forum discussions, the descriptions of worlds and cultures, the invention of language, the playful spoofing, the in-role poetry, the meta-textual allusions to sound effects, movie techniques and so on—all contribute to the narrative fantasy world they have created and indeed in which they themselves exist.

Abbott's (2002) distinction between story and discourse contributes a helpful point here. Abbott claims:

> we never see the story directly, but instead we always pick it up through the narrative discourse. The story is always mediated—by a voice, a style of writing, camera angles, actor's interpretations—so that what we call the story is really something that we construct. We put it together from what we read or see, often by influence (Abbott 2002, 17).

The story, then, emerges from reading the corpus of texts created by Tiana and Jandalf. Our understanding is mediated by the variety of voices, styles and actions of each of them. Because they keep separate character journals we hear their separate voices, and can see the story through the eyes of both characters. We gain insight into the thoughts, feelings, histories, hopes and dreams of each character through their internal monologue, and we understand their individual interactions outside of the central plot through the recounts of events, conversations and descriptions entered into their Livejournal blogs (known by users as simply, "livejournals").

In the forums and role-playing we see the central plot as a dramatic unfolding of events. We also see a richness and intricacy of narrative form, as they weave together elements from their plotting, their diaries, the backstories, the images and descriptions they have created about the culture of their worlds, as well as a host of intertextual references from books, movies, and from their own personal identities.

Reading and viewing the range of narrative discourses constructed by Tiana and Jandalf allows the reader to construct the story; a story seeped in mythology, fantasy, mystery, romance, tragedy and intrigue. The familiarity experienced when reading it is in small part attributed to the use of *Star Wars* and Middle Earth as launching points for the narrative, but is also related to our recognition of narrative form. Furthermore, our understanding is constructed through our recognition of Tiana and Jandalf's adolescent angst, echoing the experiences of young people we see mediated through popular culture teen movies or even, possibly, reflecting elements of our own youth.

I now want to return to my earlier claim that Tiana and Jandalf appeared to be pushing limits and blurring boundaries in many ways, and to consider more closely the limits of narrative. Abbott argues that role-playing games are *not* in fact narrative, because their form is "like life itself" (Abbott 2002, 32). Events unfold on their own, as a collaborative enterprise that could not otherwise exist. He claims that life, theatre improvisation and role-playing games are all alike in this respect [for an alternative take on role-playing and narrative, see Hammer, this volume]. They exist *in the moment*, rather than in true narrative form, as a representation to convey story. Ludologists have been debating over the differences between ludology and narratology for years now (see, for example, Ludology.org). I agree that role-playing and a piece of fiction are distinctly different, and support Abbott's argument that these forms are not narrative but, rather, are "the seed-ground of stories" (Abbott 2002, 33).

Yet, as I have noted, Tiana and Jandalf don't just role-play, nor do they just write fan fiction narratives; they engage in all of those other literary practices outlined earlier (e.g., poetry writing, character journals, artwork). And when they are engaged in the role-play, they are not entirely living and improvising in the moment. Instead they have an initial think-out time, and are subsequently still talking, planning, reflecting and musing in *out-of-character* chatter, denoted by the remarks enclosed by double parentheses in the transcript. They are also inevitably drawing upon what they have learned—from reading each other's livejournals, re-reading their already uploaded previous chapters, discussions within the fan fiction community, comments by parents (and researchers!) and friends about the storyline to date, and from the posts they have each made to their online forum discussing the setting, customs, clothing and culture in which they are situated. The intent too is different—the role-play is not performed and left in that instance. It is intended as a vehicle for their fan fiction.

To think about this more carefully it is helpful to think about genre. Texts are designed for social purposes, to perform various social functions. Genre theorists argue that any text forms a social function, and uses a range of specific linguistic features to achieve this function (e.g., Briggs and Bauman 1992, Cook 1989, Johns 2002, Kellner 1980, Paltridge 2001, Swales 1990, Thwaites, Davis and Mules 1994). Each genre has a unique set of features. In defining genre, Swales, for example, states:

> A genre comprises a class of communicative events, the members of which share some set of communicative purposes. These purposes are recognized by the expert members of the parent discourse community, and thereby constitute the rationale for the genre. This rationale shapes the schematic structure of the discourse and influences and constrains choice of content and style. Communicative purpose is both a privileged criterion and one that operates to keep the scope of a genre as here conceived narrowly focused on comparable rhetorical action. In addition to purpose, exemplars of a genre exhibit various patterns of similarity in terms of structure, style, content and intended audience. If all high probability expectations are realized, the exemplar will be viewed as prototypical by the parent discourse community. The genre names inherited and produced by discourse communities and imported by others constitute valuable ethnographic communication, but typically need further validation (Swales 1990, 58).

Swales observes that certain sets of linguistic features form common patterns that are recognized in texts by their audiences, who understand and engage in the discourses or in the underlying belief systems and assumptions of such texts. Swales argues also that the scope and sequence of a particular genre are typical of all texts with the same social purpose. Hence, we should pay close attention to the social purpose of a text in order to classify it, and a text will have patterns that are recognizable by audiences who engage in them. Using this as a guide, I would argue that the social purpose of the role-playing which Tiana and Jandalf engage in through Yahoo! Instant Messenger is actually a *rehearsal* of the narrative. It doesn't stand alone in any form but is used as a guide for transformation into the fan fiction narrative.

Of course, using Yahoo! Instant Messenging is not the only form of role-playing of which they avail themselves. Tiana and Jandalf also engage in asynchronous role-playing on their online discussion forum called, *Yoda Clones*. This form of role-playing may in fact stand alone. Envisaged initially as a means of convenience because the girls were unable to be online at the same time, the forum provides a space where the role-play can be written in a carefully thought out and reflective mode, rather than in the heat of the moment as can be done with Yahoo! Instant Messenger. The forum-based role-playing seems to serve two purposes: it may be used as a rehearsal for a fan fiction piece, or it may simply exist as a stand-alone narrative form. The audience for this form of role-play is much wider than the quirky instant messaging role-playing form—a quick search for the term "role-playing forums" on Yahoo! for example yields over 2 million results—so this genre is much more recognizable as a narrative form.

Figure 7.1 shows a sample of forum role-playing. In terms of genre, it closely resembles the girls' fan fiction, with identical linguistic features. The difference is that because each girl enters her contribution to the forum role-play one at a time across a period of time the forum texts have more of an episodic nature, without a clearly established sense of complication and resolution. Further, it is at the level of the schematic structure of the text that these forum-based role-plays differ from the overall coherence of their fan fiction and are somewhat more similar to the instant messaging structure; that is, they have an obvious turn-taking structure. Each girl takes a "turn" to input their response to the other, and must wait for the other to post before the narrative can continue.

Padawan Tiana Elas   s
Administrator

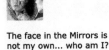

member is **offline**

The face in the Mirrors is not my own... who am I? I'm... Tiana. Aren't I?

Re: Temple Cafeteria
« Reply #28 on: Feb 5th, 2005, 03:02am »

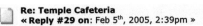

"Intensive colors wouldn't go over that well on me either, Master," Tiana said, honestly. "But color is nice every now and again." She followed Jandalf into the living area unconsciously, and flopped down on one of the larger chairs in a mockery of a meditative position.

She paused for a moment. "Who was your Master anyway?" The question was honest-- she didn't know very much about Jandalf's past... though there was the side point of getting off the previous topic.

Master Jandal f
Administrator

member is **offline**

PH34R t3h doom, Mr. Anderson... Ph34r it good.

Re: Temple Cafeteria
« Reply #29 on: Feb 5th, 2005, 2:39pm »

Jandalf's focus drifted for a moment, no doubt the effect Tiana had desired. "Elachi Kyrie. He was a Kuati human." She closed her eyes, then shook her head. "But that's not what we're here to talk about." Eyes snapping back open, she centred her attention on her Padawan.

Figure 7.1. Role-playing at the forum *Yoda Clones*

In this forum, as with all other role-playing forums I have visited, there are numerous storylines happening concurrently, often located in different geographical or temporal locations of the spaces that make up the fantasy world of the narrative. This allows a user to make multiple entries while waiting for the next person to respond in turn to each of the storylines. Although Tiana and Jandalf have a forum designed solely for the two of them for the purpose of this specific fan fiction (i.e., the *Yoda Clones* series of fan fictions), both of them are active in other role-playing forums that have multiple users.

It should be noted that Tiana's question to Jandalf, "Who was your Master anyway?" was prompted after reading Jandalf's livejournal the previous day, in which Jandalf had made the entry shown in Figure 7.2. These livejournals, as well as providing back story for the narrative, also provided a resource for both girls to think about the other's respective characters, and were an invaluable means for further developing not just the narrative of the fan fiction, but the entire diegesis of their fantasy world.

The Journal of Jandalf the Orange

Date: 2005-02-07 09:24
Subject: Padawan Years

Mood: quixotic
Music: something that I'm only half-listening to, anyway

Yup. Sometimes my sister's so weird, it's funny. Heh...I should talk. But anyway.

Take today, for example. We were comparing notes on a project when my Master came in and asked us what we were up to. I swear, Auddie positively *beamed* at him (something she doesn't do very often) and somehow deflected the question in a roundabout way, ending on the note of...bear slippers. Of all things.

I have never seen Master Elachi turn red. It was hardly there at first, but I definitely noticed it. His voice turned gruff and he asked her "*exactly* what was that supposed to mean?!"

My twin's certainly got a way of getting underneath his skin, and I wonder if I'll ever understand it. To make matters more complicated, he doesn't seem to mind. I'm not sure I'll ever completely understand Audreidi *or* my Master. They're both complex in their own ways, and maybe that's what they see in common with each other.

Upon consideration, though...my Master is Kuati, and they're rather notorious for being complicated, even if he was never brought up with them to begin with. Not only a Kuati, but trained by Master Yoda as well. In that respect...well, I can't really expect him to be anything less than complicated.

And then Audreidi...what with Mirrors and parallel universes and reflections and Force knows what else...I've given up. She's my twin sister and that's good enough for me.

Figure 7.2. An entry from Jandalf's livejournal

The genre of both the role-playing forum and the girl's livejournals can only be described as complex. Both contain a hybridity and blurring of text types that include: recounting current events, recounting events from the character's history, writing descriptions, recounting observations and writing descriptions of people, places and times, publishing and discussing the results of internet quizzes about identity that were done in role, writing out-of-character comments to each other, and to me, writing poetry, and commenting on current politics. Entries are sometimes in first person, sometimes in second person, and other times in third person. Literary devices such as flashbacks, premonitions, and questions posed to the reader are employed.

As mentioned earlier, any discussion of narrative and genre requires insight into the purpose of the text. In discussing the purpose of her livejournal (and using two of Tiana's other character names, Ariane and Eowyn), Jandalf said:

> I expand upon what my character was like when she was an adolescent, a teenager, a young woman. It's character extrapolation, really; that's the most appropriate term I can think of. The background created there not only helps to develop the character, but events that occur in these backstories can also be incorporated into the current plot. For example, there's the story I did where, on a whim, I made Master Elachi have a phobia of lizards. For the mere sake of our amusement, that's carried on into LotG [*Lord of the Garlic*—another role-play narrative series of theirs] and may or may not have had a small part to play in discovering one of the hidden cities of the Shadow Realms, depending on whether or not Ariane actually remembered the way. But my Padawan would know. Heh. I hope reading my livejournal helps Eowyn in some small way.

This establishes the articulated purpose of the livejournal as twofold: first, it is a means for exploring and writing back story for their fan fiction; second, it is designed to be read by the other. That the journal also fulfils other (more unconscious) purposes, such as allowing the girls to both have a therapeutic outlet for the expression of their everyday angst and a safe space in which to rehearse their desires and fantasies as young adolescent women, is a subject I take up later.

In addition to exploring the scope of the narrative worlds of the fan fiction, it is important to note that the girls also produce multimodal texts to enhance their fan fiction, making avatars (images to represent themselves) for role-playing, making visual signatures as can be seen at the side and end of each post on the forum (see Figure 7.1 earlier), finding icons to reflect mood, creating music bytes, making fan fiction posters in the form of an advertisement and teaser, and creating mini movie trailers using their own spliced together combination of existing movie clips, music, voiceovers and text. They also draw maps and room plans of their world, draw and paint scenery, and sketch images of their many characters. As well as hand drawn sketches, they create digital images, digital colorizations or enhancements of their

Figure 7.3. Jandalf's sketch of Jamaei

sketches, or purely digitally created images. Figure 7.3 shows the character Jemaei, as sketched and enhanced by Jandalf.

Tiana and Jandalf both move in and out of media type, text type, form, style and literary device with an ease and poetry of linguistic dexterity that is truly exceptional. I will focus now more directly on the literary distinction of their words.

Breaking through Boundaries: Literacy

Jandalf chose an excerpt from her fan fiction *The Artist's Way* as a piece of which she felt especially proud. She stated that in this fan fiction she wanted the voice of the narrating character to be very frank and honest, and claimed, "the best way for me to do that was to basically make her *me*." She begins by telling of the frustration when inspiration is lacking. Joking about the irony of writing about writer's block, she explains, "as the character progresses through the story, I tell of my own common personal frustrations with small distractions, sudden realisations of the situation, and my insecurities as an artist." An excerpt from this piece of fan fiction follows:

> The night breeze drifted through the park, stirring the early summer leaves to rustle and my long loose hair to stir on either side of my face as I stared down at the blank flimsy in front of me.
>
> I wasn't sure why it was still blank. Perhaps it reflected my state of mind, at the moment. My right hand was curled under the sheet of flimsy, one finger tapping expectantly. But my left hand, holding the inkstick in a death grip, didn't move.
>
> The bench was hard beneath me, an old wooden thing that had likely been sitting here before I was born. The lacquer was worn down but the wood, probably grown with some sort of chemical, refused to rot.
>
> I should know. I sat there every evening, watching the sun go down, waiting for inspiration to arrive over the Corellian horizon and set my left hand in motion, scribbling furiously under the streetlights as the daylight faded, writing something the local news would make a killing for the next morning.
>
> No such luck tonight. There hadn't been for weeks. A few months, really. Little did I know that I didn't really need to think of a good story, though, because one was about to happen to me. It might not have ultimately determined the fate of the entire universe, or even anyone other than me, but it was my tale, my *personal* narrative. My world. Nothing the media could ever really understand.
>
> I must have looked really stupid, my lips parted, eyes staring through the void, posture sagging . . . but he picked me anyway; I was the only one there. Spaced as I was, I didn't see or hear him coming.

In this excerpt, Jandalf uses language expertly to convey her real sense of frustration. Talking of her real experiences which influenced this part, Jandalf said that her character, just like her real self, loves to dabble in art but she "is tormented by her inner critic, a negative voice somewhere in the head that all artists share. . . . I like to experiment with sketching and . . . well, writing fiction, obviously." The imagery she creates in the language of her descriptions clearly mirrors this inner critic.

The drifting of the breeze is metonymous with the drifting of her thoughts and inability to concentrate, the rustling of the leaves and the stirring of her hair are sounds and senses which serve to distract. Her use of terms like "blank" and "flimsy" provide a sense of helplessness. The imagery of her "holding the inkstick in a death grip" and later "eyes staring through the void" further adds to the sheer futility of the exercise. Lexical items such as, "blank," "void," "waiting" and "sagging," echo the inner listlessness of the character, and effectively capture the essence of an artist's frustration. In a sense, the modality of these terms seems exaggerated—the parted lips, sagging posture and vacuous "spaced as I was" give an impression of mental illness rather than mental alertness—yet isn't this the essence of teenage angst?

The feelings of hopelessness and insecurity are articulated perfectly through the use of hyperbole here.

We also recognize here the literary technique of foreshadowing, starting with "little did I know" [that a good story was about to happen to me]. This is widely used in books, TV and other media to signal to the audience that an important event is on the horizon, allowing anticipation to build. The later clause, "I didn't see or hear him coming," serves to create suspense and excitement. The fact that the man is a Jedi knight, although obviously important in some senses, is neither here nor there from the standpoint of identifying this piece of writing as a well crafted narrative that uses narrative devices and literary techniques in a musical and poetic way, and that far exceeds the storytelling skills one might expect from a writer of "fan fiction," if one were to adhere to the notion that fan fiction is something second rate or less than a genuine and authentic writing form.

The concept of intertextuality (Kristeva 1986) provides a further useful lens. Barthes (1977) explains intertextuality thus:

> We know that a text is not a line of words realising a single "theological" meaning (the message of the Author-God) but a multidimensional space in which a variety of writings, none of them original, blend and clash. The text is a tissue of quotations drawn from the innumerable centres of culture . . . the writer can only imitate a gesture that is always anterior, never original. His only power is to mix writings, to counter the ones with the others, in such a way as to never rest on any one of them. Did he wish to express himself, he ought at least to know that the inner "thing" he thinks to "translate" is only a ready-formed dictionary, its words only explainable through other words, and so on indefinitely (p. 146–147).

Texts, then, are made from other texts, and the way a reader interprets a given text will depend upon their prior knowledge and recognition of the connections from this text to those other texts from which it is composed.

To illuminate how Tiana and Jandalf are extending beyond a superficial retelling of a known fantasy story, it is valuable to analyze the intertextual references they draw upon. Reading one of their fan fiction pieces, *Lord of the Garlic*, I found an image Tiana had posted on their fan fiction forum *Yoda Clones* to reflect a visual sense of what the world was like. This photo image shows a deep mauve sky and indigo clouds—possibly a dawn or sunset somewhere, but not likely on earth as we know it—reflected in a deep pool, high in a mountain range. The overall effect is other worldly, mystical and somehow a little poignant.

Underneath the image Tiana had written:

> At night, when the orange moon is covered (there's two moons, one rather orange red, and the other a silver *like earth's*. But the orange one circles the silver moon, and it's

only seen once a week. It causes strange fluctuations in the waters. You DID know that the sun was dying out, right? And it's a rather odd scarlet color?)

Later, Jandalf used this same concept to write the following vivid description of a "dying sun:"

> The diffuse orange-red morning light slowly crept into the room from the single high-placed window, dim from the star that would not show itself above the horizon as if in shame or fear.
>
> *Even the sun is dying here*, thought Obi-Wan, cradling the tiny form of his daughter upon a single forearm, resting her against his body.

When I asked Jandalf about what inspired her to write these words exactly, she replied:

> In that scene I wanted to convey a sense of how the sun's difference from what the characters know influences their feelings and behaviour, just like how many people from my area, used to the open prairie and the clear skies, will quickly become afflicted with a form of depression because of the closed-in feeling the mountains give them, and the constant rainy skies during winter instead of a bright sun and snow. Of course, I pretty much grew up there, so it doesn't take as much of a toll on me (besides the fact that I absolutely love the mountains). So in that scene where Obi-Wan's holding his newborn daughter and reflecting, I wanted to give the impression that the Shadow Realms are very different from what he and most of our other characters there are used to. Having people like this in my personal experience gives me a much better grasp of reactions to strange environments. There was also the part in *The Magician's Nephew* where the boy Digory carries across a profound sense of astonishment as well as silent, foreboding awe at the sight of an abandoned stone city that stretches beyond the horizon, lit only by the dying red sun.

Although the character of Obi-Wan is familiar to *Star Wars* fans, the level of thinking and piecing together of a depth of emotion and physicality for the character is not something Jandalf could possibly have copied from watching the movie. Instead, she has drawn upon her rich literary background with classics, like C. S. Lewis's *The Magician's Nephew*, and her own experiences of growing up in the prairies of Canada. She also demonstrates a keen awareness of the subtleties of human behaviour as it shifts and bends according to space, confinement, and weather conditions, demonstrating an understanding of the semiotic, psychological and interpersonal meanings of the physical landscape. Yet Jandalf would likely not have conceived the idea had Tiana not been collaborating with her on the fan fiction and had she not produced the visual image of the dying sun.

Similarly, Jandalf acknowledges being influenced by the humor of Douglas Adams and Monty Python, saying that when she writes spoof fan fiction she takes great pleasure in having relatively normal and random incidents, words, or events recur in a weird and silly manner. She illustrates with an example from their fan fiction, *Insanity Prevailing*:

> Han the Squirrel began explaining the game of sabacc to them.
>
> "Aaaaaahhh," they said after he was done, now understanding (if you the Reader want to know how sabacc works, ask me. I'll give you a printout or something).
>
> "Of course," grated Obi-Wan, "the last time I played sabacc was on campus."
>
> "If I recall correctly," remarked Jandalf, "I not only won three hand pots, but the sabacc pot as well. Naturally, that was after I bombed you out with the Idiot's array, after everyone else had the smarts to fold."
>
> Now everyone looked confused. The wizards just shrugged and told them to forget about it.
>
> Han the Squirrel thought. "So . . . is it that game that made you two hate each other?"
>
> The wizards glanced at each other.
>
> Obi-Wan coughed. "Umm . . ."
>
> "Let's just say it didn't help matters any," put in Jandalf. "Actually, he was the one that taught me how to play sabacc in the first place, so it was indirectly his fault that he lost, for teaching me so well."
>
> He scowled. "All I did was give you a printout."

Jandalf pointed out to me that I should "notice how the 'printout' concept pops up from a character shortly after the narrator helpfully mentions something about it in brackets. I like doing that, and I don't know why."

This fan fiction is a spoof and might be considered trivial or silly by some. But the literary awareness Jandalf has about the construction of the humor and the use she makes of shifting an element from the heterodiegetic narration (i.e., the narrator speaks from outside the world of the story) to the homodiegetic narration (through a character within the world of the story) suggests a high level of craftsmanship.

In-role poetry is another form of writing in which both girls engage. Figure 7.4 comprises a poem Tiana wrote that has to do with what her character was going through, and which she described as an "angst-drama-type" poem. It further elucidates the command of linguistic features the girls have as a result of wanting to create rich, in-depth narratives.

Tiana explained that the poem was about her character struggling again with her dark side, and calling out to both her (Shadow) and her Master, Jandalf. What is quite remarkable is the range of interpersonal linguistic resources used to convey this depth of angst to the reader. Using what Martin (2000a, 2000b, 2002) calls the "appraisal" system (a way of understanding how words are used to convey affective meanings to the reader), I will briefly summarize the resources Tiana uses in her poem.

Calling

I'm stuck within a tangled web of mist and betrayal,
Looking in a mirror of me, I wonder of this portayal.
Who is this shadow that I see,
This isn't how this has to be...

Standing here, I wonder how to take this,
No longer can I see myself in happiness or bliss.
Once upon a time I loved,
What's happened to my beloved?

There's nothing left but answerless questions,
What's happening, do you have any suggestions?
I'm losing myself,
You're losing yourself...

Don't make me lose what I've only just gained,
Can't you see the expressions, all so pained?
Once I drew away from all,
At least I returned at your call.

Why can't you hear me when I cry,
Why can't you hear my heart's sigh?
Don't leave again,
Must I remain?

Alone in the darkness I walk once more,
I'm searching for a way to open the door...
The Light is calling...
Again I'm falling...

Even the darkest shadow can be reborn,
But now I'm stuck between the two—torn.
Is this then the end?
Don't leave me, my... friend.

Figure 7.4. Tiana's poem written from her character's point of view

The range of material processes (and circumstantial qualifiers) include: "stuck here," "standing here," "losing myself," "drew away," "searching," and "falling." The repetition of the process "stuck" is a further means of highlighting this fearful state. These processes work together in the poem to emphasize the nightmarish quality of experience that her character is having—the sense of being frozen, unable to move and of falling into nowhere, all reminiscent of a horrible dream. She also uses the verbal process of "cry," and "heart's sigh," and these are made particularly poignant because nobody hears or recognizes these pained expressions. The detailed nominal group, "a tangled web of mist and betrayal," is a complex combination of the metaphor of the mist and the abstract concept of betrayal. Mist is usually associated with confusion and a lack of clarity, providing insight into Tiana's innermost thoughts. Furthermore, the use of the word "tangled" as a classifier of the "web" has the effect of signifying Tiana's insecurity and unhappiness. The constant use of questioning such as, "What's happened?", "Must I remain?", and "Is this the end?", clearly portrays Tiana's pain, insecurity, fear and anxiety. Although this brief analysis represents only a portion of a full linguistic analysis, it is sufficient to illuminate the complexities of literacy proficiency Tiana has demonstrated.

I have, then, argued that Tiana and Jandalf are both pushing the boundaries of narrative *and* of literacy. They have created truly hybrid forms of literacy, combining multimodal elements in new ways, and using an extensive repertoire of communication means to create their fan fiction worlds. They have blurred genres, invented a new rehearsal genre, transformed, manipulated and designed old texts into new, written across diverse literary genres, in many different styles, to produce final pieces of fan fiction writing that are of the highest level of sophistication, drawing on the full scope of linguistic resources to reach out to their readers.

Blurring and Breaking through Boundaries: Identity

Cyberspace has been credited with opening up new and liberating spaces for adults: to explore aspects of identity (Turkle 1995), to become empowered by affiliating themselves with world wide organizations, and to gain the strength and knowledge for political activism to bring about change in society (Wakeford 2000, Wolff 2003, Wood 2001). Such uses of cyberspace are also thought to have been a catalyst for challenging the artificial boundaries of the subject as defined by dominant cultures (Shaw 1998, Stone 1995). It doesn't take grand involvements in political activism to challenge the artificial boundaries of the subject. Nor does it take adult participation in global affiliations. Rather, it simply takes two girls with a passion for writing. In concluding I will explore ways in which Tiana and Jandalf are challenging the boundaries of the subject, beginning with a brief discussion of the concept of identity.

I have argued elsewhere (Thomas 2004) for theorizing identity as a blend between the self as a social being, the self as experienced phenomenologically, and the self as a subject of the discourses of language and power. I have argued that when considering identity in, around and on the screen, that we should carefully attend to psychoanalytic theory as it applies to visual and film culture, using understandings drawn from Hall (2000), Mulvey (1989), and Riviere (1986). By doing so, we can consider how the nature of viewing oneself acting inside the screen might create a disjunction, which blurs the boundaries between on and off screen. Further, it is necessary to rethink the idea that cyberspace is a disembodied space, since the lived

experience of participating in virtual worlds becomes an embodied phenomeno-
logical experience. Additionally, Butler's (1997) and others' theories about performativity and how gender may be formed in virtual contexts also influence our
thoughts about identity as it performed. Butler understands gender not as a result
of who people (already) are but a result of, among other things, the way they talk
and what they do (see Cameron 1999). From a Lacanian perspective (e.g., Lacan
1977), identity is also intimately connected to unconscious desire, which can be
manifested through both the body and through discourse. I will return to these ideas
in my discussion below.

It is common for fan fiction writers to insert versions of themselves into their
characters—known, among other things, as "fusing identities" (Black 2004, no
page). Tiana and Jandalf emphasize that their characters are very much adaptations
of their own identities, made all the stronger through both their role-playing,
which relies upon a considerable degree of instinct and their livejournals. This
allows a more introspective reflection into ways in which their characters might be
facing issues and angst-ridden insecurities similar to those they face in their real lives.

The fusion of identity can be observed in this comment by Jandalf, as she
describes the characteristics that her real self and her fictional character share in
common:

> I do have something of a temper myself, but she shows it a lot more. I made her put a
> little less focus on tact, sometimes, just to make things interesting. Like me, she's
> extremely observant about most things and painfully obtuse about some others, she
> forms very strong bonds with a few people, and she usually isn't afraid to speak her mind
> to those people and others that she doesn't know. Like me, she's discarded caring
> about what strangers think about her, as it really is a waste of time but takes some getting
> used to. Like me, she's got leadership qualities, but I tend to hide mine a little more.
> Like me, she's deeply spiritual and idealistic, although we can cover up those traits when
> we don't wish for them to be seen by others.

In discussing the way she relates to other people through role-play, Jandalf claims
that she can reveal much more of her inner self through role-playing in comparison to casual conversation. She explains:

> roleplaying brings a whole different depth, especially when you're playing a character
> that directly reflects yourself. Besides which, getting into character can lessen your
> limitations and emotional defenses that you usually have over your own self. If I
> was talking to someone about my hopes and dreams, I probably wouldn't reveal much
> more than what I'd like to see in the next year of my life. The person I converse with
> can't see past my words and my expression, either. An onlooker simply won't see into
> my mind, into my thoughts. But when I'm roleplaying, the thoughts and inner reac-
> tions of my character and how that relates to her own hopes and desires are clear for

the sake of the story. I don't want to have a wooden character, so I illustrate that in a definite way if some of the focus is on her. And of course, if she is an essential spin-off of me . . . reading into my character can by and large reveal a lot about who I am, myself.

Tiana discusses the ways her character deals with adolescent issues like growing up and peer pressure.

Of all the characters I role-play, Tiana is the most like me. Tiana is my biggest character, as I role-play with her and write with her voice the most, so she's the most like me. I've kind of fused Tiana into my internet identity completely. Her looks and all that, not to mention personality. Tiana's a bit more headstrong than I am. She's more willing to jump into things. However, she's almost other than that completely like me. Does/says is what I'd do and say.

Now, what you'll see of me in Shadow is the side of me that is searching. This side of me reflects what I was going through earlier in the year. At the time I was searching—for God (rolls eyes), a purpose in my life, and all that. If that makes any sense.

Both girls use their livejournals to recount early character memories. When I asked Tiana what the source of inspiration for her fictional memories were, she responded that she infused some of her own memories of being teased and picked on by an older boy:

I shall admit that of a lot of my part of *Lord of the Garlic* IS based on reality. Too much of it is. The memories I write in my livejournal are based on what Tiana went through as a crecheling, but a lot of it is based on the [real] distant memories I have. I'm like Tiana, I have holes in my memory, and I can only clearly remember when I was older than 7, really . . . so . . . yeah. I admit that I base her memories on my own, at least, what I have clearly . . . and not so clearly. There was a Kylan, yes—not by the name of Kylan, I couldn't recall the name if you asked me. There was more than one Kylan. Like LT (little Tiana) I was picked on. I was a little girl, small, and I looked younger than I was. I often ran away and hid, crying in a corner, or whatever. Trying to escape reality, I suppose.

It is fascinating that Tiana had drawn on her own childhood pain to develop her character. One way of thinking about this draws on Foucault's (1977) explanation of how the events and discourses that shape our histories are physically inscribed on the body.

The body is the inscribed surface of events (traced by language and dissolved by ideas), the locus of a dissociated self (adopting the illusion of a substantial unity), and a volume in perpetual disintegration. Genealogy, as an analysis of descent, is thus situated within the articulation of the body and history. Its task is to expose a body totally imprinted by history and the process of history's destruction of the body (Foucault 1977,148).

McNay (1994) argued that the body was "always already" constructed and regulated by discourses and discursive practices. Malson (1998) also believed that Foucault had explained well the way in which discourses and discursive practices can construct the body. Tiana has masterfully recalled those events which left a lasting impression on her, and has used the pain she experienced through her own body to infuse her character's body, which is then transformed into the livejournal entry which recaptures that pain.

Although I have so far discussed the ways in which the girls have both infused aspects of their "real" selves into their characters, the opposite is also true: the fictional characters are also a means for the girls to fashion new and emerging identities for themselves as they develop into adulthood. The characters allow the girls a freedom and power to author an identity (Bakhtin 1998) which plays out their fantasies and desires: of their physical bodies, their hopes and dreams for the future, and their ideas of romance. Their characters are a rehearsal of who they want to become, and in role-playing that ideal self, they can grow closer to becoming that ideal.

Here it is necessary to emphasize the significant role of the image of their characters in the discursive positioning of self. The duality of their real self as being "self," and the "self" they see reflected in the fictional "other" of their character, is embedded in the domain of images. We might think of this as both the images constructed through words or the artwork that the girls produce to reflect their characters, but more so their own imagining of themselves inside their characters. Grosz (2001), emphasizes the imaginary identifications of self through this domain,

> [r]elations between the self and the other thus govern the imaginary order . . . this is the domain in which the self is dominated by images of the other and seeks its identity in a reflected relation with alterity . . . Imaginary relations are thus two-person relations, where the self sees itself reflected in the other (Grosz 2001, 46).

The imaginative possibilities of their fictional characters empower the girls' belief to imagine these same possibilities for their real selves.

Tiana, reflected on the dialectical nature of her real self and her characters, stating:

> I model bits of myself into my characters by just letting go, per se. It's really the other way around: I infuse the characters into myself, more. You let the characters become a part of you, let yourself be able to think like they would, and it works the other way around. You can't have a character who doesn't have some of your personality without losing yourself. A good role-player will let go of their thoughts when RPing—Jandalf was the one who said it. "When RPing my mind goes blank, you don't really think to do it." or something of that accord. I have to agree—I can't think as myself when thinking as Tiana.

Online, it's like the movie *the Matrix* because we become digital variations of ourselves, and when we're unplugged, who knows what'll happen? Roleplaying online is almost akin to *the Matrix* because you're taking on a digital avatar of yourself and becoming that person to the point where you're nearly going to believe that it's all real—the biggest difference is that going online is the trip down the rabbit hole and not the other way around. Unplugging yourself from those characters online is just as tricky as unplugging yourself from a digital world, because, in theory, you *are* unplugging yourself from a digital world—and, if you've got in too deep, you're going to find yourself drowning in that rabbit hole.

You can get so into a character that pulling yourself out hurts—that when you're not in that world you wonder—you find yourself thinking as that character would at the oddest moments . . . I often think "All right, do you really think that would be a good idea if Jandalf was around?" Or "Wow, that's a cool quote, it reminds me of such and such scene online." Tiana, my online identity, does influence my thoughts a lot.

Tiana's statement provides a lucid insight into the blurring of the fictional and real spaces in which she exists, both as herself and as her characters. She talks of always being "plugged in" to her characters, and as a consequence her real self is blended with the characteristics of the fictional Tiana. Her thoughts are influenced by her role-playing and by the literacy practices she engages in with Jandalf. Her friendship with Jandalf, forged by their joint passion for fantasy, has become one of the most valued friendships in her life, even though they have only met "physically" on one occasion. Her view of the world is colored always with the words and worlds of her fan fiction, so much so that as she hears a "cool" quote, she relates it to her fantasy world. She observes the world through a writer's eyes, and her identity as a writer is highly significant to her sense of self.

Jandalf, too, talked about the ways in which her character influenced her own sense of self, and impacted her real identity, so much so that she claimed, "I've found that since I've been using her as one of my main characters, I have been . . . well . . . rubbing off on myself, in a way. I'm more outgoing than I used to be, and Jandalf's creation and use does figure in that." What both girls have done in fact is to write themselves into a new identity, empowering their realities through their fiction.

Jandalf freely wrote about her crush on Obi-Wan Kanobi and revealed that her character was able to explore a romance that she herself had not.

I've never had a boyfriend, as I said, and there's really nothing else to my romantic life. Jandalf is way ahead of me romantically, simply because she's older. I do imagine I'll get married and all that someday . . . and so I paired Jandalf up with my favourite *Star Wars* male character. Heck, Obi-Wan always was my favourite character period, even before I saw the prequels. I really liked him as an old guy, and when *TPM* came out . . . well. Good-looking, too. That's always a bonus. Heehee.

The fictional Jandalf is able to play out the real Jandalf's fantasies of femininity, exploring what it might mean to be romantically involved, to maintain a relationship, to experience a first kiss, and to enjoy the world of love. Her coy giggle ("heehee") at describing her romance reflects her youthful naïveté and her obvious pleasure in this narrative storyline. The giggle at first glance seems superficial and shallow, and it would be easy to dismiss. However, here I want to draw upon the work of Riviere (1986), who emphasized the notion of masquerade to describe the shallow surface represent-ations of women. She argued that femininity could in fact be constructed as a mask, and performed like a mimic. Riviere (1986, 38) stated:

> Womanliness could therefore be assumed and worn as a mask, both to hide the posses-sion of masculinity and to avert the reprisals expected if she was found to possess it—much as a thief will turn out his pockets and ask to be searched to prove that he has not stolen the goods. The reader may now ask how I define womanliness or where I draw the line between genuine womanliness and the "masquerade." My suggestion is not, how-ever, that there is any such difference; whether radical or superficial, they are the same thing.

Jandalf, through her giggle, is mimicking and performing a mask of femininity, yet from Riviere's perspective, this mask is reflective of the real female inside the mask. Danet (1998) makes a similar point but with respect to online spaces, arguing that the internet offers a space for playing and performing gender under the mask of anonymity. The fictional and cyber-mediated Jandalf is engaged in a romance which in fact is a rehearsal of the desires of the real Jandalf as she imagines she can be.

Conclusion

I conclude by urging educators to recognize the value of writing fan fiction and par-ticipating in the texts of pop culture. Jenkins claims, "participating in pop culture may help kids to master traditional literacy skills" (2004, no page). Marsh and Millard (2000) argue that teachers are too quick to judge pop culture harshly. They call for teachers to take notice of the pleasure, motivation and pure joy of children and young people as they engage in the various activities of pop culture. They exhort:

> Educators need only to draw on small elements in this intertextual universe in order to enliven their literacy curriculum. Not to do so runs higher risks in that children may not only be less motivated within school, but left feeling that literacy practices outside of school are meaningless and irrelevant (Marsh and Millard 2000,185).

Who decides what knowledge is legitimate and authentic, which literacies are privileged and which are stigmatized, and which literacy practices are valued while others are trivialized? In my work as an English educator and researcher of pop culture I have become acutely aware of what young people are capable of in their own "affinity spaces" (Gee, 2000) when they share a common passion and have opportunities to collaborate, play and explore new worlds of possibilities, as Tiana and Jandalf are doing online.

The skills Tiana and Jandalf have mastered far exceed traditional literacy and, indeed, go beyond talk of "skill." Tiana and Jandalf negotiate the affordances of the internet and exploit them to their fullest extent, to collaboratively construct rich narrative worlds and deeply satisfying friendships. They can work through their adolescent angst using their fictional characters as a safe means for both confronting and distancing themselves from painful experiences.

It would be a travesty indeed if Tiana and Jandalf were left feeling that their fan fiction writing was meaningless and irrelevant.

References

Abbott, H. 2002. *The Cambridge Introduction to Narrative*. Cambridge: Cambridge University Press.

Bakhtin, M. 1998. *The Dialogic Imagination*. Austin, TX: University of Texas Press.

Barthes, R. 1966. Introduction to the structural analysis of narratives. In S. Sontag (Ed.), *A Barthes Reader*. New York: Hill and Wang. 95–150.

Barthes, R. 1977. *Image, Music, Text*. London: Fontana Press.

Bhatia, V. 1999. Integrating products, processes, purposes and participants in professional writing. In C. Candlin and K. Hyland (Eds), *Writing: Texts, Processes and Practices*. London: Longman. 21–39.

Black, R. 2004. Access and Affiliation: The New Literacy Practices of English Language Learners in an Online Anime-based Fanfiction Community. Paper presented to the National Conference of Teachers of English Assembly for Research, Berkeley, CA.

Briggs, C. and Bauman, R. 1992. Genre, intertextuality, and social power. *Journal of Linguistic Anthropology* 2(2): 131–72.

Butler, J. 1997. *Excitable Speech: A Politics of the Performative*. New York: Routledge.

Cameron, D. 1999. Communication skills as a gendered discourse. In S. Wertheim, A. Bailey and M. Corston-Oliver (Eds), *Engendering Communication*, Berkeley, CA: Berkeley Women and Language Group.

Cook, G. 1989. *Discourse*. Oxford: Oxford University Press.

Cope, B. and Kalantzis, M. 2000. Designs for social futures. In B. Cope and M. Kalantzis (Eds), *Multiliteracies: Literacy Learning and the Design of Social Futures*. Melbourne, AU: Macmillan. 203–34.

Danet, B. 1998. Text as mask: Gender, play and performance on the internet. In S. Jones (Ed.), *Cybersociety 2.0: Revisiting Computer-Mediated Communication and Community*. London: Sage Publications. 129–58.

Foucault, M. 1977. *Discipline and Punish: The Birth of the Prison*. London: Penguin.

Gee, J. P. 2000. Identity as an Analytic Lens for Research in Education. Department of Curriculum and Instruction. Madison, WI, University of Wisconsin-Madison. Mimeo.

Grosz, E. 2001. *Jacques Lacan: A Feminist Introduction*. London: Routledge.

Hall, S. 2000. Who needs "identity"? In P. Du Gay, J. Evans and P. Redman (Eds), *Identity: A Reader*. London: Sage Publications. 15–30.

Jenkins, H. 1992. *Textual Poachers: Television Fans and Participatory Culture*. New York: Routledge.

Jenkins, H. 2004. Why Heather Can Write. *MIT Technology Review*. February. technologyreview.com/articles/04/02/wo_jenkins020604.asp?p=1 (accessed 2 July, 2006).

Johns, A. 2002. *Genre in the Classroom: Multiple Perspectives*. Mahwah, NJ: Lawrence Erlbaum Publishers.

Kellner, D. 1980. Television images, codes and messages. *Television*. 7(4): 74.

Kress, G. 2003. *Literacy in the New Media Age*. London: Routledge.

Kristeva, J. 1986. *The Kristeva Reader* (ed. Toril Moi). Oxford: Blackwell.

Lacan, J. 1977. *Agency of the Letter in the Unconscious or Reason Since Freud. Ecrits: a Selection* (trans. A. Sheridan). London: Routledge.

Lewis, C.S. 1955. *The Magician's Nephew*. Middlesex: Puffin.

Lewis, D. 2004. Understanding the power of fan fiction for young authors. *Kliatt*. March, 2004. findarticles.com/p/articles/mi_m0PBX/is_2_38/ai_114326743 (accessed 2 July, 2006).

Luke, C. 1997. *Technological Literacy*. Melbourne: Language Australia.

McNay, L. 1994. *Foucault: Critical Introduction*. Cambridge, Polity Press.

Malson, H. 1998. *The Thin Woman: Feminism, Post-Structuralism and the Social Psychology of Anorexia Nervosa*. London: Routledge.

Marsh, J. and Millard, E. 2000. *Literacy and Popular Culture*. London: Paul Chapman.

Martin, J. 2000a. Appraising Discourse: Co-constructing Genres. Paper presented at the Scaffolding Language and Learning in Educational Contexts, University of Technology Sydney.

Martin, J. 2000b. Beyond exchange: APPRAISAL systems in English. In S. Hunston and G. Thompson (Eds), *Evaluation in text: Authorial stance and the construction of discourse*. Oxford: Oxford University Press. 142–175.

Martin, J. 2002. Fair trade: Negotiating meaning in multimodal texts. In P. Coppock (Ed.), *The Semiotics of Writing: Transdisciplinary Perspectives on the Technology of Writing*. Bloomington, IN: Brepols and Indiana University Press. 311–38.

Mulvey, L. 1989. *Visual and Other Pleasures*. Bloomington, IN: Indiana University Press.

Paltridge, B. 2001. *Genre and the Language Learning Classroom*. Ann Arbor, MI: University of Michigan Press.

Riviere, J. 1986. Womanliness as a masquerade. *International Journal of Psycho-analysis* (10): 303–13.

Riviere, J. (1986). Womanliness as a masquerade. In V. Burgin, J. Donald and C. Kaplan (Eds),. *Formations of Fantasy*. New York: Methuen. 35–44.

Shaw, D. 1998. Gay men and computer communication: A discourse of sex and identity in cyberspace. In S. Jones (Ed.), *Virtual Culture: Identity & Communication In Cybersociety*. London: Sage. 133–45.

Snyder, I. (Ed.) 2002. *Silicon Literacies: Communication, Innovation and Education in the Electronic Age*. London: Routledge.

Sontag, S. (Ed.) 1982. *A Barthes Reader*. New York: Hill and Wang.

Stone, A. 1995. Sex and death among the disembodied: VR, cyberspace, and the nature of academic discourse. In S. Star (Ed.), *The Cultures of Computing*. Oxford: Blackwell. 143–155.

Swales, J. 1990. *Genre Analysis*. Cambridge: Cambridge University Press.

Thomas, A. 2004. Digital literacies of the cybergirl. *e-Learning* 1(3): 358–82.

Thwaites, T., Davis, L. and Mules, W. 1994. *Tools for Cultural Studies*. Melbourne, AU: Macmillan.

Turkle, S. 1995. *Life on the Screen*. New York: Simon and Schuster.

Wakeford, N. 2000. Networking women and grrrls with information/communication technology: Surfing tales of the world wide web. In D. Bell and Kennedy, B. (Eds), *The Cybercultures Reader*. London: Routledge. 350–59.

Wolff, J. 2003. Reinstating corporeality: Feminism and body politics. In A. Jones (ed.), *The Feminism and Visual Culture Reader*. London, Routledge. 414–25.

Wood, A. 2001. Fresh kill: Information technologies as sites of resistance. In S. Munt (Ed.), *Technospaces Inside the New Media*. London: Continuum. 161–74

CHAPTER EIGHT

Looking from the Inside Out: Academic Blogging as New Literacy

JULIA DAVIES AND GUY MERCHANT

Introduction

This chapter draws on an ongoing ethnography of blogging which centers on our lived experiences of digital writing and online publishing, tracing how this maps onto and extends social networks, and contributes to an emerging affinity group or online community (Gee 2004). The production and consumption of blogs is seen as a new form of social practice, dependent upon specific genres of writing and meaning making—a practice which reconfigures relationships and can engender new ways of looking at the world. Our autoethnographic approach provides an insider view of blogging as a new and popular screen-based literacy practice. In this chapter, we reflect on the processes involved in the production and consumption of blogs as well as blogs as textual material in their own right. We have become interested in exploring the way in which blogs work as *interactive* texts; as texts which are jointly composed and which are interwoven with other texts, texts for which authorship is often multiple and unpredictable.

We have found that an autoethnographic approach has allowed us to experience at first-hand, and therefore to understand more closely, how blogs work as a new type of text. Furthermore, the nature of the inquiry itself repositions the researcher, as both subject and object, and in this way breaks with the more separate stance of traditional cultural ethnographers. Here we comment on some key features emerging from our data, beginning with an overview of blogging as a social practice. This leads into an exploration of methodological issues raised in the study of online textual practices. We then focus on three key themes. The first of these is concerned with the experience of self-publishing online; the second with the nature and fabric of blogs as texts; and the third with the development of social networks through blogging.

Blogging as a Social Practice

The growing popularity of blogs that use relatively simple publishing tools that allow users—at little or no cost—to publish on the web, is of particular interest to us; we have been keen to understand how blogging has become such a seductive activity so quickly, and for so many. New blog technologies provide new affordances which can be at once both simple and complex; simple because they share some of the characteristics of paper-based texts (such as typographical conventions, spelling, paragraph, layout and so on) and complex because of the capabilities offered by hypertext. New affordances include textual connections with others on and offline; the facility to comment on others' blog posts and the possibility of replying to comments on one's own; hyperlinks to information sources; site meters which monitor "visits" from others; RSS feeds, which alert subscribed readers to other newly updated sites; the facility to embed other texts within one's own and the possibility of including a range of modalities, from audio podcasts to video streams. We have come to think about the "depth" of a text in this regard; the fabric and nature of the text seems to foster a stronger articulation of the social. Blogs which have "frequent commenters" often develop a strong sense of audience, yet there is also a sense of a potential wider audience being considered within blog texts, too. Blogs seem to be embedded in a social context related to both local and global discourses with the notion of participating in a network of bloggers being a strong drawcard for both readers and bloggers themselves. We have also found that these dynamic connections challenge our conceptions of what it means to be writers and readers, and even unsettle our ideas of what constitutes a text in online environments.

Blogs are essentially online journals which are regularly updated, often with fairly brief postings (Merchant 2006). The most recent post is usually shown at the top of the screen, with previous posts listed below and older posts are archived and hyperlinked, all in date-of-posting order. Requiring relatively little specialized technical knowledge, blogs have become a very popular way of producing digital text (Mortensen 2004). In fact, experts estimate that there are literally millions of blogs worldwide (Blogcount.com 2005) serving the needs of a wide range of individuals and affinity groups.

Blogs, as an emerging genre of digital communication, are characterized by a tendency to blend the personal with the public. The similarities with more conventional journal writing are reasonably clear, but yet, to write a blog is a little like displaying a personal journal in a shop window, for friends and passers-by to read at their leisure. Similarly, blogs often blur distinctions between the serious and the frivolous. Although multiple ownership of a blog is possible, most blogs are produced by individuals, although this is a complicated concept, since most blogs allow comments from readers so that blog posts can develop over time by means of multiple authorship.

There may be as many different reasons for blogging as there are blogs, and the range of blogs we have seen has been immense; everything from cookery blogs with detailed recipes, tried and tested (e.g., Kramer Bussel et al. 2005); to knitting patterns and experiences (e.g., Carrieoke 2005); to blogs which advertise (e.g., Nokia 2005); to blogs which satirize (e.g., adbusters 2005); to blogs which showcase obsessions (e.g., Manolo 2005); and through to blogs which share professional stories (e.g., Scott 2005), to name just a few examples. Nevertheless, whatever the articulated purposes of a blog, academic deconstructions of blogs have, among other things, discussed the social and personal *affordances* of these new literacy activities. Bortree (2005), Stern (1999) and Scheidt (2006), for example, have all written about teenaged girls' blogs or homepages as providing spaces where these girls can self-present and explore aspects of their identity. Bortree describes the "dual use" of a blog "as a tool for interpersonal communication and mass communication" (Bortree 2005, 25). Bortree's work reflects on ways in which girls' online writing is often specifically targetted at known readers, yet social complications occur when there is a wider readership. This multi-purpose dimension of blogs can also be seen, for example, in the work of "Riverbend," the pseudonym used by a young Iraqi woman who blogs her political views as well as her mundane experiences as a young woman living in a war zone (see Riverbend 2005). She writes in English to include an audience beyond Iraq, but her posts are also filled with references to and for local bloggers as well.

Indeed, while a blogger may write for a specific readership, often also known personally off-line, there is also the knowledge that the audience for a blog potentially exists beyond these known readers. Accounts of online affinity spaces have been useful in defining the coming together of like-minded interactants with shared interests (Davies 2005, Gee 2004, Knobel 2005) yet it is not altogether clear how one might define the parameters of such affinities and this, as has been discussed by Bortree (2005), can be problematic to the blogger; knowing whether one is communicating beyond an immediate group or with unknown others can cause at best stylistic difficulties, or at worst, offence. As will be exemplified later in this paper, discovering one's readership can be a disconcerting—as well as a gratifying—experience.

The complexity of audience and authorial positioning, as well as the blending of these roles, is of particular interest to us in this chapter.

Mortensen (2004) has written extensively about academics blogging, not least in her own blog. Her awareness of the potential influence of readers who comment was shown through her recent decision to disable the comment facility on her blog in order to think about her writing in a new way (Mortensen 2005). Farrell (2005, 1), also online, writes of the academic blogger:

> Academic bloggers differ in their goals. Some are blogging to get personal or professional grievances off their chests or, like Black, to pursue nonacademic interests. Others, perhaps the majority, see blogging as an extension of their academic personas. Their blogs allow them not only to express personal views but also to debate ideas, swap views about their disciplines, and connect to a wider public. For these academics, blogging isn't a hobby; it's an integral part of their scholarly identity. They may very well be the wave of the future.

This is certainly something others have found—that blogging can promote discussion of ideas in embryo:

> Through my blog and engagement in my blogging affinity spaces, I have been afforded the opportunity to build, refine and sharpen my intellectual ideas. By simply having a web presence I have found other like-minded colleagues who enter into dialogue with me about my work on a regular basis. This new type of networking has been and continues to be, for me, an invaluable force in shaping my thinking and my career choices (i-anya 2005).

The presentation of self in a particular way, as showcased through our own blogs, has been a focus of our recent academic work and we have been interested in the range of social practices we have been able to enjoy as a result of our blogging. As such, we have drawn on the New Literacy Studies and its emphasis on a social account of literacy. We suggest that this theoretical orientation is particularly helpful in analyzing new meaning-making practices associated with information and communication technologies (ICTs). As we shall show in our data, not only do new ICTs such as blogging tools fundamentally change the ways in which we write and communicate, they also change *how* we interact and *who* we interact with. And, thus, as Nixon (2003) also argues, a theoretical perspective that focuses on literacy as a social practice is likely to be most helpful. The work of Barton (1994) and Barton and Hamilton (1998) is particularly influential in this respect. Their explorations of literacy as a social practice show how specific literacy events are linked to the wider social structures in which these events are embedded and which these events in turn help to shape (Barton 1994). Specific "situated" literacy acts or events can then be analyzed; for instance, by examining the participants and settings, and the particular artifacts, activities and technologies that are used within the event (Hamilton 2000). These events are aspects of literacy practices which are linked to broader sets of values, attitudes, feelings, and relationships (Street 1993). We have observed that the online practices and events in which we have been involved via our blogs are frequently not confined to specific online literacy events and practices but are rooted in, or developed by, additional associated social events and practices beyond the internet (e.g., within our academic or private lives). This suggests that we need to expand our definition of a literacy event to include surrounding contextual factors and also to acknowledge the fact that the "situatedness" of a specific event is more complex online. Furthermore the notion of "event" seems to suggest that it is temporally and spatially bounded—clearly this does not apply in the same way to a blog. This is, of course, because of the way in which the text is never complete and readers can add to the text at any point and from any location.

Another useful perspective on blogging as a social practice comes from paying closer attention to text, design and communication. New digital technologies invoke new ways of meaning-making, and these challenge the authority of the book and the printed page as dominant sites for representation (Kress 2003). The socio-semiotic approach developed by Kress (1997, 2000, 2003) has led us to careful consideration of the characteristics of screen-based communication. His work has highlighted the affordances of the screen and the facilities of different media. And this in turn has helped us to understand the *visual*—and not just the alphabetic— nature of the texts displayed on a computer screen, and how the characteristics of these screen texts differ from those of the page. A growing academic emphasis on the materiality of new textual forms has shifted our attention to the multimodal design features of screen texts as primarily visual constructs. For example, reading a blog includes much more than simply reading the printed text of each blog post, but paying attention to layout, colors, images, and even sound. Thus, descriptions of literacy practices and events (Barton 1994) combined with a socio-semiotic approach (Kress 1997) usefully enable us to demonstrate the intricate connections between textual production and consumption, and to explore social interactions within particular discourse communities.

The research presented in this chapter draws on recent work in digital literacy including that of Markham (1998), Mortensen and Walker (2002), and Sunden (2003), as well as the theoretical overviews of Lankshear and Knobel (2003) and Herring (2004). In addition to our interest in blogs on their own terms as new literacies, as researchers, we are interested also in exploring methodologies for studying digital writing which need to account for the multiple perspectives of readers and writers of blogs, as well as encompass methods of analysis that do justice to the complexities of blog texts.

Methodological Issues in Researching Online Texts

There are a number of approaches that can be taken in the study of new forms of digital literacy and online practice. Textual analysis is an obvious starting point, and certainly, the history of research within the social sciences provides many blueprints for this, along with a rich tradition of working with print-based texts. But even print-based textual material can be problematic as research data at times (Hodder 2003), and the sheer complexity of digital environments presents whole new sets of problems. Hodder (2003, 156) reminds us that, "texts have to be understood in the contexts of their conditions of production and reading," and underscores how a single text can be read in many ways. While this is true of all texts, the complex configuration of digital texts which are often multimodal, hyperlinked and dynamic in character, make even partial readings increasingly problematic. In looking at a blog, for instance, we need to accept that the text is seldom static, it is regularly updated and interactive via the comments function attached to each post, and that a visitor to the blog is highly unlikely to follow all the available hyperlinks or explore all of the archived posts, and that multiple visitors are unlikely to follow these links in exactly the same way anyway, and so on. Instead, readers will make choices about what to read and what to ignore, designing their own reading path (Kress 2003) through the text. These features conspire to make traditional textual analysis problematic because the different paths that readers take will inevitably impact on meaning.

As mentioned earlier, recent theorizing in the domain of literacy studies has been dominated by a social account of literacy. Street's concepts about socially embedded literacies (Street 1997), along with literacy practices and events (Barton 1994) and the social semiotic approach to text analysis (Kress 1997), all demonstrate the intricate connections between processes of textual production-consumption and social interaction within discourse communities. Therefore, a methodology for the study of digital writing would need to explore at least some of the multiple perspectives and relationships between readers and writers along with analyses of the complex texts thus produced. This suggests that researching digital writing needs to be informed by a robust theoretical position that can capture the complexities of relationships and identities; interaction, text production and consumption; and the role of the mediating technologies that are used.

If the complex interactions between people and machines lie at the heart of communication through digital writing, methodological questions about the nature of enquiry and the position of researchers are equally important. Existing work in the field of digital writing shows researchers adopting a variety of relationships to digital culture. It is useful at this point to identify some of these specific research positions as we ourselves see them. The list of positions below captures our own "take" on the various methodological positions available in the research literature, although we recognise these positions may overlap, shift, disappear or expand over time.

- Researcher as identifier of new tropes (Ito 2004; Lankshear and Knobel 2003; Rheingold 2003)
- Researcher as insider (Markham 1998; Sunden 2002)
- Researcher as analyst (Werry 1996; Shortis 2001; Burnett et al. 2003)
- Researcher as both subject and object (Mortensen and Walker 2002)
- Researcher as activist (Prensky 2001; Gee 2004)

Our own methodological position can be classified as "researchers as both subjects and objects." That is, we are both authors of the texts (our respective blogs)—which offer a range of narratives about our lives, experiences and thoughts as well as researchers of our own blogging activities.

Lankshear and Knobel (2003) draw our attention to the importance of "insider research"—research of and by people who are immersed in the use of new media. This kind of research is needed in order to complement and enrich the important work that they and others have done in keeping up with new developments in digital literacy. We may recognize in this kind of work an attempt to capture and document new practices and, in the case of Rheingold, for example, even to predict the future (Rheingold 2003). There is perhaps also an unspoken concern here that age and scholarship may combine to create the distance of an outsider, as the researcher becomes remote from the practices she or he is studying. From this perspective, even detailed ethnography of the textual worlds of Japanese schoolchildren have the potential for being read as deconstructions of "exotic" practices (Ito 2004). By exotic, we mean practices which are innovative, culturally located, often marking the emergence of a new trend. These particular research positions seem to condense around a conception of researcher as identifier of new tropes and memes.

While a focus on new tropes and memes provides a starting point for the systematic study of the role of textual production and consumption within digital culture, there is clearly scope for development, revision and synthesis. The inter-relationship between the unit of analysis and the mode of data collection, for example, provides fruitful ground for rethinking the methodologies needed for effectively investigating digital writing practices. A common characteristic of popular digital writing is the way in which onscreen text mediates a social relationship between two or more people. From this it seems that a more rigorous approach would involve the study of digital writing in its broader social context, uncovering the nuances of local settings and their interplay with the different perspectives of participants. So for example in Julia's post (digitalliteracies.blogsome.com/2006/07/31/things-that-make-me-go-hmmm/) on defining digital literacies one would need to have access to a range of sources of information in order to attempt a thorough analysis of this text. This would include a knowledge of who the participants were, their previous familiarity with the topic and with each other, the degree to which their settings were similar or shared and an understanding of their purposes for posting and commenting. To clarify, some of these commenters had been discussing definitions of digital literacies at a conference, another is a doctoral student and another is a complete newcomer; all came to the text with differing degrees of knowledge of each other, with differing shared experiences and discussions. Their backgrounds would be clear to some readers and not so apparent to others. This in turn would have implications for modes of data collection. Keeping with our example above, specific data collection methods might include an understanding of the topic under discussion, its progeny and the social networks of the commenters and their social location. A researcher's options might include entering into the blog discussion and/or contacting the individual participants for further clarification. Ways of describing the dynamic nature of onscreen communication are needed in order to understand collaborative text construction, movements between reading and writing, and the changing, visual nature of screens (Kress 2003).

It is important to ask to what extent the study of practices within digital culture could (or should) influence ways of conducting and disseminating research. As Facer argues, we could easily see new literacy practices as:

> a phenomenon existing "out there" in the world of research subjects rather than a set of practices that might reciprocally alter the ways in which researchers interact with research subjects, each other and the wider audience for [. . .] research (Facer 2002, 3).

Here, there is the suggestion that studying digital culture in daily life may not only lead us to rethink how we do research but also how we present data, involve participants and disseminate our findings. Clearly we need more work in this area and, as Nixon (2003) observes, more focus on *how* we research as well as *what* we research.

In our work we have adopted an innovative approach by drawing on Markham's (1998, 2004) ideas about autoethnography as one potentially fruitful way of addressing methodological issues in studying digital writing. While Markham's work offers a close account of her involvement in an online community, our own collaborative work traces the overlapping, yet distinct, experiences of two individuals engaged in online events and practices. This researcher-as-subject-and-object analysis has enabled us to capture the similarities as well as the differences in our lives on- and off-line and to extrapolate from these certain degrees of commonality and areas of difference. Analysis examines the ways in which our own blogs have reflected the intersections of our academic lives with our personal, social and cultural worlds (cf., Ellis and Bochner 2003). Our position as research subjects-and-objects affords us maximum "insider" access to the online and offline nuances and complexities entailed in producing-consuming our blogs.

Turning Inside Out: Our Study of Blogging

From November, 2004, through to November, 2005, we used our own activity of blog-posting (drjoolzsnapshotz.blogspot.com and myvedana.blogspot.com) and associated digital practices such as reading, linking to and commenting on other blogs as a focus for reflection and analysis. This included our engagement with Flickr.com, an online photo-sharing service which was initially used to publish images to our respective blogs, but subsequently developed for each of us as a semi-autonomous digital practice in its own right. Our blogging and Flickr posting began some time before November 2004, so our blogs were reasonably well established at the start of our autoethnography. The data we collected for this autoethnography included: blog design, posts and comments, and the use of the multimodal affordances of blogging software. Part of our subsequent methodological work included comparing and contrasting the different ways in which we conceived of, designed and composed our blogs. Unstructured fieldnotes were published on a regular basis on a shared metablog, Blogtrax (Blogtrax.blogsome.com) using a webhost which allowed each writer to categorize postings through the use of tags. Tags are keywords or search terms a user can append to a post (or image) that enables like things to be grouped by the user or found by readers/viewers. Initially an in-common list of tags was generated in quite a rough way, drawing on areas of interest we already shared in our academic work; some of these were broad themes, such as 'identity', while others were very specific, such as "Flicker," which referred to a specific website and hosting service. Because our Blogtrax blog was a formative text, and was used to record our thinking as we went along, it was difficult to predict in advance which categories we would use and which ones might be redundant, too vague, or too broad. As such, our initial list of tags was not used to confine our thinking, but we hoped that these early tags would help us sift through the information on the blog at a later date. As we wrote each post, we ascribed one or more tags to that post in order to help order and review the data later. As a result, the metablog became a denser, more overtly co-constructed text which cross-references to our personal blogs as well as to other relevant sites, and in this way contrasted with our respective personal blogs. These published fieldnotes and reflections thus were simultaneously a record of research-in-progress and a product in themselves; the metablog constitutes both data and analysis.

The list of tags or categories we used on the metablog gradually developed over time, reflecting both our shared and our individual interests; we found the affordance of tags useful in our qualitative research. In terms of specific data analysis methods, we adapted Wolcott's system of interpretation and analysis (1994) and grouped our final categories into wider themes. Specific examples from within each of these grouped blog categories were used to illustrate these themes. The themes we identified are described briefly below, and provide a framework for the following three sections.

1. *Publishing the self* which includes specific issues about performing online identities, our sensitivities as bloggers to impression formation and our decisions about what to post and what not to post. In considering the content of our blogs, we look at how postings can work on the boundaries between private and public life. We also include the affective dimension of blogging in this category (such as feelings of pride, embarrassment and so on) and their relationship to respect and reputation in blogging communities.

2. *The nature and fabric of the text* as an interlinked and constantly evolving work, that is fluid, visual and, at least in part, created by readers, other bloggers and the comments that are added. *The fabric of the text* is concerned with the tools used to construct meaning. Predominantly this is about the use of multimodal text to signify group membership, reference to shared understandings and humor. However, we are also keen to show how the visual mode is used and, particularly focus on the use of photographic images. This section talks about the way in which medium, modality and semantics connect.

3. *Social networks* looks at how interactivity gives rise to the notion of blogging as a shared endeavour, a network than can lead to the development of a community of practice or an affinity space and how this relates to other platforms for online interaction (email, Flickr, MSN, shared blogs, others' blogs) as well as to offline interaction.

1. Publishing the Self

One of the attractions of blogging is the potential for immediate publication and opportunities to communicate with a multi-faceted audience—one which is potentially wide, diverse and dispersed, but also one which is known and familiar (Bortree 2005). What is communicated through blogs varies enormously from political and journalistic material to niche interest and personal or family information. While blogs can serve a wide range of purposes, they are ultimately an arena through which we communicate about ourselves.

As academics, we are no strangers to the world of publication, and are familiar with the formal and informal procedures that constitute gatekeeping when we publish, or attempt to publish, our work in high-status academic journals and books. For instance, we know well that it is part of the function of referees and peer-reviewers to determine the boundaries of what is acceptable to put into print. Our institutional and professional lives often guide the sort of topics that we write about. Furthermore, we are keenly aware of the time that it can take for our ideas or our research to finally make it through to publication—not to mention some of the gains and losses that occur on the way (e.g., editorial changes beyond our control; conversion of standard UK English into US English which affects word choice, idioms, punctuation and spelling; helpful reviewer suggestions).

For some academics who blog, the opportunity to write outside the boundaries of traditional academic publication is appealing (Mortensen 2005). One of the features of our experience of this is the manner in which our own blogs became a way to explore a wide variety of ideas and other material, thus constituting an alternative way of presenting the self. As Guy suggests in a post on Blogtrax:

> the blog is more than a showcase of themes, or random interests. It gives me a space, albeit a limited one, to explore what I want to explore. I enjoy composing posts and I like writing. And in contrast, I often feel constrained by the writing games we have to play as academics. Constrained by the scope as well as the genres we write in (Blogtrax 2005a).

Our initial analysis shows a high level of boundary-crossing in our immediate blogging networks as we seamlessly blend personal with professional worlds, seriousness with frivolity, addressing popular as well as academic concerns. References to developments in new digital technology feature alongside personal jokes, popular culture, critical theory, photography and the visual arts; the self is performed through an amalgam of discourses so that the blog becomes a textual expression of how discourses are appropriated from so many spheres and used to perform the self.

Private Lives in Public Spaces

As we began to reflect on our own experiences of blogging, the idea of "authoring the self" (Holland et al. 1998) often came to the fore. Not only were we pushing at the boundaries of academic self-publication, we also became aware of broader issues of identity in our online writing. As described above, threading through our posts were stories of our lives. Our notions of identity are informed by social theory, and perhaps best captured in the work of Giddens:

> The existential question of self identity is bound up with the fragile nature of the biography which the individual "supplies" about herself. A person's identity is not to be found in behaviour, nor—important though this is—in the reactions of others, but in the

capacity to keep a particular narrative going. The individual's biography, if she is to maintain regular interaction with others in the day-to-day world, cannot be wholly fictive. It must continually integrate events which occur in the external world, and sort them into the ongoing "story" about the self (Giddens 1991, 54).

This idea of keeping a particular narrative going, building a dynamic story of oneself in our social worlds, is explored and developed in one of Julia's comments posted on Blogtrax:

> I have an ongoing story. But I think we have several ongoing stories. I also think that if we bear in mind a particular audience, we change our story to suit them and ths [sic] change our notion of who we are according to our audience (Blogtrax 2005b).

So here we see the idea that identity is *produced* through action and performance (Grosz 1994). A plural narrative begins to develop, and our perception of an actual or imagined audience prompts us to think about what we wish to show. Identity performance, involves a sense of audience—an audience to whom one is presenting a particular narrative (or narratives) of the self. A perspective on this is offered by Guy, writing on Blogtrax, who suggests one way in which this can work:

> I wouldn't wish to bore readers with unfiltered outpourings. So there are some, admittedly fuzzy, boundaries. There's also some themes—gadgets; footprints; web's wonders; new literacy; music; and me—although, interestingly enough, I've never consciously decided on these, they've just emerged over time I guess I've constructed and performed a blogger identity which overlaps at points with my social/professional worlds (Blogtrax 2005c).

Here, Guy uses the idea of themes to explore the way particular threads weave in and out of his own blog (myvedana.blogspot.com). This is described as being quite an organic process, as these narrative threads or interests "emerge" in successive posts. These threads comprise the fabric of the textual self or persona that is being performed. Julia captures the sense in which active identity performance leads to a distinct "Dr Joolz persona" in which she is engaged in the activity of writing the self—as distinct, but not entirely separate, from other aspects of her lived experience. In this way, in *blogging* DrJoolz, she *becomes* DrJoolz, even to the extent that this influences real world actions such as collecting images to blog and so on.

> [I] have been thinking about how in some ways I have developed a DrJoolz persona who is a little bit different from my identity as a researcher at work, as a colleague, as someone at home with family relationships. Maybe on the blog I present myself as having some kind of coherence; some sort of joined upness. In writing about myself I am somehow writing myself. I am subject and object of the work; and interestingly because I am

writing about blogging I sometimes do stuff so I can blog it. In this way the blog influences my life; it does not simply record aspects of it (Blogtrax 2005d).

This leads us to consider the emergence of a particular kind of blogger identity; an identity that has a symbiotic relationship with other aspects of the self. Within the context of our blogging, both of us are engaged in self-disclosure; as Julia reflects, "I have even told the world my feelings in a very uncharacteristic act of openness" (Blogtrax 2005e).

The tension between self-disclosure and public performance seems to be quite central to our experience of blogging. What has become clear to us is that while we are both sensitive to this tension, we explore it in characteristically different ways in our own blogs. Guy, for instance, aspires to a way of writing that is exploratory and not overtly interested in maintaining readership. He explains his view that:

> The inner workings of jottings, musings, impressionistic thoughts and emotions go down, go public prior to substantial reworking. And as they go along they collect and discard readers, comments, and other links (Blogtrax 2005f).

But of course, in online environments even the most intimate revelations of one's private life can be constructed or perceived as a carefully managed process of self-presentation. And indeed, what for the individual blogger may be a tension between private and public worlds, may for the reader merely seem like authentic (or inauthentic) communication, as Julia's comparison with television chat show environments illustrates:

> this strange thing of chat shows where they [are] pretending they are in a lounge at home or something, and refer to interviewees as 'guests' (they are paid after all)—(sofas; drinks; flowers on the table; some 'guests' even bring presents)—Yes, I think the blog has a lot in common with that; this sort of pretense at exclusive views on the 'real' thoughts and so on of a guest; and it is presented as if to a group of friends—even though it goes totally public, is not exclusive etc etc. Except that people *do* sometimes choose to reveal a lot of their 'private lives' both on chat shows and on their blogs. In this way that 'private/public' thing is shared by blogs and by chat shows (Blogtrax 2005g).

The chat show analogy is helpful in conveying the idea of a public performance space, that, no matter how contrived it may be, does contain real "personalities" in a real location (or locations). From time to time, bloggers give us a sense of their experience in relation to the space they are in, even though in fact they report to us from within a shared cyberspace. Despite the fact that they could be anywhere, we still can get a sense of their location through their blogs. Guy writes about how this background can be helpful, "Even the trivial stuff—S. blogs there's snow in New York . . . —can turn out to be interesting" (Blogtrax, 2005h).

Through the accumulation of information about bloggers' lives, readers build a richer picture and an understanding of how multiple discourses make up complex selves. When such details are offered and reciprocated across a plurality of blogs, a sense of a shared social history is acquired, especially where comments are made about others' lives and views. In turn there is a new sense of self, as it is woven into a joint narrative text across the blogs; a sense of a new self in a new and complex internet space.

Bloggers Have Feelings, Too

A recurrent theme in our blogging activity relates to the affective aspects of onscreen writing. We cannot control or limit our audience, and so once our blog is "live," it exists in a more or less public arena and can attract praise or criticism, support or derision. And perhaps because blog posts are relatively quick and straightforward to publish, humiliating errors of judgment are always possible. In a sense, we put ourselves "on the line" when we go public; we have found that we need to be brave to blog! As cited above (Blogtrax, 2005e), Julia expresses regret about a particular posting, worrying that it may have seemed like a "rant," and ends her post with the note, "(. . . *Must not use blog to rant as this can be very offensive to others. Have learned valuable blogging lesson.*)" (Blogtrax 2005e). Here, Julia is wary of a common criticism of bloggers: encapsulated in the idea that they "rant" or use their blog as a soapbox to indulge and proclaim their particular pre-occupations. Here the self-criticism is evident in the way she describes her own post as an "unprecedented outburst" and the concern that this may be "offensive" to others.

In a more introspective posting, Guy writes about his feelings about his blog (see Figure 8.1).

Here Guy uses the image of an eye in order to emphasize his feeling of being under surveillance as he writes, "My blog is watching me, staring out from the screen at me, and just the other side through the darkness of the pupil, visitors peer in at me" (Blogtrax, 2005i). This seems to communicate the sense of a vulnerable author who in some ways feels under scrutiny, or that he is being judged by imagined readers. More often though, our analyses suggest this sort of self-consciousness manifests itself in a concern that things may look wrong on screen or be misinterpreted.

The sense in which one is publicly exposed via one's blog is mentioned quite often on Blogtrax, My Vedana and DrJoolz. Indeed, we found that we both commented on feelings of nervousness and apprehension about particular posts. This suggests that alongside anxieties about public exposure through blogging, there is, as suggested above, also the risk of being misunderstood or misinterpreted. Both of us have had experiences of this. A specific example occurred when Guy posted a link to a blog to which someone subsequently added pornographic images in the

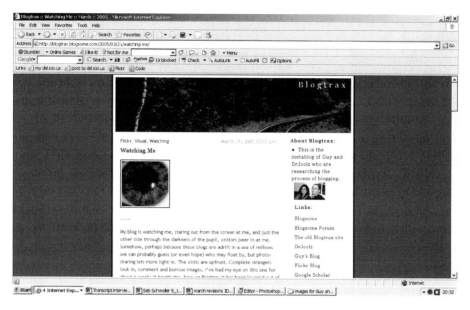

Figure 8.1. Watching me

comments section. This led to Guy being upset because he felt he had inadvertently put pornography on *his* blog because of the hyperlink. As Julia observed, "He felt he was tainted by association." (Blogtrax, 2005e). Through this incident, we saw more sharply how texts were so closely woven together online, that in some ways another person's words and actions, become part of one's own text. Authorship and identities can become blurred as texts intertwine and merge.

The affective dimension of blogging is nonetheless more subtly nuanced than these examples of anxiety and embarrassment suggest. In fact, we should be quite clear that our initial enthusiasm for the research we report here stemmed from the pleasure and excitement that we found in our own early experiences of blogging. Feelings of freedom from being constrained in what we wrote seemed to combine with the pleasure of seeing our texts on screen, and this in turn generated a very real attachment to our respective blogs.

In this section we have reflected on ways in which our own blog publishing has provided a vehicle for us to narrate ourselves and to present our different social identities. This aspect of blogging is one we have found both challenging and, in turn, liberating. As academics we feel we have been able to make contacts with others in ways we have not previously experienced. We explore this social aspect of blogging in later section (see Section 3). Within the current section, we have seen how our presentations of identity have often been influenced by the nature and fabric of the text, in a familiar "medium is the message" manner. In the next section we offer further details of this and of other affordances of the blog modalities.

2. The Nature and Fabric of the Text

Blogs are designed to be read and used on screen rather than on paper, but perhaps like newspaper readers, blog readers tend only to regard the most recent entries as worthy of their attention. These recent entries appear first, at the top of the screen, with older posts generally archived in monthly groups, and as such, made peripheral to the central part of the blog. Despite this, the idea of archiving does suggest that a blog is a cumulative text, one with a present and a past history. This customary layout, negotiated easily with experience, is an online textual convention to be learned (see Figure 8.2).

This layout is presented to most bloggers as a ready-made template; the dating system, the archiving and the comments sections, all appear "magically" once a new blog has been set up. While the default template can be left as it is, many bloggers customize the basic shape after a while, and sometimes even move on to using more complex hosting systems than they began with as they become more experienced and discriminating about what they want from their blog. For example,

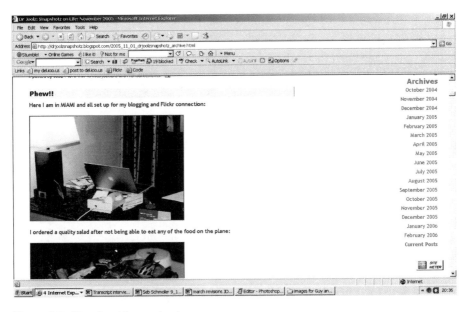

Figure 8.2. Dated archives and a site meter

Julia moved Blogtrax (first set up on Blogger.com) to another host (Blogsome.com) so that posts could be tagged and categorized as they were being written. In describing this on Blogtrax she wrote:

> Have spent quite a while today moving all the posts over from Blogtrax (one) to its new home here. Hopefully this will help Guy and I in the long run when we use it as a data-base to help us write.
>
> The next big task, (and the whole thing will have been pointless without this next step) is to categorise all the posts.
>
> This in itself is of course an analytical process (Blogtrax 2005j).

The categories facility, as described earlier, provided by some hosts such as Blogsome, allows flexibility in the organisation of the database of posts beyond the date-only ordering available on most blog hosting services. As described earlier, this tagging facil-ity enables posts to be collated under any category that a blogger wishes to create and subsequently tag posts with. Hyperlinks to each category or set of posts appears in the blog's sidebar. Thus in Blogtrax, categories include affinity spaces; learning; and communities of practice. Clicking on one of these hyperlinked categories means that posts allocated to that category will move to the "front page" of the blog. Posts may be allocated to more than one category so that multiple appearances across categories are possible. The software that drives this categorizing function thus requires some new skills to be learned in order to use the function effectively. At the same time, this function also provides important new textual affordances with respect to more easi-ly following threads of interest across a blog's entire set of posts. Many of these skills are what make the difference between a non-dynamic text that is intended to be kept as "flat"—something which when printed on paper, loses no affordances—in contrast to the more densely layered and flexible hypertext. In this way the skills to be learned, while involving digital technology, have implications for literacy.

The blogroll, also a common feature of blogs in general, is a hyperlinked list of other blogs, and allows bloggers to signpost sites that are of interest to them. Such a list could of course, be hidden on the blogger's own computer under "favorites" or "bookmarks" on their internet browser interface of choice. The public display of blogrolls, then, sets out affinities clearly for readers, allowing the blogger to publicize and share her interests and priorities. Furthermore, blogrolls allow bloggers to con-textualize for themselves and for others their space within the "blogosphere." So through blogrolls, bloggers can stake out an interest, an identity and even loyalties to others; through blogrolls a certain "character" for the blog can be established. Blogrolls are also known as blog "referrals" and are often mutual (e.g., Guy's *My Vedana* blogroll includes a link to DrJoolz's blog, and *vice versa*). Being on a high-profile blog's blogroll confers instant high-level status to one's own blog and may lead to one's blog appearing on multiple strangers' blogrolls. Networks thus are drawn out with inter-woven threads of often reciprocal patterning (of course, including a high-profile blog in your own blogroll does not ensure that your blog will be listed in this high-profile blogger's blogroll). In this way the affordances of the blog medium promote interaction between bloggers and increase their potential for social networking.

This phenomenon can be seen in the blogrolls of My Vedana and DrJoolz Snapshotz, that each contain links to other academics' blogs, literacy sites and related research sites. These lists reflect our dovetailing interests as well as our divergences (see Figure 8.3).

The way that links on blogs can be used to establish allegiances has already attracted the attention of researchers. Van House (2004), for example, writes about the mutual linking and blogrolling of bloggers in this way:

> While much blogging is a form of personal expression, when the bloggers in question are a community of mutually-referenced topical bloggers . . . [they] see their work as collaborative (Van House 2004, 2).

Van House, like us, argues that the norms of blogging promote a high degree of self-disclosure, but also that the closeness woven through online links means that blogging allows close collaboration and knowledge sharing. Visits to one's blog can be moni-tored closely by means of add-ons such as site meters. Site meters allow bloggers to

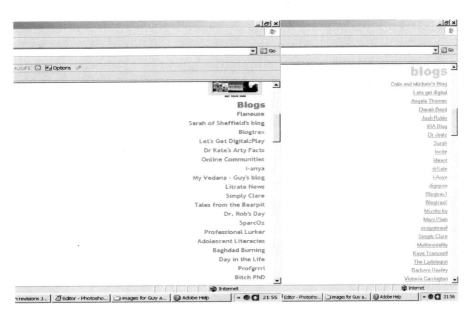

Figure 8.3. Blogrolls on My Vedana and DrJoolz (as at November 18, 2005).

track from where "visitors" have come (i.e., the referring URL), what page on the blog they enter by and where they exit, as well as the number of pages they have looked at, and so on. All this information might motivate the blogger to keep writing, or even to visit the sites of those who have looked at their blog. This is another route through which connections can be reciprocated and deepened.

The feature of any hypertext which most obviously distinguishes it from other kinds of texts is the hyperlink; it gives the onscreen text a kind of "depth," a richer texture than a printed page generally has. This facility allows readers to jump from one text to another and back again, to trace a journey across the web from one text to another, or simply to ignore the links altogether. In composition, hyperlinks make it possible for bloggers to easily reference other work; jackdaw-like, they can gather threads of texts in one place, weaving these texts together by means of hyperlinks. By including the URL of a website into a blog post, a blogger enables readers to choose to "click on" and move to cited texts on other sites in order to read more about a topic, issue or event, etc. In this way, blogs are partially composed of other texts, gaining the Bakhtinian buzz of "double voicing" and "ventriloquism" (Bakhtin 1981). To clarify, by inserting hyperlinks and thereby incorporating other texts into one's own, the words of other writers are read within the context of the host text. Within the words and images produced by the blogger, there will be importations from elsewhere, giving the text a rich diversity of voices.

For example, in My Vedana, Guy uses a series of links to make a point about regulation, self-regulation and ethics on blogging,

> After serving her time as blurker [i.e., a blog lurker; someone who just visits and reads posts] and blog commenter, Kate now has her own blog and so, in celebration drkates artyfacts (Kate 2005) is top blog. I really liked the agenda setting statement in her first posting:
>
> *"Commenters may be interested to know the themes in advance, so they can adjust their comments accordingly.*
>
> *For now the themes are:*
>
> *rucksacks*
>
> *lost tickets*
>
> *lost items"*
>
> I liked it because I've been reflecting on regulation, self-regulation and ethics in blogging. So, Kate's provisional agenda reminded me of this, and what Torill does not write about on her blog. And then, from another point of view Danah Boyd writes about other people wanting to control what she blogs. "*I want the right to control my voice*", she says, and that's a theme that's emerged for me through this last week.
>
> // posted by guy @ 2:33 PM

Comments:

That's funny, I read both Torill and Danah's posts the same day and noticed similar themes too. And yippeee, isn't it wonderful that Kate is blogging, now she can be a 100% insider too! *applauds*

posted by Anya : 11:06 PM

Strange to be wandering around in the same territory, leaving footprints in cyberspace. Off to see Kate now, must dash!

posted by guy : 9:45 AM (My Vedana 2005)

It is possible here to understand the text quite well without following all the links (i.e., all those words in Guy's post that are underlined are links to sites outside his blog), yet it is nonetheless clear that to fully understand the gist of Guy's post, one must go and see the sites to which Guy refers or links. The text of his post is not self-contained and one can in a way see a history of his thoughts by visiting the same texts he read prior to making this post. In this way, the text of his post is to some extent dependent on these other texts. However, hypertextual reading confers particular degrees of freedom to the reader who is able to determine not only the reading path taken, but also the level of attention and depth of reading allotted to a text. While academics are well accustomed to citing and quoting widely (and in the example above, Guy cites Kate's words for emphasis), blogs can also link directly to the other texts, so that these other texts can be read at source, in context, and all at one "sitting." The relationship goes two ways; the other texts gain an extra dimension too, in that they are now linked to another text or site. Julia talks about this on Blogtrax:

And our blogs' fabrics are constituted of our links as well as our words and pictures (etc). *Other people's texts become part of ours*, because we weave them in. . . . our blogs are continuous texts with each other; our links tie us together and are mutually constitutive (if I can say that). So in building texts we constantly re-affirm and regenerate what the group is. We are our associations (Blogtrax 2005e).

Here Julia discusses how others are drawn into an affinity, as they can see from their site-meters, feeds and "trackback" functions that show where links have been made to their work. The originators of texts that have been linked to, can visit a blog and read and comment back, and meanings can be developed, shared or disputed. Multiple links can be made into and out of any online text; some texts will gain renown through such multiple links and of course, the more visits that such texts receive, the higher up a search engine's set of returns for key words they will move.

There is a sense on both Julia's and Guy's respective blogs and on their shared Blogtrax, that there are some regular readers and commenters. Again Julia remarks:

> We have found each other through common interests through a series of links, through degrees of separation. We have traced paths via each other and kept within a group with some pretty high status cultural capital. No wonder we love the web; we talk to people 'like us' and we go through the links on many people's blogs in this way. Our network is safe (Blogtrax 2005e).

Just as with the blog roll, commenters are valued; Anya's comment on Guy's post on p.185, indicates that commenters play a constitutive role in text making. While bloggers—ostensibly at least—seem to set up their blogs in order to serve their *own* purpose, it has become clear that certain aspects of blogs are responsive to comments by and declared interests of others. At times, questions are asked of readers; references are made as to who might be interested in a post; sometimes bloggers will post entries that mirror those of others. For example, on August 26 2005, Julia posted a photograph of a cake she had made and linked to cakes made by other academic bloggers, such as, SimplyClare (SimplyClare 2005) and MaryPlain (MaryPlain 2005). These three bloggers had made cakes and posted photographs of them. Through their blogs they were able to demonstrate a certain synchronicity of life rhythms with each other and to show shared interests beyond the academic field of their professional lives. In this way affinities were declared and boundaries were perhaps also set. There is also an unspoken irony which works across these blogs; the three academics had met recently for the first time in "real space" at an academic conference. The blogs were allowing them to take risks in showing aspects of their private lives, but which indeed seemed to also help them take risks in the way they discussed new ideas on their blogs. Allowing the boundaries between seriousness and play, between home and academic lives to blur is a new way of writing that blogging promotes.

As a screen-based form, a blog is a distinctively visual text and bloggers quickly become aware of the multimodal semioses at work (Kress, 2003). Both of us, in turn, became pre-occupied with the look of our blogs. In order to include images on our blogs, we made use of the photosharing site, Flickr.com. By doing this, we became members of separate communities within Flickr itself with each becoming involved in Flickr to varying degrees, with Julia taking more of an interest in images as a digital medium and in the Flickr community. In this way we saw how the technology itself began to influence relationships and activities; we also saw how blogging could impact on ways in which bloggers spent their time offline. Julia began to search for photographs to contribute to Flickr and this, in turn, directly influenced what she wrote about on her blog.

For example, in the post presented below, we see evidence of Julia's involvement in the Flickr community, her interest in academic debates about play and learning, and the treatment of dolls. She refers to an academic paper she has written, as well as links to another blog she is involved in within the academic community. She uses an image from Mohawk (see Figure 8.4), a Flickr member (Mohawk/Limbert 2005a) as an integral part of the post, and discusses the image within this—and elsewhere (DigitalPlayer 2005). In this post, Julia also refers to Guy and his daughters, revealing information about his offline life, and to a photo he has posted on Flickr. The responses of readers equally blend playful, serious and personal comments (underlined words and phrases denote hyperlinks):

Mohawk

claims to be <u>lazy and confused</u> (Mohawk/Limbert 2005a) as well as aged 31.

I am interested in the exciting artifacts he uses in his photographs.

'What an interesting juxtaposition!!!!',

I hear you say.

And others call out:

'Check out the semiotics in that!!!'

thanks so much to Mohawk [Mohawk/Limbert 2005b] for showing us <u>this</u> [Mohawk/Limbert 2005c] too.

You must see the discussion <u>here</u> [DigitalPlayer, 2005] of what is going on.

Figure 8.4. Mohawk/Tea (Mohawk/Limbert 2005b)

Aaaanyway at the weekend (when I was working) a student told me she had read my Babyz paper here. [Davies 2003]

She told me she had to stop reading after a while as the thought of cyber babyz being tortured upset her so much. When I told her this was just girls (gurlz) playing experimentally and it was only pixels being manipulated not Babyz being tortured, she explained that many murderers had been found to have brutalised their dolls when younger.

So I now worry about Guy's daughters' futures. See here. [on-the-run, 2005]

posted by Joolz : 10:40 PM

Comments:

I once wrote an essay for Peter Smith (yes I was his student once) on The Little Mermaid as an example of bricolage.

My son was very attached to Barbies (so there all you gender determinists) but also liked to cut their hair off and mutilate them (he was 3 at the time)

So my essay for my MA was on the Little Mermaid as bricolage.

The final version that my son played with had a pink punk haircut, and wore an attractive ensemble of clothing including some tattered Cinderella outfit but sadly the legs had been amputated for unknown reasons.

He is obviously in danger of being a mass murderer.

I will go and tell him now (he is sick at home).

posted by Kate : 9:06 AM

-

When I was nine, I brutalised my Girlsworld head. It had to be done: the makers provided makeup and extending/retracting hair. Perhaps all doll manufacturers can be held accountable for the mass murderering tendencies of mass murderers.

I also bit my cat's tail once. He bit me first.

posted by Simply Clare : 5:07 PM

-

I had Sindy's little sister Patch (I was a Sindy girl not a Barbie girl) and I cut her hair, made a right mess of it..

posted by Mary Plain : 8:49 PM (DrJoolz 2005/10)

The meanings of this post are inscribed within the complex image, a sophisticated visual joke, as well as through the posted words and links. The blog entry itself grows with the addition of comments and becomes multi-authored—and as a result new meanings develop. It reflects aspects of the academic world as well as making references to personal lives. No attempt is made within the comments to explain to others beyond the group and in this way meanings are kept closed; the group is in some ways exclusive despite the fact that the discussion is taking place online. While the post could be understood by a wider audience, some of the readers who commented created quite specific meanings anchored to discourses located in shared online and offline worlds (e.g., the concept of "gurlz," "gender determinists," "bricolage" as a concept within literary analysis, the difference between Sindy and Barbie dolls). So there is a sense of intimacy in this exchange, despite the potential readership being much broader. The social and the academic networking are blurred and the academic and playful are both evident. This illustrates how the blogging software is structured in such a way that makes this kind of textual interaction and semantic development possible.

3. Social Networks

Throughout our study of blogging, we have been grappling with ways of describing the social dimension of this popular new literacy practice. As the previous sections have shown, our blogs overlap with and expand on pre-existing networks and more established modes of communication. So, for the two of us at the centre of this study, blogging has certainly enriched our familiarity with each other, both as academics and in more general terms. For two academics working in the same field in the same city, but in different institutions, occasional face-to-face meetings and email exchanges would not be atypical. However, "meeting up" and "interacting" through blog posts and comments has changed and enriched this professional relationship.

At the same time as our blogs are professionally and textually related to each other, however, these blogs are also located in a wider network of academics who work in the literacy field in the UK. They constitute a small group of colleagues who are more geographically dispersed than we two are and with whom we would normally have less frequent contact; perhaps at most meeting up bi-annually at seminars or UK-based research conferences. Beyond this, our blogs are also linked in with academics in Australia and the U.S.; colleagues who we meet occasionally, that one or the other of us has met, or those who we have yet to meet face-to-face. Wellman (2002) describes these sorts of social networks as being *glocalized* in the sense that they blend local and global communication and interaction. So, although blogging is the focus of our ethnography it becomes impossible to separate it as a practice from the contexts and networks in which it is embedded. Furthermore, it is quite apparent that with this kind of blogging there is no clean separation of online and offline activity. As Leander observes,

> It is increasingly less tenable to hold onto a vision of culture, identity and literacy prac-
> tice in which the "offline" and the "online" are held radically apart in the ways that they
> are practiced and signified (Leander 2003, 392)

As we have seen above, blog comments often pertain to both offline and online
discourses and practices. This blending of worlds perhaps makes it even more
problematic to describe online inter-relationships. A sense of this is captured by
Julia, who comments on Blogtrax that

> although I write with a group of people in mind, I am always hoping for more like mind-
> ed people to listen—and join in. Thus the use of links for people to follow up on previ-
> ous conversations, allows them to 'catch up'. Many links will not be read by 'regulars' as
> they refer to old stuff. In this way it is like explaining a family joke, or a bit of social his-
> tory to a new member of the group. And this of course brings us yet again, back even
> closer to a need to refine 'Affinity Spaces' as a concept. The drive to involve more peo-
> ple, comes from my constant desire to interact with others; to be social; to find more like
> me; so I can learn from them, with them, find out stuff. Anything. I love to follow their
> links; I love to have a reaction from others. I like to see *them* (Blogtrax 2005g).

In our work, we have both been exploring the concepts of "affinity spaces" (Gee
2004) and "communities of practice" (Lave and Wenger 1991) in order to try to
describe our relationship with others who blog and who seem to operate within a
similar "constellation of sites." Affinity spaces, according to Gee (2004), are guided
by purpose and content. Thus the endeavor or interest around which the space is
organized is, for Gee, the primary affinity; it is thus less about interpersonal relationships. According to this definition, blogs *could* provide an affinity space, but yet
apart, perhaps, from Blogtrax itself, our own blogs do not easily condense around
a clear-defined "endeavor" or "interest." Rather it is almost as if the shared point of
contact—perhaps broadly described as an enthusiasm for new literacies—has
become the point of departure, from which we begin to explore other interests and
other dimensions of our lifeworlds. In this sense, our personal blogs seem to be a
way in which we function as networked individuals, keeping and creating contacts
and links between a diverse group whose varied interests reflect our own.

For a personal blog, it is the individual rather than the place that becomes the
locus of connectivity, and in previous sections of this chapter we have developed an
account of how this occurs. We can and do access, post and comment on blogs from
anywhere where we can be online. This enables us to publish ourselves, and to use
the textual and social affordances of the blogging software to remain active in our
social networks. From this point of view, blogging constitutes a new literacy
practice (Lankshear and Knobel 2003), albeit one which we suggest can only be
properly understood within the context of other forms of interaction. This may go

part way to account for the reaction of some colleagues and friends who will visit a blog and later comment that they "just don't get it." "Outsiders" may not only fail to understand how the blog works, but also how it is located in new webs of communication.

Conclusion

In a special edition of *Reading Research Quarterly*, Hagood (2003) urged literacy educators to engage with new technology as a way of understanding the characteristics and potentialities of communication in the new media landscape. She suggested that:

> researchers who attempt to explore research questions that address how new media and online literacies affect youngsters' constructions of identities and notions of self need also to apply such questions to themselves as they engage these same media technologies in their lives (Hagood 2003, 389).

In following this, the autoethnographic study we have reported here has brought to the fore a number of features of our own online writing and text-making practices and opened up further avenues for exploration. Although the nature of the study has revealed a number of key differences in the way we approach writing online as individuals, it has also enabled us to identify some key aspects of blogging as a new literacy practice.

First, blogging seems to be closely tied up with self-presentation and impression formation. On our pages we perform our identities in a particularly public arena, one which can be accessed by friends or rivals, family or strangers, colleagues at work, those from our own professional networks and those from the wider academic community. In this sense our blogs are texts for self-presentation which we hope will "be accepted as appropriate and plausible performances" (Hine 2000,122). Through this unfiltered self-publication we are potentially vulnerable, open to misinterpretation or even ridicule. Yet at the same time our blogs, by making us visible, can also develop respect and reputation. In our metablog, we traced the theme of identity performance and the ways in which it mirrors multiple and shifting perceptions of audience. Writing online provides us with the opportunity to "author the self" (Holland et al. 1998), to sustain a narrative of identity (Giddens 1991), and even to explore a number of different stories of the self, but these identities always are forged through our connection with others. So, although we have identified different ways in which we, as individuals, conceive of and respond to audience, how we imagine our readership is important to us. As Hine argues, a webpage:

> is made meaningful primarily through the imagining of an audience and the seeking of recognition from that audience (Hine 2000,136).

How we position ourselves in relation to our imagined or actual audience informs and is informed by the nature of the texts that we produce and consume in our blogging lives.

Second, we have shown how the social software used by blog hosts (Blogger, Blogsome, Xanga etc.) facilitates particular kinds of textual practice and supports the development of online relationships. The salience of visual style and regular blog updates provide a sort of invitation to those in a social network to visit regularly. In this social world the visitor or reader has considerable freedom and is able to determine not only the reading path but also the level of attention paid to the text, depth of reading and degree of interactivity. At the same time the blogger uses the genre to signal allegiances and affiliations through various textual and hypertextual moves. Bloggers, whether at any one time they are producers or consumers, navigate their way around a thickly interwoven fabric of online and offline texts, which often blend serious and more frivolous discourses.

Third, we have explored how blogging is characteristic of a particular kind of social networking. Borrowing from the work of Wellman (2002), we have described this in terms of glocalized and networked individualism. We have traced how those particular social networks operate in both online and offline spaces and how at times the blurring of those boundaries which demarcate the public/private spheres of our lives is a strong characteristic of our blogs, as well as of blogs in general.

Finally, in the context of this ethnographic study we have adopted an approach which places the focus on the social and cultural aspects of being a blogger and shows the overlap of private, personal and interpersonal worlds. This enquiry has repositioned us as central, as part subjects, part agents and part observers within an autoethnographic process. This contrasts with the more separate stance of traditional ethnographers. Online ethnography has presented us with new opportunities that force us to reconsider the linear trajectory of research design that until now has followed a simple timeline from the identification of subjects, materials and context through to analysis and publication. In this way our study adds to the understanding of new literacy practices and signals the emergence of new epistemological approaches. Of particular interest here is the metablog Blogtrax which not only became a place in which we stored our fieldnotes, but also provided us with the opportunity to interact with our research audience and fellow bloggers throughout our study. Blogtrax also used a tag and search facility which enabled us to code and classify our fieldnotes as they were written. As a result, the traditional authorship boundaries were relaxed, as commenters became involved in ongoing discussion and debate. This shows the possibility of a more transparent research process which in turn places researchers in a new relationship with participants and user-groups, who can view, comment on and even help shape the research as it unfolds. As blogging itself offers new opportunities for networking and encourages new relationships between readers and writers, so using new technologies can encourage new relationships between producers and consumers.

References

Adbusters 2005. Adbusters. adbusters.org (Accessed 27 October, 2005).

Bakhtin, M. 1981. Discourse in the novel. In M. Holquist (Ed.), *The Dialogic Imagination* (C. Emerson and M. Holquist, Trans.). Texas: University of Texas.

Barton, D. 1994. *Literacy: An Introduction to the Ecology of Written Language*. London: Blackwell.

Barton, D., and Hamilton, M. 1998. *Local Literacies: Reading and Writing in One Community*. London: Routledge.

Blogcount.com 2005. Blogcount. dijest.com/bc/ (Accessed 3 March, 2006).

Blogtrax 2005a. Porous. blogtrax.blogsome.com/2005/01/27/porous/ (Accessed 7 August 2006).

Blogtrax 2005b. The Reflexive Project of the Self. blogtrax.blogsome.com/2005/08/24/the-reflexive-project-of-the-self (Accessed 3 March 2006).

Blogtrax 2005c. Longhand. blogtrax.blogsome.com/2005/08/19/longhand-2/ (Acessed 7 August 2006).

Blogtrax 2005d. Meta stuff at last. blogtrax.blogsome.com/2005/05/16/meta-stuff-at-last/ (Accessed 6 August 2006).

Blogtrax 2005e. Paths through the net. blogtrax.blogsome.com/2005/07/29/paths-through-the-net (Accessed 7 August 2006).

Blogtrax 2005f. Outside In. blogtrax.blogsome.com/2005/10/14/outside-in (Accessed 7 August, 2006).

Blogtrax 2005g. Life Blogging Life. blogtrax.blogsome.com/2005/07/25/71/life-blogging-life (Accessed 7 August 2006).

Blogtrax 2005h. Vanity Blogging. lbogtrax.blogsome.com/2005/10/01/vanity-blogging (Accessed 7 August 2006).

Blogtrax 2005i. Watching Me. blogtrax.blogsome.com/2005/03/21/watching-me (Accessed 7 August 2006).

Blogtrax 2005j. New Blog. blogtrax.blogsome.com/2005/05/22/new-blog (Accessed 7 August 2006).

Bortree, D.S. 2005. Presentation of self on the web: An ethnographic study of teenage girls' weblogs. *Education, Communication and Information* 5(1): 25–39.

Burnett, C., Dickinson, P., McDonagh, J., Merchant, G., Myers, J. and Wilkinson, J. 2003. From recreation to reflection: Digital conversations within educational contexts. *Educational Studies in Language and Literature* 3: 149–67.

Carrieoke 2005. Carrieoke's Knitting Blog: Im a crafty Schmoo. carrie.prettyposies.com (Accessed 29 October, 2005).

Davies, J. 2003. Negotiating Femininities On-Line. Paper presented to The University of Sheffield ESRC funded seminar series on Children's Literacy and Popular Culture. shef.ac.uk/literacy/ESRC/pdf/papers/davies_4.pdf (Accessed 3 March, 2006).

Davies, J. 2005. Nomads and tribes: Online meaning-making and the development of new literacies. In J. Marsh and E. Millard (Eds), *Popular Literacies, Childhood and Schooling*. London: Routledge. 160–75.

Digitalplayer 2005. Playing with Dolls. letsgetdigitalplay.blogspot.com/2005/10/playing-with-dolls.html (Accessed 3 March, 2006).

DrJoolz 2005. Mohawk. drjoolzsnapshotz.blogspot.com/2005/10/mohawk.html (Accessed 5 March, 2006).

Ellis, C. and Bochner, A. 2003. Autoethnography, personal narrative, reflexivity: Researcher as subject. In N. Denzin and Y. Lincoln (Eds), *Collecting and Interpreting Qualitative Materials*. London: Sage. 199–259.

Facer, K. 2002. Beyond Language: Exploring the Potential of Multi-Modal Research. Paper presented to the International Federation for Information Processing conference, Manchester, July 2002.

Farrell, H. 2005. The Blogosphere as a Carnival of Ideas. chronicle.com/free/v52/i07/07b01401.htm (Accessed 29 October, 2005).

Gee, J. 2004. *Situated Language and Learning: A Critique of Traditional Schooling*. London: Routledge.

Giddens, A. 1991. *Modernity and Self Identity: Self and Society in the Late Modern Age*. Oxford: Polity.

Grosz, E. 1994. *Volatile Bodies: Towards a Corporeal Feminism*. Bloomington, IN: Indiana University Press.

Hagood, M.C.2003. New media and online literacies: No age left behind. *Reading Research Quarterly* 38(3): 387–391.

Hamilton, M. 2000. Expanding the new literacy studies: using photographs to explore literacy as a social practice. In D. Barton, M. Hamilton, and R. Ivanic (Eds), *Situated Literacies: Reading and Writing in Context*. London: Routledge. 16–34.

Herring, S. 2004. Slouching toward the ordinary: Current trends in computer-mediated communication. *New Media and Society* 6(1): 26–33.

Hine, C. 2000. *Virtual Ethnography*. London: Sage.

Hodder, I. 2003. The interpretation of documents and material culture. In N. Denzin and Y. Lincoln (Eds), *Collecting and Interpreting Qualitative Materials*. London: Sage. 155–76.

Holland, D., Lachinotte, W., Skinner, D. and Cain, C. (1998) *Identity and Agency in Cultural Worlds*. Cambridge MA: Harvard University Press.

i-anya 2005. Commenting on Academic *blogs*. anya.blogsome.com/2005/10/25/commenting-on-academic-blogs/#comments (Accessed 28 October, 2005).

Ito, M. 2004. Personal Portable Pedestrian Lessons from Japanese Mobile Phone Use. Paper presented to "Mobile Communication and Social Change," the 2004 International Conference on Mobile Communication in Seoul, Korea, October 18–19. itofisher.com/mito/publications/personal_portab.html (Accessed 3 March, 2006).

Kate 2005. *Dr Kate's Artyfacts*. drkatesartyfacts.blogspot.com (Accessed 3 March, 2006).

Knobel, M. 2005. Technokids, koala trouble and Pokémon: Literacy, new technologies and popular culture in children's everyday lives. In J. Marsh and E. Millard (Eds), *Popular Literacies, Childhood and Schooling*. London: Routledge. 11–28.

Kramer Bussel, R., Alizinha and Nichelle 2005. Cupcakes Take the Cake. cupcakestakethecake.blogspot.com (Accessed 28 October, 2006).

Kress, G. 1997. Visual and verbal modes of representation in electronically mediated communication: The potentials of new forms of texts. In I. Snyder (Ed.), *Page to Screen: Taking Literacy into the Electronic Age*. London: Routledge. 53–79.

Kress, G. 2000. Multimodality. In B. Cope and M. Kalantzis (Eds), *Multiliteracies: Literacy Learning and the Design of Social Futures*. London: Macmillan. 182–202

Kress, G. 2003. *Literacy in the New Media Age*. London: Routledge.

Lankshear, C. and Knobel, M. 2003. *New Literacies: Changing Knowledge and Classroom Learning*. Buckingham, UK: Open University Press.

Lave, J. and Wenger, E. 1991. *Situated Learning: Legitimate Peripheral participation*. Cambridge: Cambridge University Press.

Leander, K. 2003. Writing travelers' tales on New Literacyscapes. *Reading Research Quarterly* 38(3): 392–6.

Manolo 2005. Manolo's Shoe Blog. shoeblogs.com (Accessed 28 October, 2005).

Markham, A. 1998. *Life Online: Researching Real Experience in Virtual Space*. London: Sage.

Markham, A. 2004. Reconsidering self and other: The methods, politics, and ethics of representation in online ethnography. In N. Denzin and Y. Lincoln (Eds), *Handbook of Qualitative Research*. London: Sage. 793–820.

Mary Plain 2005. Tales from the Bearpit. talesfromthebearpit.blogspot.com (Accessed 3 March, 2006).

Merchant, G. 2006. A sign of the times: Looking critically at popular digital writing. In J. Marsh and E. Millard (Eds), *Popular Literacies, Childhood and Schooling*. London: Routledge. 93–109.

Mohawk / Limbert, S. 2005a. Profile on Flickr. flickr.com/people/Mohawk (Accessed 3 March, 2006).

Mohawk / Limbert, S. 2005b. Tea. Image as part of a set, *Somnambule*. flickr.com/photos/mohawk/13599814/in/set-237158 (Accessed 3 March, 2006).

Mohawk / Limbert, S. 2005c. Rewind-Button. Image as part of a set, *Somnambule*. flickr.com/photos/mohawk/13598396/in/set-237158 (Accessed 3 March, 2006).

Mortensen, T. 2004. Personal Publication and Public Attention. *Into the Blogosphere*. blog.lib.umn.edu/blogosphere/personal_publication.html (Accessed 26 February, 2005).

Mortensen, T. 2005. Comments. *Thinking with my Fingers*. torillsin.blogspot.com/2005/10/comments.html (Accessed 19 October, 2005).

Mortensen, T. and Walker, J. 2002. Blogging thoughts: Personal publication as online research tool. In A. Morrison (Ed.), *Researching ICTs in Context*. Oslo: Intermedia Report. 249–79.

My Vedana 2005. New Online. myvedana.blogspot.com/2005/10/new-online.html (Accessed 3 March, 2006).

Nixon, H. 2003. New research: Literacies for contemporary research into literacy and new media? *Reading Research Quarterly* 38(3): 407–13.

Nokia 2005. The Nokia 7710 VIP Blog. rodrigo.typepad.com/nokia7710 (Accessed 28 October, 2005).

On-the-run 2005. Barbie Pierced. Image on Flickr. flickr.com/photos/71313784@ N00/34530976 (Accessed 3 March, 2006).

Prensky, M. 2001. *Digital Game-Based Learning*. New York: McGraw-Hill.

Rheingold, H. 2003. *Smart Mobs: The Next Social Revolution*. Cambridge MA: Perseus Publishing.

Riverbend 2005. Baghdad Burning. riverbendblog.blogspot.com (Accessed 28 October, 2005).

Scheidt, L. 2006. Adolescent diary weblogs and the unseen audience. In D. Buckingham and R. Willett (Eds), *Digital Generations: Children, Young People and New Media*. Mahwah, NJ: Lawrence Erlbaum.

Scott 2005. This Teaching Life. thisteachinglife.blogspot.com (Accessed 28 October, 2005).

Shortis, T. 2001. *The Language of ICT*. London: Routledge.

SimplyClare 2005. Simply Clare. simplyclare.blogspot.com (Accessed 3 March, 2006).

Stern, S. 1999. Adolescent girls' expression on homepages: Spirited, somber and self conscious sites. *Convergence*, 5: 22–41.

Street, B. (Ed.) 1993. *Cross-Cultural Approaches to Literacy*. Cambridge: Cambridge University Press.

Street, B. 1997. The implications of the New Literacy Studies for education. *English in Education* 31(3): 45–59.

Sunden, J. 2002. *Material Virtualities: Approaching Online Textual Embodiment*. New York: Peter Lang.

Van House, N. 2004. Weblogs: Credibility and Collaboration in an Online World. Paper presented to the Computer Supported Cooperative Work Workshop, October, 2004. sims.berkeley.edu/~vanhouse/Van%20House%20trust%20workshop.pdf (Accessed 28 October, 2005).

Wellman, B. 2002. Little boxes, glocalization, and networked individualism. In M. Tanabe, P. Besselaar and T. Ishida (Eds), *Digital Cities II: Computational and Sociological Approaches*. Berlin: Springer. 10–25.

Werry, C. 1996. Linguistic and interactional features of Internet Relay Chat. In S. Herring (Ed.), *Computer Mediated Communication: Linguistic and Social Perspectives*. Amsterdam: Benjamins. 47–63.

Wolcott, H. F. 1994. *Transforming Qualitative Data: Description, Analysis and Interpretation*. London: Sage.

CHAPTER NINE

Online Memes, Affinities, and Cultural Production

MICHELE KNOBEL AND COLIN LANKSHEAR

Introduction

This chapter explores social practices of propagating online "memes" (pronounced "meems") as a dimension of cultural production and transmission. Memes are contagious patterns of "cultural information" that get passed from mind to mind and directly generate and shape the mindsets and significant forms of behavior and actions of a social group. Memes include such things as popular tunes, catchphrases, clothing fashions, architectural styles, ways of doing things, icons, jingles, and the like.

To introduce this discussion it is important to distinguish the level at which we will be talking about memes in this chapter from the way memes are talked about in the formal discourse of memetics. There are some broad surface similarities between theorized conceptions of memes within memetics and "popular" appropriations of "meme" as a word to describe particular "infectious" phenomena (and which tends to conflate the message/idea and the idea "carrier" or "vehicle" under the same term). These similarities, however, do not run very deep. It seems to us very unlikely that many, if any, so-called internet memes of the kinds we talk about in this chapter will have even remotely the kind of shelf life and cultural influence that serious memeticists assign to memes. By the same token, participants in popular practices of online "meming" would not typically be interested in buying into the deep issues that engage serious students and theorists of memes, such as whether or not memes are actually associated with physical neural manifestations in human brains, or have a kind of independent agency in terms of replication, etc. Nonetheless, there are some very interesting and worthwhile points to be discussed around online memes, and these points resonate structurally—even if on a rather superficial level—with "hard core" conceptions of memes. It is these points that are of interest to us here.

In this chapter we focus on online memes as a distinctively contemporary category of (popular conceptions of) memes. We identified a pool of successful online memes reported in mainstream media venues such as newspapers, television, online magazines and news-based forums over the 5-year period between 2001 and 2005. These online memes were examined using methods of discourse analysis (e.g., Fairclough 1992, Gee 1996, Kress 2003) and the concept of "affinity spaces" (Gee 2004) to address three purposes:

1. To identify and examine the qualities that seem to constitute each exemplar as a *successful* online meme. Working from this base, we aimed at considering the extent to which successful *online* memes reflect the same or additional defining characteristics to those listed as the definitive set identified by Richard Dawkins in 1976—that is, at a time prior to the emergence of online memes—as constitutive of successful memes.
2. To establish some key categories of successful online memes so as to better understand the online "memescape" in terms of purposes, uses and appeal.
3. To explore possible ways teachers might take up memes as a "new" literacy within school-based learning contexts.

Memes: The Concept

Occasional talk of "memes" as contagious or inheritable units of cultural information first appeared more than 80 years ago in biological studies of memory persistence in organisms (Semon 1924), and later within "diffusion of innovations" theory in the 1960s (cf. Rogers 1962). The current interest in memes and contemporary conceptual and theoretical development of the idea, however, dates back to ideas advanced by the geneticist Richard Dawkins in 1976. In his ground-breaking book, *The Selfish Gene*, Dawkins proposed a substantial evolutionary model of cultural development and change grounded in the replication of ideas, knowledge, and other cultural information through imitation and transfer. His definition of "memes" posited actual biological changes in brain neurons when minds became infected with memes. He also allotted agency to memes, too, and argued that memes have "some influence or power over their own probability of replication" (Dawkins 1999, xvi). Dawkins's position is controversial among those who formally theorize and study memes, and has triggered a range of "mutations" in the ways memes are conceptualized and formally studied. For example, biological conceptions of memes tend to focus on the effects memes have on behavior (Aunger 2002, Brodie 1996). Psychological and cognitive conceptions of memes tend to pay closer attention to decision-making processes *prior* to action (Aunger 2002, 37). Sociological and cultural definitions of memes of the kind informing the study discussed in this chapter downplay any suggestion that memes have physical neural presence. Rather, they emphasize the roles memes play within particular cultural spaces. (For more on different conceptions of "memes" see Knobel 2006.) This latter orientation informs the present study.

Memes as Objective and Distinct Social Phenomena

A cursory search of the internet is enough to show that "meme" is a popular term for describing "catchy" and widely propagated ideas or phenomena. Marketing strategies from the late nineteenth century can be described retrospectively in terms of selling memes to consumers. Today's advertisers use the term "viral marketing" to describe successful advertising campaigns. To reduce the study of memes to marketing strategies alone is, however, to miss the potential fruitfulness of this concept for understanding mindsets, new forms of power and social processes, new forms of social participation and activism, and new distributed networks of communication and relationship—among other social phenomena (cf. Blackmore 1999, Brodie 1996, Downes 1999).

The varying accounts of memes that can be found in the literature convey a sense of discreteness or boundedness attaching to memes. Memeticists use terms like "unit," "pattern," "idea," "structure," and "set" when describing memes. This suggests memes have "edges," even if these edges are blurry in practice. This accords with our approach in this chapter, which views memes as recognizable, bounded phenomena that have material effects in the world and that can be scrutinized. Dawkins's original examples of memes—tunes, good ideas, catch-phrases, clothes fashions, ways of making pots or building arches—still serve as useful guides for identifying and analyzing memes.

Characteristics of Memes

Dawkins (1976) identified three key characteristics of successful memes: fidelity, fecundity, and longevity. These remain the definitive set of characteristics and provide a useful starting point for studying online memes. Fidelity refers to qualities of the meme that enable it to be readily copied and passed from mind to mind relatively intact. Fidelity has very little to do with truth *per se*, and memes are often successful because they are *memorable*, rather than because they are important or useful (Blackmore 1999, 57). Ideas that make intuitive "sense" and are meaningful to individuals in ways that allow the ideas to be imitated or reproduced readily stand a much better chance of becoming memes than do ideas that are not easily copied or understood by a large numbers of people.

Fecundity refers to the rate at which an idea or pattern is copied and spread. The more quickly a meme spreads the more likely it is to capture robust and sustained attention and be replicated and distributed (Brodie 1996, 38). Susceptibility is an important dimension of meme fecundity as well, although Dawkins himself did not address it. Rather, susceptibility is indicated in the work of memeticists who build directly on his work and is now widely recognized as a factor in meme fecundity (cf. Brodie 1996, Vajik 1989). Susceptibility refers to the "timing" or "location" of a meme with respect to people's openness to the meme and their propensity to be infected by it. Susceptibility is enhanced by the meme's relevance to current events, its relation to extant successful memes, and the interests and values of the people using the spaces in which the meme is unleashed. Ideal conditions of susceptibility will let the "hooks" and "selection attractors" built consciously or unconsciously into the design and function of a meme take hold more easily and in ways that maximize the possibilities for the meme to "catch on" and be transmitted rapidly from person to person without being hindered or slowed by mental filters or other forms of cultural immunity (cf. Bennahum in Lankshear and Knobel 2003).

Longevity is the third key characteristic of a successful meme. The longer a meme survives the more it can be copied and passed on to fresh minds, thereby ensuring its ongoing transmission. Longevity assumes optimal conditions for a meme's replication and innovation.

Internet Memes

The concept of a "meme" itself has become something of a meme online. Among internet insiders, "meme" is a popular term for describing the rapid uptake and spread of a particular idea presented as a written text, image, language "move," or some other unit of cultural "stuff." This use of the term begs the question of longevity— since in terms of serious meme time the internet has not been around long enough for any kind of evolutionary longevity to have been established. Indeed, using "meme" to describe online phenomena of the kind discussed in this chapter can blur the distinction between a meme *per se* and a new vehicle for an old meme, as the Nigerian letter scam meme attests. The email versions of this letter vary in terms of contextual details, but the gist remains constant: a relative of, or an ex-government official associated with, a deposed dictator of an African country needs to launder an enormous amount of misappropriated funds through a mediating bank account and offers the reader a generous proportion of the total sum for providing a temporary holding account for the money. Victims provide bank account numbers and soon find their own accounts are emptied and the "relative" or "dignitary" is nowhere to be found (Glasner 2002, Wired 2002). The purpose of the Nigerian letter scam meme itself is as old as recorded time: to get rich quick. What is new is the vehicle; dressing the old meme up in contemporary garb which, in this case, ranges from using email to trading on money laundering as a high profile everyday focus.

Notwithstanding such slippages, which doubtless incline some serious students of memes to frown on populist appropriations of a concept that should be taken altogether more seriously, it is interesting and informative from the standpoint of literacy practices to consider some examples of relatively successful memes carried on the internet. Many of these memes have become internet lore, and even though all of them are relatively "new" in terms of longevity, all of them draw deeply on popular internet culture where, after all, 10 nanoseconds might be quite a long time, and 5 minutes—as the saying goes—can seem like more or less forever.

Memes as a New Literacy Practice

Memes have always been a part of human cultures; however, as discussed briefly above, it is only relatively recently that the concept has been developed and accepted as having descriptive and explanatory power with respect to cultural development. When we first identified memes as a "new" literacy (Lankshear and Knobel 2003), we sketched some possible significance memes might have for literacy educators with respect to enacting active/activist literacies (i.e., "If *we* don't like *their* contagious ideas, *we* need to produce some of our *own*," p. 37, original emphases). Subsequently (Knobel 2006, Knobel and Lankshear 2005, Lankshear and Knobel 2006a), we have begun exploring memes more closely with a view to better understanding them as cultural phenomena and as new literacy practices, and to more carefully consider what they might "mean" for literacy education. The study we report in this chapter is part of this ongoing work.

Methodology

The data set for this study comprises a "meme pool." To generate this we began by using different kinds of well-known online search engines. Our assumption was that successful online memes would have the kind of presence that registers with such search engines. The search engines used to generate this "meme pool" were selected on the ground that they would obtain maximum coverage of likely meme conduits (e.g., website archives, blogs, broadcast media sites). We mainly used Google.com, to search websites in general, and Technorati.com, to search weblogs in particular. These wide-ranging searches were supplemented by targeted searches. We trawled Wikipedia.org, a collaborative, open-access online encyclopedia that has excellent coverage of popular culture phenomena (Scholz 2004). We also searched through popular image and animation archives and forums like Somethingawful.com, Milkandcookies.org and Fark.org for mention of popular internet phenomena. Selection criteria for finalizing the data set began with Dawkins' characteristics of successful memes (fidelity, fecundity and susceptibility, and longevity). We also made selections on the basis of whether

- the meme was more or less wholly transmitted via electronic vehicles (e.g., email, websites, online discussion forums, chat spaces); and
- could be deemed "successful" in respect of being sufficiently strong and salient to capture online and offline broadcast media attention in the form of full-blown reports through to side-bar mentions in newspapers, television news reports or talk shows, widely read trade publications or general-audience magazines.

With respect to the latter criterion we employed three databases to verify broadcast media reports of memes generated by the first phase of searching the internet: Proquest (ABI/Inform), Lexis-Nexis, and WilsonWeb. All three survey broadcast media items, require paid subscription and, to this extent, are considered reliable indices to and archives of mainstream media reports and articles.

The initial data pool was bounded by a 5-year period (i.e., 2001–2005) to ensure a robust set of online memes that post-dated the widespread take-up of online internet practices by the general public (at least within developed countries), or the more widespread possibilities of access to the internet that can be dated from roughly 2000 onwards (cf. demographic reports published by Nielsen-Netratings.com). This meant, however, that certain popular but early online memes like the Dancing Baby (c. 1996) and Dancing Hamster (c. 1999) animations, along with Mahir Cagri's "I Kiss You" website (c. 1999), were excluded from the pool. These *types* of successful memes are, however, amply represented within the final pool. Hence, their exclusion does not compromise this study.

Data Set

General and focused searches identified a total of 19 instances or sets of instances that seemed to be regarded by the internet community as distinct and popular memes or contagious ideas that began much of their "life" online and which became well enough known to have been reported in broadcast media venues (see Table 9.1).

TABLE 9.1. The set of online memes identified for this study

Memes are ordered from least recent to most recent.

- Oolong the Rabbit (2001)
- Nike Sweatshop Shoes (2001)
- All Your Base Are Belong To Us (2001)
- Bert is Evil (2001)
- Tourist of Death (2001)
- Bonsai Kitten (2002)
- Ellen Feiss (2002)
- Star Wars Kid (2002)
- Black People Love Us (2002)
- "Every time you masturbate . . . God kills a kitten" (2002)
- "Girl A"/Nevada-tan (2003)
- Badger, Badger, Badger (2003)
- Read My Lips' "Bush-Blair Love Song" (2003)
- The Tron Guy (2003)
- Lost Frog/Hopkin Green Frog (2004)
- JibJab's "This Land is My Land" (2004)
- Numa Numa Dance (2004)
- Dog Poop Girl (2005)
- Flying Spaghetti Monster/Flying Spaghetti Monsterism (2005)

All 19 memes received mentions in regional and/or national newspapers and magazines. The Star Wars Kid was mentioned in *Time* and *Wired* magazines, BBC reports, Canada's *Globe and Mail* newspaper and the U.S.'s *New York Times* newspaper. The Numa Numa Dance video meme was the focus of several *New York Times* articles, was mentioned on CNN (a major U.S. news broadcast network) and also played on the *Today Show* and *Countdown* television shows in the U.S. Each meme in the final data pool has generated a range of homage or spoof websites or other artifacts (including themed merchandise).

While meeting our criteria for selecting online memes for this study, the final meme pool nonetheless remains selective and non-definitive. In several cases, establishing a date for a meme was difficult. Some memes lay dormant online for a period before becoming truly contagious. In other cases dates are disputed. We triangulated dates as best we could in these instances, or else appealed to Wikipedia as the source likely to have the most reliable information. For example, the "All Your Base Are Belong To Us" meme is difficult to pin down in terms of a "starting" date, but at the time of writing, Wikipedia identified it as an "internet phenomenon" beginning in 2001, although it may have been copied and uploaded to the internet before then.

Moreover, pinning down precise criteria for something counting as a meme is close to impossible, as witnessed in the long-running debates and lack of consensus in articles published in the *Journal of Memetics* (jom-emit.org/past.html). Indeed, much of the memetics literature has been dominated by arguments concerning what is and is not a meme. Criteria bickering seems to have been a dead end as a field of engagement within memetics, and has produced few empirical studies of actual memes (exceptions include: Butts and Hilgeman 2003, Chattoe 1998, Gatherer 2003). The present paper is not interested in contributing further to debates over what memes are and are not. As such, we did not develop a definitive set of criteria to use in judging what are memes and what are not memes. Rather, we are invested in identifying key characteristics of successful online memes—and which are often referred to explicitly by others as "memes"—and understanding these memes as new literacy practices. Focussing on what appear to be reasonably well-defined, widely dispersed, and wildly successful memes helps us to better understand how memes operate in everyday life. This position echoes that of Charles Simonyi, a key figure in software development and an early programmer with Microsoft. Simonyi chided Richard Brodie, now a well-known memeticist, for originally missing the point with respect to useful analyses of memes:

> "Come on!" exclaimed Charles. "You are asking the wrong question! Who cares if a yawn is a meme or not! The right question is, 'What are the interesting memes?'" (Brodie 1996, 25).

This sentiment drives the present study.

Data Analysis

Each meme was scrutinized using three general axes of analysis found in discourse studies: namely, the referential or ideational system, the contextual or interpersonal system, and the ideological or worldview system as represented by a given discursive move. This analysis was facilitated by prompt questions, summarized in Table 9.2 on page 207.

One of the risks associated with discourse analysis studies is that phenomena are often inadvertently reduced to static texts or that the analysis becomes too text-centric (cf., critiques in Knobel 1999). In order to address this potential issue, Gee's concept of "affinity spaces" (2004) was used to ensure that analysis also focused on the meme as part of larger sets of social interactions and ways of achieving things or of getting something done. Gee uses the concept of an "affinity space" to focus on learning, but our interest here is wider than learning *per se*. Nonetheless, some of the key features of affinity spaces that enable learning are the very stuff of how literacies—and new literacies especially—are constituted and experienced more generally by people engaging in them. Gee (2004, 9, 73) describes affinity

TABLE 9.2. Prompt questions for discursively analyzing online memes

Referential or ideational system	The focus is on the meaning of a meme:
	• What idea or information is being conveyed by this meme? How do we know?
	• How is this idea or information being conveyed?
	• What does this meme mean or signify (within this space, for certain people, at this particular point in time)? How do we know?
Contextual or interpersonal system	The focus is on social relations:
	• Where does this meme "stand" with respect to the relationship it implies or invokes between people readily infected by this meme? What tells us this?
	• What does this meme tell us about the kinds of contexts within which this meme proves to be contagious and replicable?
	• What does this meme seem to assume about knowledge and truth within this particular context?
Ideological or worldview system	The focus is on values, beliefs and worldviews:
	• What deeper or larger themes, ideas, positions are conveyed by this meme?
	• What do these themes, ideas and positions tell us about different social groups?
	• What do these memes tell us about the world, or a particular version of the world?

spaces as

> specially designed spaces (physical and virtual) constructed to resource people [who are] tied together . . . by a shared interest or endeavor . . . . [For example, the] many many websites and publications devoted to [the video game, *Rise of Nations*] create a social space in which people can, to any degree they wish, small or large, affiliate with others to share knowledge and gain knowledge that is distributed and dispersed across many different people, places, Internet sites and modalities (magazines, chat rooms, guides, recordings).

Among various other features concerning learning in particular, affinity spaces instantiate participation, collaboration, distribution and dispersion of expertise, and relatedness. Our focus on new literacies is interested in social practice as a whole, of which learning and sharing knowledge and expertise are a part. Our point is that the "logic" of new literacies embodies general features and qualities highlighted by Gee's account of "affinity spaces." These features and qualities emphasize the relational and social aspects of any literacy practice and draw attention to various social and resource configurations within which and through which people participate and learn. Prompt questions for analyzing affinity spaces—developed as part of this study—include:

- What is going on here and who is involved? How do we know?
- Who would recognize this meme as part of, a resource for/within, or relevant to a particular affinity space and what tells us this? Who would not recognize this meme and what might be some of the consequences of this?
- What kinds of affinity spaces might most readily embrace this meme, and what suggests this? What (shared) interests or endeavors might this meme resource? What do people "learn" as a result of engaging with this meme?
- What ways of doing, knowing and using resources (i.e., social practices) seem to be part and parcel of this meme?

Outcomes

As stated at the outset of this chapter, the purpose of this study was three-fold. First, the study aimed at examining successful online memes in order to see whether features in addition to those first outlined by Dawkins could be added to a substantive definition of this kind of meme. Second, the study aimed at developing a typology of memes in order to look for possible patterns of purpose, use and take-up within and across different affinity spaces. Third, the study aimed at exploring possible worthwhile uses teachers might make of memes as a new literacy within school contexts. The remainder of this chapter is given over to discussing each of these aims in turn.

(i) In Relation to the Characteristics of Successful Internet Memes

The analysis suggested no radically different characteristics pertaining to online memes that set them apart from other kinds of memes. What the analysis did arrive at, however, was a number of broad features that contribute additional insights into the "make-up" of online memes as a distinct category of meme practice.

What was apparent after studying these memes was that Dawkins's "fidelity" feature of memes is perhaps better understood in terms of "replicability" where online memes are concerned. Many of the online memes in this study were not passed on entirely "intact" in that the meme "vehicle" was changed, modified, mixed with other referential and expressive resources, and regularly given idiosyncratic spins by participants (e.g., All Your Base, Lost Frog, Star Wars Kid). While the meme or contagious idea itself remained relatively intact, the "look" of the meme wasn't always held constant. In many ways, these "mutations" often seemed to help the meme's fecundity in terms of hooking people into contributing their own version of the meme. A concept like "replicability" therefore needs to include remixing as an important practice associated with a many successful online memes, where remixing includes modifying, bricolaging, splicing, reordering, superimposing, etc., original and other images, sounds, films, music, talk, and so on (see Lankshear and Knobel 2006a).

With respect to the life of these online memes, as distinct from longevity in a strict sense, the search and selection process that generated the final data set showed how easy it was to find ample online archives of original texts, images, and video clips and other footage, as well as detailed accounts of the origins and spread of many of these memes and their various permutations. It certainly seems that the internet itself greatly facilitates meme longevity (not to mention meme distribution, as well). The blogosphere, in particular, appears to be an ideal vehicle for transmitting memes, with weblogs now replacing email and discussion forums—which were dominant meme conduits in the late 1990s and early 2000s—as a primary way of spreading memes (see especially memes emerging in 2002 and after). This resonates with the ongoing work of Eytan Adar and his colleagues at the Hewlett Packard Dynamics Lab which focuses on tracing what they call "information epidemics" spread via weblogs, which they see as potent fields for spreading contagious ideas (Adar et al. 2004, 1).

Analysis of the contextual or social "systems" of the memes in this study also suggested three distinct patterns of characteristics that, we argue, are likely to contribute directly to each meme's fecundity. These characteristics include:

- Some element of humor, ranging from the quirky and offbeat, to potty humor, to the bizarrely funny, to parodies, through to the acerbically ironic, and/or
- A rich kind of intertextuality, such as wry cross-references to different everyday and popular culture events, icons or phenomena, and/or
- Anomalous juxtapositions, usually of images.

Space precludes a close examination of each meme in the pool with respect to all three of these characteristics, so indicative examples will be used instead to illustrate each.

(a) Humor

Humor is a key component in at least 17 of the 19 memes in this study (acknowledging that humor is always open to interpretation on a reader's or viewer's part). Perhaps the most famous and enduring meme within this study's data set is the All Your Base Are Belong To Us meme. The meme began with someone uploading to the internet a video clip of the opening sequence of the Japanese video game, *Zero*

```
In A.D. 2101

War was beginning.

Captain: What happen?

Mechanic: Somebody set up us the bomb.

Operator: We get signal.

Captain: What !

Operator: Main screen turn on.

Captain: It's You !!

Cats: How are you gentlemen !!

Cats: All your base are belong to us.

Cats: You are on the way to destruction.

Captain: What you say !!

Cats: You have no chance to survive make your time.

Cats: HA HA HA HA ....

Captain: Take off every 'zig' !!

Captain: You know what you doing.

Captain: Move 'zig'.

Captain: For great justice.
```

Figure 9.1. English version of the opening sequence of *Zero Wing*
(Source: planettribes.com/allyourbase/story.shtml)

Wing. The syntactic and semantic hiccups within the English subtitles of this sequence seemed to tap directly and immediately into what a *Time* magazine article about this meme identified as "geek kitsch" humor (Taylor 2001; see Figure 9.1). In short, this sequence aims at establishing the context for the game, which is set in some future time beset by warring factions. It involves the sudden appearance of Cats, an evil-doer, on a monitor screen inside a military space craft. Cats announces that he is the victor in this war, but the Captain of the space craft responds valiantly by calling for the ZIG fighters to be launched. The Captain explains to these ZIG fighters that all of earth's fate is in their hands, and then the game begins, with the game player working to help the Captain defeat Cats and his fighters.

The seriousness of the dialogue about a threatened global takeover coupled with language translation glitches struck a chord online. The clip quickly caught on among video game players and software programmers first, and later within wider audiences (especially when a voice track and sound effects were added to the clip). The original clip itself then sparked a remixing epidemic, with active meme participants generating a range of new, very funny, photoshopped takes on the "All Your Base" catchphrase. This included a reworking of the iconic Hollywood sign, road signs, high-profile advertisements, official documents, food products and toys, and so on to announce to everyone that, "All Your Base Are Belong To Us" (see planettribes.com/allyourbase/index.shtml). These remixes are in many ways funnier than the original clip due to the creative uses of key phrases and the celebration of quirkiness that they embody. The catchphrase, "All your base are belong to us," now regularly appears in news or political reports in the broadcast media or the blogosphere, and is used to describe clumsy, heavy-handed take-over bids for positions of power and the like. The longevity of this meme seems assured, and recent remixes of this meme include the Danish production: "All Your Iraq Are Belong To Us" (mb3.dk/ayiabtu).

As another example, the Ellen Feiss meme began as a television advertisement by Apple for its campaign to entice PC users to "switch" to Apple. When the advertisement aired on television, 14 year-old Feiss appeared to be quite "out of it" (she later claimed filming had occurred close to midnight when she was very tired and that she had taken a strong dose of anti-allergy medication for her hayfever just before filming began). Her awkward eyebrow lift, uncoordinated hand movements, and her use of sound effects to describe her computer crashing, coupled with lengthy pauses in her monologue, caused riotous laughter around the world. Apple cancelled the advertisement as soon as it was realized why the ad had become so popular, but not before the ad had been digitized and archived on multiple websites. Ellen quickly reached iconic status among young, male programmers, Apple Mac users, and college students (see: ellenfeiss.net) and her story was reported in at least one book and a range of newspapers. In response, Ellen worked at keeping a low profile and turned down numerous invitations to appear on major talkshows within the U.S. Nevertheless, three years after the meme began, a number of t-shirts celebrating Ellen Feiss are still available for purchase online and numerous tribute and remix sites remain active (see, for example, ellenfeiss.gloriousnoise.com; jeffwilhem.com/files/ellen1.mov). In 2006, Ellen appeared in a French short film, *Bed and Breakfast* (listen: theflux.tv/files/podcasts/fluxradio27.mp3). She was invited to play the lead female despite having no previous film acting experience. It seems the director had seen her Apple Switch television advertisement and felt she was perfect for the role.

In addition to quirky and situational kinds of humor, five of the memes examined in this study put humor to use in generating biting social commentary memes. The Nike Sweat Shop Shoes meme is a good example of this. In January 2001, Jonah Peretti forwarded to friends a series of email exchanges he had had with the Nike company concerning Nike's iD campaign that allows customers to customize their shoes (Peretti 2001). Peretti's request to have "sweatshop" embroidered on his new shoes had been denied and came at a time when Nike was under fire for exploiting workers in under-developed countries. Despite persistent questions on Peretti's

```
From: "Personalize, NIKE iD"
To: "'Jonah H. Peretti'"
Subject: RE: Your NIKE iD order o16468000

Your NIKE iD order was cancelled for one or more of the following reasons.
1) Your Personal iD contains another party's trademark or other intellectual property.
2) Your Personal iD contains the name of an athlete or team we do not have the legal right to
use.
3) Your Personal iD was left blank. Did you not want any personalization?
4) Your Personal iD contains profanity or inappropriate slang, and besides, your mother would
slap us.

If you wish to reorder your NIKE iD product with a new personalization please visit us again at
www.nike.com

Thank you,
NIKE iD


From: "Jonah H. Peretti"
To: "Personalize, NIKE iD"
Subject: RE: Your NIKE iD order o16468000

Greetings,
My order was canceled but my personal NIKE iD does not violate any of the criteria outlined in
your message. The Personal iD on my custom ZOOM XC USA running shoes was the word "sweatshop."
Sweatshop is not: 1) another's party's trademark, 2) the name of an athlete, 3) blank, or 4)
profanity. I choose the iD because I wanted to remember the toil and labor of the children that
made my shoes. Could you please ship them to me immediately.

Thanks and Happy New Year,
Jonah Peretti


From: "Personalize, NIKE iD"
To: "'Jonah H. Peretti'"
Subject: RE: Your NIKE iD order o16468000

Dear NIKE iD Customer,

Your NIKE iD order was cancelled because the iD you have chosen contains, as stated in the
previous e-mail correspondence, "inappropriate slang". If you wish to reorder your NIKE iD
product with a new personalization please visit us again at www.nike.com

Thank you,
NIKE iD
```

Figure 9.2. An excerpt from the "Nike Sweatshop Shoe" meme
(Source: snopes.com/business/consumer/nike.asp; accessed 7 March, 2005).

part, the company hid behind company policy statements and did not provide a logical rationale for the cancelled order. Peretti gathered these exchanges together in a single email and sent it off to a few friends (see an excerpt from the exchange in Figure 9.2).

The satiric humor and social commentary contained in this set of email correspondence caught popular attention and soon reached thousands of people via email networks. This in turn sparked mainstream broadcast attention, and Peretti's meme was the subject of a range of news and magazine reports, including *Time* magazine, and Peretti himself was interviewed on the *Today Show*, a popular news events talk show in the U.S.

Other examples of humor in the meme pool include the oft-linked-to website known as Black People Love Us! (blackpeopleloveus.com), which is a wry, if not scathing, commentary on white American liberal paternalism towards black Americans (as a side note, this meme was also created by Jonah Peretti, in collaboration with his sister). This faux "personal" website comprises a series of "testimonials" from a middle-class white couple's black friends that emphasize much of the condescension that can occur in naïve liberal positions on social and cultural difference (e.g., references to "being articulate," white people demonstrating "solidarity" by speaking Black English and claiming a preference for rap music). Another well-known social commentary meme that makes effective use of sardonic humor is the Bush-Blair Love Song meme created by the Swedish group, Read My Lips (atmo.se/zino.aspx?articleID=399). Read My Lips spliced together dozens, if not hundreds, of fragments of news videos of George Bush and Tony Blair, and synched their lip movements and onscreen actions with the love song, "Your Eyes," to produce a text suggesting an intimate romance between the two. The resulting video stands as a clear indictment of the Bush-Blair alliance in the invasion of Iraq and is a popular clip within affinity spaces shaped by people critical of the invasion of Iraq and/or critical of the militarist alliance between Bush and Blair.

(b) Rich intertextuality

Cross-references to a host of popular culture events, artifacts and practices also characterize many of the successful memes in this study. Perhaps the most widely known intertextual meme is the Star Wars Kid. This meme began when schoolmates of a 15-year-old, heavily-built Canadian schoolboy, Ghyslain Raza, found a video recording he had made of himself. The tape showed him inspired by *Star Wars* movies to somewhat awkwardly mime a lightsabre fight using a broomstick-like golf ball retriever. His friends uploaded the footage to Kazaa—a now-defunct person-to-person file sharing service—where it was found by millions of viewers, many of whom added music, special effects and highly recognizable *Star Wars* sounds (e.g., the light sabre "swoosh-hum") to create the now-famous Star Wars Kid meme (e.g., screamingpickle.com/humor/legends/StarWarsKid/). Subsequent remixes of this video clip include Ghyslain cast as Gandalf in *Lord of the Rings*, as William Wallace in the movie *Braveheart*, and as Neo from the *Matrix* movies, among others. One version mixes the Dancing Baby meme and Ghyslain in a faux trailer for a Hollywood buddy movie, while another mixes the clip with Tetris, an enormously popular, early video game. These cross-references to popular movies, movie genres, and games clearly tap into an affinity space that recognizes and appreciates this intertextuality, while at the same time they serve to blur the line between an ordinary life and the extraordinary lives of characters in movie and game universes. The popularity of the Star Wars Kid remixes even produced an online petition to Lucasfilm to include Ghyslain himself as a character in *Episode III* of the *Star Wars* prequel series (petitiononline.com/Ghyslain/petition.html). The Star Wars Kid meme has in turn become a popular culture touchstone and regularly appears as a reference in animated cartoon series and video games.

Figure 9.3. The original Hopkin Green Frog flier (Source: lostfrog.org)

The Lost Frog meme also alludes to a range of popular culture phenomena as it remixes and mutates the text of a lost pet announcement. The lost pet flier (see Figure 9.3) was found posted in Seattle streets.

A member of a popular image sharing forum scanned the found text and uploaded it to the forum archive, where members of this group quickly picked up on the pathos and determination in the child's language and hand-drawn images and used image editing software to manipulate or "photoshop" the original image. The remixed images produced by this group, and later, by others around the world, are always humorous, yet often touching. Collectively they narrate massive, albeit fictional, citizen mobilization in the ongoing search for Hopkin Green Frog. The remixed images include typical "missing persons" announcement vehicles (e.g., broadcast media news reports, milk cartons, road signs), crowd scenes seemingly devoted to spreading the news about the lost frog (e.g., "lost frog" banners at a street march and at a crowded soccer match), and a host of other "remember Hopkin" scenarios (e.g., lost frog scratch-it lottery tickets, Hopkin's ID on someone's instant message buddy list, Hopkin as a "not found" internet file image). As with the Star Wars Kid meme, references to popular culture artifacts and practices abound, and include reworked book covers, music album covers, video games, eBay auctions, and so on. Other images spoof advertising campaigns (e.g., an Absolut Vodka spread becomes "Absolut Hopkin"; a Got Milk? advertisement becomes "Got Frog?"). Many of the lost frog images refer to other memes as well. For example, an aeroplane pulling a lost frog announcement banner also appeared earlier in an All Your

Base Are Belong To Us remixed image, as did photoshopped highway signs. This rich layering of cross-references appears to help the fecundity of a meme by encouraging subsequent photoshoppers to make their own engaging cross-cultural references that add layers of meaning for "those in the know" to an already humorous contribution.

(c) Anomalous juxtaposition

In addition to humor and intertextual references, over half of the memes in the data set for this study included what could be called anomalous juxtaposition as part of their "hooks" for maximizing the susceptibility of the idea being passed from mind to mind (i.e., Oolong the Pancake Bunny, Bert Is Evil, Bonsai Kitten, Tourist of Death, Nevada-tan, Numa Numa Dance, God Kills a Kitten, All Your Base, Lost Frog, and Star Wars Kid). The kind of juxtaposition found in these memes includes incongruous couplings of images (e.g., the Tourist of Death figure originally set against a backdrop of a wide range of tragic events, beginning with New York City's Twin Towers attacks, and including the Titanic, a number of hurricanes, and ferry accidents), deliberately provocative (e.g., the faux Bonsai Kitten website that presents "illustrated"—i.e., photoshopped and very fake—step-by-step instructions for altering the shape of pet cats), and the simply quirky (e.g., Oolong the Rabbit who was taught to balance on its head objects like film canisters and different food items by Japanese photographer, Hironori Akutagawa. Akutagawa documented these "head performances"—as he called them—in photographs posted to the internet; or the Numa Numa Dance clip of a North American male lipsynching and dancing to a Romanian pop song while remaining seated in his chair throughout).

The Bert Is Evil meme is a good example of this kind of anomalous juxtaposition. This meme was spawned by an actual event. It began with a photograph of the muppet, Bert, a character from the popular and long-running children's television show, *Sesame Street*, being photoshopped into a picture of Osama bin Laden and uploaded as a joke to an online photoshopper forum. The image was subsequently downloaded and used in Bangladesh on street march banners by supporters of Osama bin Laden. The creators of the banners either did not notice Bert in the picture they downloaded or did not know who Bert was. The banner image caught wide broadcast media attention and rapidly prompted different people to create remixed images that added evidence to the claim that Bert was indeed evil, rather than a harmless children's television character (see: bertisevil.tv). These photoshopped and animated images show the muppet involved with the Ku Klux Klan, as part of President Kennedy's assassination, as connected with the Charles Manson murders, and the like. The overall tenor of these remixed images tends to be one of "moral bankruptcy," with an almost paparazzi feel to most of the images in that many are staged to look as though they were taken by hidden cameras or in off-guard moments. The juxtaposition of horrible, tragic or seedy scenarios with an innocuous puppet from a children's television show generates a kind of gallows humor by presenting documentary evidence that clearly cannot be true. The fecundity of this meme may also be due in part to real-life stories concerning the public airing of hidden seedy or immoral lives of some movie and television stars, and, particularly, stars of children's television.

A non-humorous example of anomalous juxaposition concerns the Nevada-tan meme. This meme was also sparked by a real-life event. In 2003, an 11-year-old Japanese school girl murdered a classmate by slashing her throat with a box cutter before returning to class, covered in her classmate's blood. The murderer subsequently became known as "Nevada-tan" due to images of her wearing a hooded sweatshirt emblazoned with the word "Nevada" released by broadcast media. Nevada-tan's age and her website full of shock animations (e.g., The Red Room) and other gruesome internet culture references and artifacts sparked national debates in Japan concerning the age limit for criminal culpability and the social effects of internet use. Nevada-tan, however, has become something of a popular culture icon among some groups and is depicted as a manga or anime character in fan fiction texts, has generated homage websites, appears as a character in cosplay (i.e., in-person character role plays often built around anime storylines), and is mentioned in a number of Japanese pop songs. It can be argued that the juxtaposition of a young, ordinary-looking girl with a gruesome murder she did not even try to hide created attention hooks that helped turn Nevada-tan's case and persona into a meme within certain affinity spaces shaped by people interested in, say, "shock humor" takes on the macrabre and/or on chilling news events.

(d) An outlier

These three characteristics of fecund online memes—humor, intertextuality, and anomalous juxtaposition—are not cut and dried, however. One meme in the set does not display any of these features. The Dog Poop Girl meme stands as an outlier and has much to say about the social power of online memes. In brief, this meme initially comprised a photograph of a young woman and her dog on a train in South Korea. The dog had fouled the train carriage and its owner refused to clean up the mess, even after being asked a number of times to do so. A disgruntled fellow passenger took a phonecam image of the offender and her dog and posted it to a popular website. It was quickly picked up by the internet community and widely circulated online, both in its original form, and in slightly remixed poster versions. It took only a few days for the woman to be identified from this photo and her personal information was published online as a way of punishing her for her failure to be a responsible citizen. The meme in effect became something of a witch hunt, and saw the woman hounded online and offline until she posted a very contrite apology for her actions to an internet forum.

This meme attracted broadcast media attention around the world due mostly to its vigilante nature and the breaching of the woman's right to personal privacy.

(ii) A Typology of Successful Internet Memes

Discursive analysis shows that the memes selected for this study can be organized into different categories of *kinds* of memes. These can be considered in terms of the principal purpose each is organized around, and in terms of type. Producing a typology of the memes in this study helps to map interesting patterns that offer additional insights into the online memescape. These patterns are summarized on page 218 in Figure 9.4.

Most of the memes in our pool seem to appeal to and draw on the creative energies of people who enjoy playful, absurdist ideas carrying little "serious" content and/or who enjoy humorous ideas carrying serious content which may be considered to be social critique and commentary (with the Dog Poop Girl and Nevada-tan memes remaining the outliers here).

Playful and absurdist ideas include dignifying the everyday or banal with epically-scaled imagined responses to some real or fantastical event, or with casting a minor event or ordinary person as having global import, as is the case with the Lost Frog and the Star Wars Kid memes. Equally, a penchant for the absurd underscores the popularity of quirky and anomalous images or video sequences, as is the case with Oolong the Pancake Bunny or Gary Brolsma's Numa Numa Dance.

Wry and satiric humor is used to good effect in the memes that serve social critique, criticism or commentary purposes within this data pool. The depiction of a coy but intimate relationship between Bush and Blair, for example, satirizes the political and military alliances between the two countries as ultimately self-serving. All the social critique memes in this study have playfully serious qualities, which may further serve to enhance their contagiousness and fecundity.

Overall, the playfulness seen in most of these online memes—whether absurdist or aimed at social commentary—taps into shared popular culture experiences and practices. This in turn helps to define certain affinity spaces (e.g., gamer spaces, photoshopper spaces, manga/anime spaces, left-leaning political spaces, "good" community member spaces, spaces created by fans of Asian popular cultures, blogger spaces) by semiotic nods and winks to those "in the know" as it were. "Outsiders" to these spaces will often have difficulty seeing the humor in or point to many of these memes. Susan Blackmore, a prominent memeticist, is right when she argues that the "effective transmission of memes depends critically on human preferences, attention, emotions and desire" (Blackmore 1999, 58). Affinity spaces clearly play an important role in the fecundity of a successful meme, especially when the meme is distributed online.

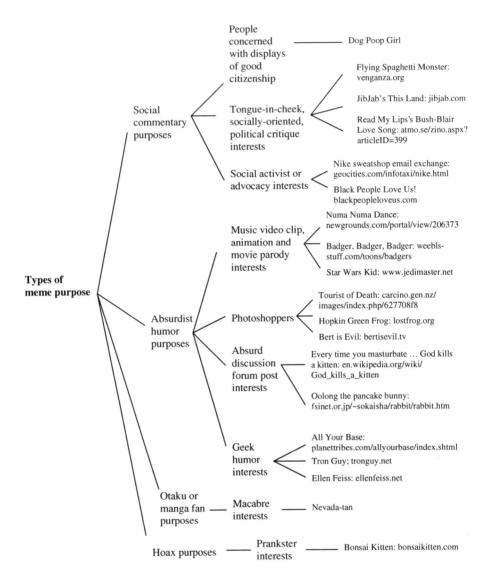

Figure 9.4. A provisional meme typology

Social commentary memes also underscore the importance of timeliness in terms of maximizing people's susceptibility to "catching" and passing on a meme. The successfulness of the five memes in the data whose purpose is to comment on or critique some aspect of society seems attributable in a significant way to the match between the meme and recognizable events or issues in the larger world (and confirmed by analysis of the contextual system invoked by or embodied in the meme). The Nike Sweatshop Shoe meme was launched into a context of existing critiques of corporate manufacturing practices that made it ripe for contagiousness. The Bush-Blair Love Song was launched during a time of growing civil disquiet over the U.S. and British military coalition in the invasion of Iraq. Anti-war protestors, in particular, were willing carriers of this meme. It may well be that participating as a carrier in passing these kinds of memes on to others marks somebody as being a person of a particular kind who has particular *desirable* characteristics and worldviews within groups or social spaces committed to critiques of power and inequity.

(iii) Memes and Literacy Education

Memes are thoroughly social in that they require networked human "hosts" in order to survive. The discursive study of online memes as a new literacy therefore needs to attend carefully to this social-ness and avoid reducing meme research to an examination of reading and production processes at the level of static, fixed-in time texts. With respect to literacy education in schools, the social dimension of meming translates into focussing on practices that are larger than reading and writing, and which can be captured by means of distinguishing between "big L" Literacies and "little l" literacies. This is, of course, a shameless remix of James Paul Gee's work which draws a distinction between D/discourse and R/reading (cf. Gee 1996, 2004), but it is nonetheless a useful way of thinking about literacies in general and new literacies in particular. For us, Literacy, with a "big L" refers to making meaning in ways that are tied directly to life and to *being* in the world (cf. Freire 1972, Street 1984). That is, whenever we use language we are making some sort of significant or socially recognizable "move" that is inextricably tied to someone bringing into being or realizing some element or aspect of their world. This means that literacy, with a "small l," describes the actual processes of reading, writing, viewing, listening, manipulating images and sound, etc., making connections between different ideas, and using words and symbols that are part of these larger, more embodied Literacy practices. In short, this distinction explicitly recognizes that L/literacy is always about reading and writing *something*, and that this something is always part of a larger pattern of being in the world (Gee, Hull and Lankshear 1996). And, because there are multiple ways of being in the world, then we can say that there are multiple L/literacies.

Using this distinction to think about *new* literacies enables us to see how producing a photoshopped image for the Bert Is Evil or the All Your Base memes is an example of literacy that involves, among other things, generating a text comprising a carefully designed montage of photographic and hand-drawn images along with written words or embedded sound effects. The multimedia dimensions of this text production are to some extent recognizably and interestingly "new"; understanding which software application to use to cut and crop and blend disparate images into a new "whole," knowing which image manipulation tools to use and for what effects (e.g., using the "blur" tool to soften the edges of imported or cut-and-pasted images so that they look more "naturally" a part of the overall scene); how to generate and fix in place layers of images; how to add a sound track or printed stretches of text; how to save the resulting file in an internet-friendly format and how to upload the file to an archive or forum, and so on. In short, contributing a multimodal "meme text" that has the maximum appearance of veracity, regardless of the actual absurdity of the content for this contribution, requires a range of finely-honed technical skills and competencies.

More important, however, are the "big L" Literacy practices associated with meming that are invested in meaning making, social significance-making, and identity-making in one's life worlds. The texts and montages produced and read as part of being infected with and propagating a meme online are never free standing. Rather, they are implicated in and generated out of networks of shared interests, experiences, habits, worldviews and the like that pick up on or use texts, events, phenomena, icons, cultural artifacts, etc., in particular if not socially idiosyncratic ways. For example, posting a picture of a rabbit with food on its head only makes sense in an online forum that celebrates quirky conversation responses. This pancake bunny meme began when an image of a rabbit balancing what was referred to as a "pancake" on its head, along with the caption, "I have no idea what you're talking about . . . so here's a bunny with a pancake on its head," was posted to a discussion forum (see kimsal.com/rabbit_pancake.jpg). Hence, analyzing the "ideational system" of a given meme needs to be carefully nuanced in order to fully appreciate that successful online memes are often heavily ironic and tongue-in-cheek, and reference multiple texts, events, cultural practices and values, so on. Looking for the meme to make "sense" in its own right would be to overlook much that is important, especially with respect to absurdist memes. Similarly, analyzing the contextual system of successful online memes also needs to be nuanced and pay close attention to the often collaborative, cumulative and distributed nature of these memes.

A "big L" conception of new Literacies recognizes that everyday life is often amplified through the participation of and interaction with people one may never meet and, moreover, that in online spaces this interaction and participation may occur in ways never before possible. The Lost Frog meme isn't simply about generating humorous images concerning the search for or the whereabouts of a child's lost frog. It plays out as a distributed collaboration that crosses national borders and languages (e.g., not all the lost frog images make use of English) and brings together people who may not know each other, but who value each other's contribution nonetheless. The "big L" dimensions of the Lost Frog meme include recognizing how amateurish or clumsy photoshopping will not prove to be as memorable or as contagious as something slick and well-crafted both in terms of design and technical proficiency. At the same time, however, it also encompasses knowing that a particularly humorous or conceptually clever version of the meme will win out over the quality of technical execution any day. It also includes recognizing clever intertextuality in the form of cross-references to other memes or cultural practices, beliefs and phenomena (e.g., conspiracy theories, alien abduction theories, the significance of computer or web browser error messages, the social role of remembrance ribbons, "missing persons" announcement vehicles, etc.).

The L̲iteracy practices of meming also involve people deciding how they will choose to read or interpret a meme and the "spin" they will give it as they pass it along to others. In the case of the Lost Frog meme, this could mean that one sees the archive of lost frog images as poking cruel fun at the 16-year-old autistic young man who was found to have posted the original flier (see Whybark 2004), or as evidence that ordinary events, such as losing a pet or toy, can take on epic proportions within a person's life and that this quality is aptly represented and dignified in the Lost Frog image archive.

Some of the other "Big L" Literacy practices discernible in the meme pool used in this study include the practices of video game playing, celebrating Japanese popular culture, being a fan (which can include writing fan fiction, setting up homage websites, linking to a meme archive via one's weblog, etc.), being privy to a plethora of online—and offline—affinity space "insider jokes," being familiar and up-to-date with Hollywood movies and with fan practices such as lipsynching to pop songs or cosplay, and so on. Ursula Franklin, writing well over a decade ago during the early years of the internet, warned against taking an "artifactual approach" to examining new technologies, and argued for focusing instead on technology use as part of a "system of social practice" (Franklin 1990). Franklin's advice applies to studying new L/literacies, as well. When we examine memes as L̲iteracy practices it is possible to see that they involve much more than simply passing on and/or adding to written or visual texts or information *per se* (i.e., l̲iteracy). Rather, they are tied directly to ways of interacting with others, to meaning making, and to ways of being, knowing, learning and doing.

The importance of teachers having a "big L" Literacy mindset on memes cannot be over-emphasized. Understanding successful online memes can contribute much to identifying the limitations of narrow conceptions of literacy and new technologies in classrooms. It can also help with understanding new forms of social participation and influence in everyday life. For example, the phenomenon of online memes challenges the growing dominance of "digital literacy" conceptions of what it means to be a competent user of new technologies and networks. Increasingly, digital literacy is being defined by policy groups and others as technical or operational competence with computers and the internet (cf., accounts in Lankshear and Knobel 2006b). The term "digital literacy" is also used by some to describe the ability to evaluate information by examining sources, weighing up author credibility, assaying the quality of writing and argument building in an online text, judging the "truth value" of a text found online, and so on (e.g., Gilster 1997). Many of the successful memes included in this study would be discounted or ignored by digital literacy advocates because they do not carry "useful" information. Digital literacy mindsets, however, do not pay adequate attention to the importance of social relations in developing, refining, remixing and sharing ideas in fecund and replicable ways, or to the important role memes themselves play in developing culture and creativity (cf., Lessig 2004).

Applying conventional information evaluation criteria and digital literacy competency checklists (see, for example, certiport.com) to website-based memes like Black People Love Us! (blackpeopleloveus.com) will make little sense because the website itself is a deliberate parody of personal web pages and is not intended to be "true" in any conventional way. The "testimonials" made by Black people about the White couple who "created" this page (and in reality, who are not a couple at all) may or may not be "true" or "authentic," but this doesn't actually matter because Peretti and his sister nonetheless use this website to convey a significant message. From a technical standpoint, the website is painfully cheesy in its design, and no doubt deliberately so. What matters most about this meme is the challenge it poses to liberal attitudes that are patronizing and that reduce historical and social inequities to superficial differences concerning, for example, skin colour, music preferences and language use.

Meming is also a fruitful practice for educators to focus on when thinking about new forms of social participation and civic action in the wake of widespread access to the internet and involvement in increasingly dispersed social networks. Brodie (1996) has argued for more attention to be paid to the memes with which we are infected, and with which we infect others, as well as to the material effects of these infections. Not all of the memes gathered for this study are benign or contribute positively to rich and productive ways of being in the world. The Dog Poop Girl meme, for example, rightly roused criticisms of the vigilante way in which the woman was identified and then publicly hounded until she apologized. The power of this meme to mobilize public censure of this woman was clearly significant in its reach and has opened a Pandora's box of issues concerning to what extent memes should be used to right relatively minor social wrongs and by what authority. In South Korea, academics and journalists alike have been openly discussing the importance of understanding the dangers of witch-hunt types of approaches to public castigation of a person. Indeed, participating in this meme by passing the woman's picture and personal details along to others is not an innocent, playful or morally clear-cut act, and provides teachers with a controversial event that promotes important discussions about the moral and civic dimensions of participating in certain memes.

The Star Wars Kid meme also provides fruitful ground for teachers and students to examine what happens when a very reluctant meme star is adopted by members of a wide-ranging cybercommunity who spend enormous amounts of energy identifying who he is in meatspace and where he lives, and who then broadcast his full name across the internet, focusing widespread media attention on the reluctant star. It turns out that Ghyslain himself did not find anything funny about the Star Wars Kid meme, and he and his parents regarded it as cruel and invasive. Ironically, a group of cybercitizens who banded together and raised money to buy him an iPod were offended when he not only refused to have anything to do with them and their iPod, but brought charges against certain meme participants on invasion of privacy and related counts. Although well intentioned in all cases of this kind, the material effects of memes are not always beneficial to meme "stars" and neither do all of these "stars" welcome the attention directed at them (cf. Ellen Feiss and her television advertisement for Apple; the father of Terry, who lost his frog; and, intially, Gary Brolsma of Numa Numa Dance fame). Examining memes like this can add new meaning to participating in memes that includes an ability to weigh up how far one's participation will reach.

Analyzing meme processes and effects as new forms of social influence can become an important part of revising critical literacy practices in classrooms to better take account of new literacy practices and new ways of transmitting both healthy and toxic ideas rapidly and extensively. Engaging in the serious study of memes can help educators to equip students with important strategies for identifying the memes that infect their minds, and for evaluating the effects these memes have on their (ethical) decision-making, actions and relations with others. *Counter-meming*, for example, is a well-established practice online, and refers to the deliberate generation of a meme that aims at neutralizing or eradicating potentially harmful ideas (see, for example, the work of Adbusters.com and strategies outlined at memecentral.com/antidote.htm and dkosopedia.com/index.php/Meme). Mike Godwin (1994), for example, documents how he deliberately began a meme to counter what he called the "Nazi-meme" that he saw operating in different online discussion boards to which he belonged. Godwin describes this Nazi-meme as the then widespread practice of discussants drawing direct analogies between what another person had written and posted to the board and Nazism, and he felt compelled to counteract this often glib and offensive analogy. So he developed "Godwin's Law of Nazi Analogies" and released this meme into discussion groups wherever he saw a gratuitous Nazi reference. His original "law" stated that: "As an online discussion grows longer, the probability of a comparison involving Nazis or Hitler approaches one" (Godwin 1994, 1). Godwin found that his meme quickly caught on and became a kind of "marker" for judging the worth of a discussion thread. The original statement of Godwin's

Law underwent a number of mutations at the word level, but the idea itself remained intact. Godwin himself recounts,

> As *Cuckoo's Egg* author Cliff Stoll once said to me: "Godwin's Law? Isn't that the law that states that once a discussion reaches a comparison to Nazis or Hitler, its usefulness is over?" By my (admittedly low) standards, the [counter-meme] experiment was a success. (1994, 1).

Godwin proposes that this kind of "memetic engineering" is an important component in contributing to the health of people's social and mental lives. He argues that once a harmful meme has been identified we may well have a social and moral responsibility to chase it down by releasing a positive counter-meme into the idea stream. Studying memetic engineering may well prove to be an important component of classroom critical literacy approaches to understanding social power and influence. At least 4 of the 19 memes collected for this study can be categorized as successful and deliberate counter-memes (i.e., the Black People Love Us! meme, The Flying Spaghetti Monster meme, the This Land Is My Land meme, and the Bush-Blair Love Song meme). These memes are generative resources that can be used in classrooms to promote discussions about each meme's contagious qualities, the ideas they convey and why, who created each meme and how it has been dispersed (e.g., via which affinity spaces). These memes can be dynamic resources for developing informed points of view on a range of social issues. It is also worth bearing in mind that researchers like Adar and colleagues are arguing that the most socially powerful or *influential* people online are not necessarily high profile persons and groups, but rather, are those people who *cause* idea epidemics (Adar in conversation with Asaravala 2004; Adar et al. 2004).

The power of memes to spread contagious ideas and to infect minds with particular ideas is widely recognized, and entire groups have begun experimenting with meme engineering and distribution on quite significant scales. This offers a range of models for working with memes from within classroom spaces. The critiques of mainstream media, marketing, and consumption memes propagated by the non-profit group, Adbusters (adbusters.org), provide excellent models of the kinds of memes students can participate actively in as part of dynamic approaches to resisting corporate-manufactured identities and consumption mindsets (see, for example, unbrandamerica.org). Non-profit community groups are also beginning to look to the grassroots mobilization that occurs around remixed or evolving multimedia memes as a viable model for mobilizing commitment to social causes (e.g., Surman and Reilly 2003).

In 2005, a meme engineering contest was hosted by Eyebeam, a non-profit digital arts and education outfit in New York City, and titled the "Contagious Media Showdown" (showdown.contagiousmedia.org). Prizes were awarded to deliberately developed, meme-based websites that proved to be maximally "contagious" as judged within one or more contest categories. These categories included: which idea generated the most unique visitors to the website (i.e., a traffic volume count); which contest website was linked to most by blogs, or which contest website scored the highest on a well-known website popularity index (in this case, Alexa.com). The content of the winning memes was more bizarre than socially aware (e.g., a hoax website advertising underwear with built-in satellite tracking devices for keeping track of loved ones was the overall winner; another winner was a website comprising video clips of people crying while eating). However, the motivation behind the contest and its outcomes (the tracker panties website attracted well over 20 million unique visitors during the three-week contest time period; collectively, the 60 entries in the contest attracted over 50 million unique visitors in the same period) are instructive with respect to the effectiveness of the internet as a meme carrier and the accessible processes by which one can generate and disseminate memes online.

Conclusion

Within literacy education, analysis and dissection of online memes can be used to explore why some ideas are more easily replicated, are more fecund and have more longevity than others, and what the consequences of this are or might be. Studying online memes that aim at promoting social critique can help educators to rethink conventional approaches to critical literacy that all too often operate at the level of text analysis without taking sufficient account of the social practices, ideas, affinities and new forms of social participation and cultural production that generated the phenomenon under examination. Engaging with online memes as examples of new L/literacies can help educators to equip students with important strategies for identifying the memes that infect their minds, and for evaluating the effects these memes have on their (ethical) decision-making, social actions and their relations with others. Well-informed and savvy online meming may well provide students with a fruitful and accessible practice for bringing about positive social changes in the ways people think and, perhaps, act towards others.

References

Adar, E., Zhang, L., Adamic, L. and Lukose, R. 2004. Implicit Structure and Dynamics of Blogspace. Draft research report for the HP Information Dynamics Lab. hpl.hp.com/ research/idl/papers/blogs/index.html (accessed 4 March, 2004).

Asaravala, A. 2004. Warning: Blogs can be infectious. *Wired*. March. wired.com/news/print/ 0,1294,62537,00.html (accessed 7 March, 2005).

Aunger, R. 2002. *The Electric Meme: A New Theory of How We Think*. New York: Free Press.

Blackmore, S. 1999. *The Meme Machine*. Oxford: Oxford University Press.

Brodie, R. 1996. *Virus of the Mind: The New Science of the Meme*. New York: Integral Press.

Butts, C. and Hilgeman, C. 2003. Inferring potential memetic structure from cross-sectional data: An application to American religious beliefs. *Journal of Memetics* 7(2). jom-emit.cfpm.org/2003/vol7/butts_ct&hilgeman_c.html (accessed 7 November, 2005).

Chattoe, E. 1998. Virtual urban legends: Investigating the ecology of the world wide web. *IRISS '98 Conference Proceedings*. International IRISS Conference, 25–17 March, Bristol UK. sosig.ac.uk/iriss/papers/paper37.htm (accessed 6 March, 2005).

Dawkins, R. 1976. *The Selfish Gene*. Oxford: Oxford University Press.

Dawkins, R. 1999. Foreword. In S. Blackmore, *The Meme Machine*. Oxford: Oxford University Press. vii–xvii.

Downes, S. 1999. Hacking memes. *First Monday* 4(10). firstmonday.dk/issues/issue4_10/downes/index.html (accessed 19 November, 2005).

Fairclough, N. 1992. *Discourse and Social Change*. Oxford: Polity Press.

Franklin, U. 1990. *The Real World of Technology*. Toronto: House of Anansi.

Freire, P. 1972. *Pedagogy of the Oppressed*. New York: Seabury Press.

Gatherer, D. 2003. A reply to the letters of Edmonds (2002) and Duthie (2004): Birth of a meme: The origin and evolution of collusive voting patterns in the Eurovision Song Contest. *Journal of Memetics—Evolutionary Models of Information Transmission*. 8. Jom-emit.cfpm.org/2004/ vol.8/gatherer_d_letter.html (accessed 6 March, 2005).

Gee, J. 1996. *Social Linguistics and Literacies: Ideology in Discourses* (2nd ed.). New York: Taylor & Francis.

Gee, J. 2004. *Situated Language and Learning: A Critique of Traditional Schooling*. New York: Routledge.

Gee, J. Hull, G., and Lankshear, C. 1996. *The New Work Order*. Sydney: Allen & Unwin.

Gilster, P. 1997. *Digital Literacy*. New York: Wiley Computer Publications.

Glasner, J. 2002. Nigeria hoax spawns copycats. wired.com/news/business /0,1367,53115,00. html *Wired*. June (accessed 7 March, 2005).

Godwin, M. 1994. Meme, Counter-meme. *Wired* 2.10. wired.com/wired/archive/2.10/god-win.if_pr.html (accessed 24 November, 2005).

Knobel, M. 1999. *Everyday Literacies*. New York: Peter Lang.

Knobel, M. 2006. Memes, literacy and affinity spaces: Implications for policy and digital divides in education. *e-Learning*. 3(3).

Knobel, M. and Lankshear, C. 2005. "New literacies": Research and social practice. *54th Yearbook of the National Reading Conference*. Oak Creek, WI: National Reading Conference. 22–50.

Kress, G. 2003. *Literacy in the New Media Age*. London: Routledge.

Lankshear, C. and Knobel, M. 2003. *New Literacies*. Buckingham: Open University Press.

Lankshear, C. and Knobel, M. 2006a. *New Literacies: Everyday Practices and Classroom Learning*. 2nd edn. Maidenhead, UK: Open University Press.

Lankshear, C. and Knobel, M. 2006b. Digital literacies: Policy, pedagogy and research considerations for education. *Nordic Journal of Digital Literacy*, 1(1).

Lessig, L. 2004. *Free Culture: How Big Media Uses Technology and the Law to Lock Down Culture and Control Creativity*. New York: Penguin.

Peretti, J. 2001. My Nike adventure. *The Nation*. 9 April. Reprinted at CorpWatch corp-watch.org/article.php?id=147 (accessed 7 March, 2004).

Rogers, E. 1962. *Diffusion of Innovations*. New York: Free Press.

Scholz, T. 2004. It's new media: But is it art education? *fibreculture: internet theory + criticism + culture*. 3. journal.fibreculture.org/issue3/issue3_scholz.html (accessed 7 November 2005).

Semon, R. 1924. *The Mneme*. New York: Macmillan.

Street, B. 1984. *Literacy in Theory and Practice*. Cambridge: Cambridge University Press.

Surman, M. and Reilly, K. 2003. Chapter 5: Mobilization. *Appropriating the Internet for Social Change*. Report commissioned by the Social Sciences Research Council, Canada. com-mons.ca/articles/fulltext.shtml?x=336 (accessed 7 March, 2005).

Taylor, C. 2001. All your base are belong to us. *Time* 157(9): 4

Vajik, P. 1989. Memetics: The Nascent Science of Ideas and Their Transmission. An Essay Presented to the Outlook Club, Berkeley, California. home.netcom.com/~cbell58/meme2.htm (accessed 18 March 2006).

Whybark, M. 2004. Hopkin explained. 22 November. mike.whybark.com/archives/ 001951.html (accessed 9 March 2005).

Wired 2002. Nigeria e-mail suckers exist. *Wired*. April. wired.com/news/culture/ 0,1284,51725,00.html (accessed 7 March 2005).

CHAPTER TEN

New Literacies

CYNTHIA LEWIS

Ironically, reading this volume on "new literacies" brought me back to 1978, when as a masters student I first read Janet Emig's 1971 classic, *The Composing Process of 12th Graders* (1971). This book, and others of that early generation of writing research (e.g., Graves, 1983) attempted to understand the process of writing by observing the process in action and by asking writers to think and talk about their processes, including their intentions, negotiations, stances, stylistic choices, and so forth. Before this time, little was known, from a research standpoint, about the actual processes writers underwent. At around the same time, academic writers began to examine and write about the writing processes of well-known writers as well as their own writing processes, what might today be viewed as auto-ethnographic research. For example, Murray's (1968) advice for teachers of writing was full of descriptions of his own writing process and suggestions for reading about the writing lives of famous writers. Another marker of the early writing process movement was its devaluing of academic or schooled writing. This was most prominent in Elbow's *Writing Without Teachers* (1973), but also evident in Macrorie's *Telling Writing* (1970), in which he refers to the "phony, pretentious language of the schools" as "Engfish" (p. 1). This focus on the writing process of actual writers and what was seen as its antithesis in schools contributed to the making of the discipline of literacy studies with a focus on writing.

I open with this backward glance to make the point that many of us writing about "new literacies" are, in fact, engaged in the making of a discipline that requires some knowledge-producing strategies similar to those taken up in the early days of writing research. We need to know what writers of new literacies *do* when they write—what they think about and how they negotiate the demands of new forms and processes of writing. Perhaps it's not surprising, then, that this sampler includes research in the three areas that marked early writing studies: examinations of writing processes as articulated and demonstrated by those who practice new literacies; an auto-ethnographic meta-account of a particular form of digital media (blogging); and, in general, a valuing of informal, out-of-school literacies and the resourceful competence of those who engage in them. I would argue that it is necessary at this time to "re-make" the discipline of literacy studies, and that these moves—to reflect, describe, categorize, document, and differentiate—are part of the generative act of re-envisioning writing in digital times.

The contributors to this volume make it clear that rethinking writing in digital times means focusing on practices over tools. In the opening chapter of this book, which also serves as the introduction to this volume, Lankshear and Knobel make the important point that new literacies aren't new unless they have both new "technical stuff" and new "ethos stuff." New technologies afford new practices, but it is the practices themselves, and the local and global contexts within which they are situated, that are central to new literacies. The logical implication, spelled out in several of the chapters, is that schools would accomplish more if, like new literacy users, they too focused on practices rather than tools. Instead, as Leander's chapter so clearly demonstrates, even schools with abundant technological resources, serving students who themselves are well resourced, lack the "ethos stuff." That is, the world of education (policies and systems more than individual teachers) has not shifted mindsets in line with those described in this book's opening chapter. Through professional development, teachers receive training in curricular uses of technology, but they do not learn about new mindsets, identities, and practices that come with new technologies, forms of communication, and economic flows.

So what are these new mindsets and practices? The authors of these chapters focus on many, including new ways of understanding and experiencing genre, identity, collaboration, authority, and sociality. I'm going to add a few of my own and take up some of these along the way. What I want to do is reflect on the 'Big L literacies' as Knobel and Lankshear refer to them, borrowing from Gee's Big D/Little d "D/discourse" distinction. Big L literacies are connected with identities, patterns, and ways of being in the world rather than solely with the acts of reading and writing. The three dimensions of practice I'll discuss—agency, performativity, and circulation—are salient across the forms and cases of new literacies discussed in this volume. I'll talk a little about these dimensions of Big L practices as they show up in the chapters and then discuss some questions and fears that these practices may raise for educators and researchers alike.

Agency

Most of the chapters point to new forms of agency that emerge through the practice of new literacies. This is perhaps most explicitly addressed by Gee and Hammer, but the potential for and limits on agency resonate throughout the book. New literacies tend to allow writers (users; players) a good deal of leeway to be creative, perform identities, and choose affiliations within a set of parameters that can change through negotiation, play, and collaboration. Gee's notion of "projective stance" articulates the nature of agency in new literacies and its appeal to the desire for play and control, but also, paradoxically perhaps, the need to understand the codes, conventions and values (or "doctrine," as he calls it) that align with particular ways of thinking, being, and acting. In this way, the learner understands the larger picture and why it might be worthwhile to be recruited into the doctrine. We've seen variations of this philosophy before, from music teaching (Suzuki method) to work in composition studies (Bartholomae's "Inventing the University," 1985), to some versions of genre approaches. What they all have in common is the belief that true agency is arrived at through a mixture of process and product, learner control and imposed limits. The most important ingredient, however, is a meta-awareness of how the domain works and how one might work the domain.

We can see a mixture of these ingredients in Hammer's description of the boundaries of agency (which often stops short of authority) for secondary authors within role-playing games. Here Hammer delineates the ways that agency is limited through collaborative negotiations of narrative plausibility, participant structures, and primary authorship. Ironically, it is these very limits that lead to complicated assertions of agency, requiring that secondary authors understand the politics of participation, features of genre, elements of story, and affordances of technological tools. In other chapters, agency is most connected to subverting genre in some way—as in the boundary-blurring practices of the girls' uses of fan fiction in Thomas's chapter. Shifting between role-playing and out-of-character discussions, and in and out of what might traditionally be thought of as narrative, the girls imaginatively remix known characters and storylines. Yet in fan fiction, insider knowledge of known characters and storylines is part of the thrill. The predictable, then, spawns agency in the production of new texts.

Performativity

Another dimension of practice that runs across many of the new literacies described in these chapters is peformativity. By this, I am referring to the individual and group identities that are constructed through repeated performances of self and in anticipation of the expectations, social codes and discourses available within a given context. We see this in Thomas's rendering of Jandalf and Tiana as they make and remake roles, narratives, and their own identities through quite phenomenal uses of writing. Their performances are, at times, rehearsals, as in the role plays that lead to their narratives, and at other times more conventional performances in the sense of working within the genre-specific conventions of narrative. They continually perform a version of self, shifting voices, drawing on the intertextual chains that exist through the textual history of each exchange and their larger social and textual networks. They interpret, invent, revise, inflect, and so on, moment-to-moment.

Performativity is also central to meming, in Knobel and Lankshear's chapter, in the sense that the memes themselves both construct and are constructed by group identities through repeated performances. And, again in this case, the performances are dependent on the intertextual chains that exist through the textual history of the meme (what the meme is drawing on from politics, music, products, etc., for purposes of humor, social commentary, fandom, and hoax).

Repeated performances are at work as well in the inscribed literacies of school that Leander discusses—repeated performances related to uses of space, time, and materials. By contrast, Leander presents an alternative relationship to time—a simultaneity—exhibited by students engaged in digital literacies at school. We see this orientation toward time in the students he describes who are engaged in online activity that reached beyond the space-time of school activities. We see it also in the exchanges of Jandalf and Tiana who perform themselves at once in role and out, for instance, and in the process of meming, which must be performed simultaneously in order to have fidelity, fecundity, and longevity.

To some degree, performative practice is built into digital technology with multiple windows, synchronicity, graphical possibilities, and what Ito (2005, p. 3) calls "hypersociality." This was evident in a study on Instant Messaging that Bettina Fabos and I conducted (Lewis and Fabos 2005). Our participants' uses of "away" messages expressed aspects of their identities and their performative practice of shifting style and tone from message to message, thus simultaneously staying in touch with a wide array of friends and acquaintances and building the social narratives of their lives. Academic blogging foregrounds performative aspects of literacy as well. Davies and Merchant discuss how blogs project particular personas, both personal and professional. They develop the theme of "publishing the self" in which they indicate how uncomfortable this kind of public performance can be. Much of the tension they describe is the result of performing the self for both a small group of like-minded colleagues (other academic bloggers who are professional colleagues and friends) at the same time that they are also projecting a persona for a much larger, amorphous audience who may not understand the inside references and jokes and may, instead, take offense. Some of these intertextual references are communicated through the blogging format itself, such as the list of favorite blogs that most blog pages include. Thus, the tools and practices are mutually reinforcing.

Circulation

In her book on young people's uses of new media. Livingstone (2002) points out that internet spaces are more often "based on bricolage or juxtaposition." This representational style, Lankshear and Knobel (2003) and Leu (2000) suggest, is keyed to new epistemologies, and to new ways of being and thinking. These new epistemologies, as I see it, are related to new practices of circulation, which depend on the cut and paste style of bricolage and juxtaposition for production and exchange. Digital texts, in part because of their simultaneity, circulate widely across time and space, are cut and pasted, edited, revised, and juxtaposed in ways that cannot be as easily accomplished in print. This can be disconcerting to some who are not in the loop. In Leander's chapter, for example, the teacher's sense of a lack of control related to how texts circulate and her non-inclusion in the process created the conditions for "closure" that he discusses. Students are asked to close their laptops to make sure that the knowledge circulated is generated in and disseminated through the classroom. Knowledge generated in and disseminated through the internet is viewed as lacking legitimacy (e.g., parodies or social interaction) or as threatening to the local community (e.g., text answers).

Circulation is the name of the game for memes, of course. They circulate widely and change—get parodied, modified, and so forth. Also, "reading" the memes involves knowledge of how they have circulated—a deep understanding of cross-references and intertextuality—where the memes have come from, what they refer to, and where the language or images have been before they became this particular meme. This is true for Thomas's participants as well, whose own highly creative work spins off of work that has come before—magical and fantasy worlds. These paths that have led to their work are important for them to know in order to write their own texts and understand each other's. Intertextual connections and circulatory routes also have much to do with the popularity of websites in Stone's research. Stone makes the important point that the websites should not be read as conventional examples of whatever genre they may on the surface seem to be. Instead, a competent reading of these sites requires an intertextual breadth and understanding of how these texts circulate. Where they have been, what they draw on, and who reads them strongly determines how they are to be read. As Stone points out, if Stickdeath were read as a straight informational text, "it would read like a guide to becoming a sociopath" rather than as sharp social commentary.

The digital texts in these chapters are widely and quickly circulated, with many receiving a multitude of hits and written comments each day. Writers of digital texts must be aware of their circulatory routes to accomplish their goals. For example, Black's study of an ELL fan fiction writer shows how Nanako's sense of audience is very much connected to an understanding of how her work circulates. Nanako's author's notes have both a public and personal voice, addressing specific readers as well as the larger affinity group. The wide circulation of blogs combined with the typically informal tone and somewhat personal content of the genre causes tensions for Davies and Merchant as they navigate the line between personal and public voice. The potential for wide circulation of blog entries suggests the need for less personal disclosure. However, academic bloggers use their blogs, in part, to speak to an affinity group of like-minded scholars, and thus imagine a smaller, more closely-knit circulatory route.

Fears and Questions

When I first began to think about the chapters in this volume, I glanced at a title of a book advertised in the magazine I was reading. The word in the title that gave me pause was "chronophobia." It seemed important that that word came my way as I was thinking about these chapters because the stark contrast between the school-based literacies represented in Leander's chapter and the Big L literacies in Thomas's and Knobel and Lankshear's seems related to a fear of time—fear of the new uses of time and space that all these chapters point to. I will admit to having this fear myself when I see students in my own classes with their laptops open, looking at their screens and smiling at times when I haven't told a joke. Apparently, I am not the only sage on the stage and, in fact, as the chapters in this book make clear, the concepts of "sage" and "stage" are seriously dismantled by the emphasis on collaborative knowledge production across time and space that new literacies bring to the fore. I've also seen up close the ways in which school concepts of time and space can interfere with well-intentioned projects involving technology. Recently, my class of pre-service English education students used Instant Messaging with middle school students as a way of communicating about the young students' writing projects. The conditions were ideal—a metro magnet inquiry-based school, adequate technology resources, interested teachers, strong connections already established between my students and the kids they had already been working with in person each week. But things fell apart, largely due to time-space problems: transporting laptops from one part of the school to another; proximity to network hubs; too little transition time between classes; preordained amounts of time designated to each curricular activity. The project worked best in those instances when students had broadband internet access at home and could arrange to connect with my teacher education students outside of school. As Leander's chapter so vividly rendered, patterns of organizing time and space in schools are firmly established and hard to disrupt even in schools with strong resources and technologically savvy students.

Another fear related to new literacies is foregrounded by the important question asked by Livingstone (2002) in her book, *Young People and New Media*:

> To the extent that we are indeed witnessing a transformation in the notion of the text, one must ask whether there are parallel changes in the user (or reader)? And if so, are such changes in young people's ways of knowing to be encouraged? (p. 229)

No doubt, many readers would agree that there are parallel changes in the user—at least this is the argument I have tried to make in this chapter and elsewhere. But the question of whether such changes are to be encouraged is a deeper one because it is about who and what we want young people to become. Anxiety about the kind of young people that we want to produce has been discussed by Luke and Luke (2001):

> The perception of crisis [over perceived loss of print literacy] is an artifact of a particular generational anxiety over new forms of adolescent and childhood identity and life pathways . . . (p. 105).

Here, they make clear that the crisis is not to be found in the child or adolescent as subject, but in the teacher, researcher, and policy-maker as the adult. As Kress, Jewitt, and Tsatsarelis (2000) point out in an article on the effects of new representational modes on educational practice, it is at the intersection of identity, knowledge, and pedagogy that social subjects are formed. Again, the question is what kind of social subject are parents, teachers, and policy makers going to be comfortable producing—at least to the point that they think they have control over the subject that gets produced.

It's not just about my generation of middle-aged teachers who are uncomfortable with new orientations to time, space, performance, creativity, and design. My pre-service teachers tend not to be comfortable with these new orientations either. Popular technologies are to be used and shared out-of-school. To do so in school challenges the materiality of what it means to be a teacher, in their minds—what Margaret Finders and I (2002) have called the "implied teacher"—the inscription of who and what a teacher should be and how a school or a classroom should work.

And, if I can play devil's advocate for a bit, maybe we have good reason to be fearful or, at least, skeptical about the kinds of literacies that are celebrated in this book. Maybe these literacies, which are already practiced and perfected outside-of-schools— at least by those who have access—should not be incorporated into school literacies. After all, where will young people learn the skills of deep reading and analysis that are the hallmark of what it means to be educated (not what is tested, of course, but what it means to be educated)? I received that kind of response in reviews of my own work on new literacies. And it's a reasonable question, in my view. I would bet that the kinds of writing that Tiana and Jandalf engage in—especially their sophisticated rhetorical analyses—would be celebrated in school as well as out. They talk about their practices in fairly school-like ways. And, let's face it, what can school teach these girls about genre? But how about young people who chat or text message most of the time or read and create memes, engaging in highly performative, simultaneous, pastiche-like activity. What kind of social subject is produced through these activities and is it one we adults will want to live with?

On the other hand, Leander points out that the modern workplace is poly-chromic. If so, then perhaps the kind of social subject we currently aim to produce in school is inadequate for participating in social worlds outside of school. Gee (2002) has argued that leaving new literacies out of school creates yet another brand of "haves" and "have-nots." Those who have access to digital worlds outside of school will be schooled in the new epistemologies that will provide them with the capital they need for participating as engaged citizens in their social futures. Those who don't will not have this opportunity because these new epistemologies, as already discussed, are not part of the "scope and sequence" (to borrow a phrase from basal readers) or the vision of what it means to be educated. The current obses-sion with testing "the basics" and the narrow definition of what counts as "basic" exacerbate the problem.

In the end, I suspect it won't matter much if parents, educators, and other adults encourage the changes or not. As these chapters so clearly depict, young people will continue to engage in a range of new literacies during their out-of-school hours. The question is whether we want to make school literacy more engaging for students and more meaningful to their present and future lives in a digitally mediated world. If so, then we need to understand the shifts in practices and epistemologies that have taken place and consider how these shifts should inform our teaching of reading and writing. This volume leads the way in helping us better understand these shifts in practice and the fears that attend them. Like the beginnings of writing research in the second half of the 20th century, this project is about the making of a discipline. As such it will involve re-envisioning what will count as literacy in our digitally mediated times and how our new conceptions should shape the teaching and learn-ing of literacy in schools.

References

Bartholomae, D. (1986). Inventing the University. *Journal of Basic Writing, 5*, 4–23.

Elbow, P. (1973). *Writing without teachers.* New York: Oxford UP.

Emig, J. (1971). *The composing process of 12th graders.* Urbana, IL: National Council of Teachers of English Press.

Gee, J.P. (2002). Millennials and Bobos, Blue's Clues and Sesame Street: A story for our times. In D.E. Alvermann (Ed.), *Adolescents and literacies in a digital world* (pp. 51–67). New York: Peter Lang.

Graves, D. (1983). *Writing: Teachers and students at work*. Portsmouth, NH: Heinemann.

Ito, M. (2005). Technologies of childhood imagination: Yugioh, media mixes, and everyday cultural production. http://www.itofisher.com/mito/archives/000074.html (accessed 9 September, 2006).

Kress, G., Jewett, C. & Tsatsarelis, C. (2000). Knowledge, identity, pedagogy, pedagogic discourse and the representational environments of education in late modernity. *Linguistics and Education, 11*, 7–30.

Lankshear, C. & Knobel, M. (2003). *New literacies: Changing knowledge and classroom learning*. Philadelphia, PA: Open University Press.

Leu, D. J. (2000). Literacy and technology: Deictic consequences for literacy education in an information age. In M. Kamil, P. B. Mosenthal, P. D. Pearson, & R. Barr (Eds.), *Handbook of reading research*, volume III (pp. 743–770). Mahwah, NJ: Erlbaum.

Lewis, C. & Fabos, B. (2005). Instant messaging, literacies, and social identities. *Reading Research Quarterly. 40*, 470–501.

Lewis, C. & Finders, M. (2002). Implied adolescents and implied teachers: A generation gap for new times. In D. E. Alvermann (Ed.), *Adolescents and literacies in a digital world* (pp. 101–113). New York: Peter Lang Publishers.

Livingstone, S. (2002). *Young people and new media*. London, England: Sage.

Luke, A. & Luke, C. (2004). Adolescence lost/childhood regained: On early intervention and the emergence of the techno-subject. *Journal of Early Childhood Literacy, 1*, 91–120.

Macrorie, K. (1970). *Telling writing*. Rochelle Park, NJ: Hayden.

Murray, D. M. (1968). *A writer teaches writing*. Boston, MA: Houghton Mifflin Co.

Contributors

Rebecca Black is an Assistant Professor in the Department of Education at the University of California, Irvine (U.S.). Her work is at the forefront of research that focuses on new literacies and English language learning. Her book on adolescents and online fan fiction will be published in 2007 by Peter Lang.

Julia Davies is a Lecturer within the School of Education at the University of Sheffield (England). Her recent research focuses on popular media and new forms of literacy practice and includes analyses of gender, learning and formal and informal education. Julia has published in a wide range of books and national and international journals.

James Paul Gee is the Tashia Morgridge Professor of Reading in the Department of Curriculum and Instruction at the University of Wisconsin at Madison (U.S.). His current research focuses on learning and literacy in video and computer games, and recent books include *What Video Games Have to Teach Us About Learning and Literacy* and *Situated Language and Learning*.

Jessica Hammer is a doctoral student at Teachers College, Columbia University (U.S.). She also works as a game designer and consultant, including stints with gameLab, LEGO, RealNetworks and on viral marketing projects aimed at both "traditional" and "non-traditional" markets. Jessica's current research focuses on narrative, and role-play gaming.

Michele Knobel is a Professor of Education at Montclair State University (U.S.), where she co-ordinates the graduate and undergraduate literacy programs. She is also an Adjunct Professor of Education at Central Queensland University, Australia. Her research focuses on the relationship between new literacies, social practices and digital technologies. Recent books include the *Handbook for Teacher Research* (with Colin Lankshear).

Colin Lankshear is Professor of Literacy and New Technologies at James Cook University (Australia) and Visiting Scholar at McGill University (Canada). His research interests include philosophical and empirical investigation at interfaces between new technologies, literacy and everyday social practices. He is co-author (with Michele Knobel) of *New Literacies: Everyday Practices and Classroom Learning* and joint editor of the forthcoming *Handbook of Research on New Literacies*.

Kevin Leander is an Associate Professor in Language, Literacy, and Culture at Vanderbilt University (U.S.). His research focuses on developing new conceptions of space-time relationships within young people's lifeworlds as they engage with new and emerging digital technologies and social spaces online within a range of contexts. He has co-edited the book, *Spatializing Literacy Research and Practice*, published by Peter Lang.

Cynthia Lewis is a Professor of Literacy Education at the University of Minnesota (U.S.). Her research focuses on literacy as a social and critical practice, and the ways in which literacy practices are shaped by social identities, new media, and the politics of classrooms and communities. Cynthia has published widely and her books include *Literacy Practices as Social Acts* and *Reframing Sociocultural Research on Literacy* (the latter co-written with Patricia E. Enciso and Elizabeth Birr Moje).

Guy Merchant is a Principal Lecturer at Sheffield Hallam University (England). His research within the field of new literacies focuses on children and adolescents and their engagement with new media. He has published in a wide range of journals in England, the U.S. and elsewhere, and writes for diverse audiences, including practicing teachers, university students, and fellow academics.

Jennifer Stone is an Assistant Professor in Language, Literacy and Culture at the University of Washington, Seattle (U.S.). Her research and publishing focuses on the literacy resources young people bring with them to classroom learning, with particular emphasis on digital literacy resources.

Angela Thomas is a Lecturer in Education at the University of Sydney (Australia). Her current research focuses on gender, identity narrative, and role playing. Angela's work is particularly notable for her longitudinal study of a group of adolescents and their narrative and identity practices. Her research focuses on collaborative narrative writing and the use of multiple media and genre as expressive resources. Recent books include *Children's Literature and Computer Based Teaching* (co-written with Len Unsworth, Alyson M. Simpson, and Jennifer L Asha).

Subject Index

Author Index

new
literacies
ꟼ

AND DIGITAL EPISTEMOLOGIES

Colin Lankshear, Michele Knobel,
Chris Bigum, & Michael Peters
*General Editor*s

New literacies and new knowledges are being invented "in
the streets" as people from all walks of life wrestle with
new technologies, shifting values, changing institutions,
and new structures of personality and temperament emerging
in a global informational age. These new literacies and
ways of knowing remain absent from classrooms. Many education administrators, teachers, teacher educators, and academics seem largely unaware of them. Others actively
oppose them. Yet, they increasingly shape the engagements
and worlds of young people in societies like our own. The
New Literacies and Digital Epistemologies series will explore this terrain with a view to informing educational
theory and practice in constructively critical ways.

For further information about the series and submitting
manuscripts, please contact:

Michele Knobel & Colin Lankshear
Montclair State University
Dept. of Education and Human Services
3173 University Hall
Montclair, NJ 07043
michele@coatepec.net

To order other books in this series, please contact our
Customer Service Department at:

(800) 770-LANG (within the U.S.)
(212) 647-7706 (outside the U.S.)
(212) 647-7707 FAX

Or browse online by series at:

www.peterlang.com